"Vintage Cybill . . . not only one of t[...]
hilarious kiss-and-tell memoirs to come[...]
of Hollywood in years, but also a moving
account of her journey of self-discovery. Such
unflinching honesty makes for one juicy book."

People

Few women in the past three decades have lit up the American imagination like Cybill Shepherd. From wholesome beauty queen to saucy cover girl, from heartbreaking movie star to one of television's most beloved comediennes, she has imbued each of her roles—right down to her current passions of devoted mother of three, champion of women's issues, and sultry cabaret singer—with an indomitable spirit that has made her, at fifty, a female icon to an entire generation. Now in this bestselling memoir, she tells her remarkable story. Whether stepping on Elvis's blue suede shoes or going toe-to-toe with Bruce Willis, Cybill has never held anything back, and it's all in *Cybill Disobedience*.

"A riveting, candid, fresh
and self-revealing book."

Liz Smith

Cybill Disobedience

How I Survived Beauty Pageants, Elvis,
Sex, Bruce Willis, Lies, Marriage,
Motherhood, Hollywood, and the
Irrepressible Urge to Say What I Think

Cybill Shepherd

with Aimee Lee Ball

AVON BOOKS
An Imprint of HarperCollinsPublishers

AVON BOOKS
An Imprint of HarperCollins*Publishers*
10 East 53rd Street
New York, New York 10022-5299

Copyright © 2000 by Cybill Shepherd
Front and back cover photograph © by Timothy White
ISBN: 0-06-103014-7
www.avonbooks.com

First Avon Books paperback printing: May 2001
First HarperCollins hardcover printing: May 2000

Avon Trademark Reg. U.S. Pat. Off. and in Other Countries, Marca Registrada, Hecho en U.S.A.
HarperCollins ® is a registered trademark of HarperCollins Publishers Inc.

Printed in the U.S.A.

10   9   8   7   6   5   4   3   2   1

This book is dedicated to my mother,
Patty Cornelia Shobe Shepherd Micci, and
my father, William Jennings Shepherd Jr.

Thanks for falling in love.

Contents

Contents

Prologue

Los Angeles, California, Oct. 30, 1999

6:27 P.M. — In 123 minutes I'm appearing onstage in my cabaret act at the Cinegrill of the fabled Hollywood Roosevelt Hotel. However, right now I'm on the Hollywood freeway in bumper-to-bumper traffic. At this pace, one inch every five minutes, I'll just make it at eight-thirty in the year 2004.

7:12 P.M. — Turning off Highland onto Hollywood Boulevard, we're rear-ended by a station wagon.

7:14 P.M. — I have no choice. Leaving my driver, Tom, to take care of that situation, I take off running, dragging behind me a rolling suitcase filled with my costume, makeup, and sheet music. I'm wearing a black leather cap, black high-tops, black jeans, and a bodywear top that I hadn't exactly planned on publicly displaying in an area of town where this kind of cleavage can either get you arrested or hired. Heading west toward Mann's Chinese Theater, a greasy-looking wino calls out "C'mon, baby, gimme some of that!" Without breaking stride, I holler back, "Normally I would, but right now I don't have time."

7:16 P.M.—Reaching the north corner of the intersection of Orange and Hollywood Boulevard, I look up and freeze in fear. My name is *not* on the marquee. This is not good. Could it be I'm here on the wrong night? I dart through traffic and leaping safely onto the far sidewalk, quickly glance down at my star on the Walk of Fame. I notice a wad of gum on it. I try to kick it off. Now I've got a glob of purple goo stuck to the bottom of my shoe. I yank off the shoe and hobble into the Roosevelt lobby.

7:20 P.M.—To my enormous relief, I see a placard that says Cybill Shepherd *is* performing here tonight. Carrying my shoe, dragging my suitcase, I hurtle across the lobby and pound on the elevator button. The doors open almost immediately, but the elevator is full. I jam myself, my shoe, and my suitcase in anyway, gasping for breath. A woman behind me squeals, "Are you who I think you are?"

"I certainly hope so," I answer, trying to maintain some semblance of composure.

7:25 P.M.—My assistant, Jason, anxiously paces at the door of my fourth-floor dressing room as I rush in and begin frantically unpacking my bag.

"Your hairdresser's stuck in traffic on the freeway,"

Jason says, taking in my disheveled appearance, ~~~ing hard to hide his horror. The eighteen-hour makeup that gives my face and arms a flawless resurfacing has leaked out over everything in my bag: brushes, rollers, makeup, hair spray. It's time for prayer. "Please God, let my hairdresser get here in the next five minutes."

7:29 P.M.—The stage manager knocks: "One hour, Cybill! Do you need anything?" I want to say yes. I need my hairdresser to be here, I need my makeup to be scraped out of the bottom of the bag, I need my sheet music to be dried out, but I can't say any of that because my cell phone is ringing.

7:30 P.M.—It's my older daughter, Clementine, calling from the car. She and my younger daughter, Ariel, are stuck on yet another freeway taking our beloved black pug Petunia to the vet. Obviously, Clementine and Ariel are going to be late for my show. I understand. They have their priorities too.

7:35 P.M.—My twelve-year-old son, Zachariah, rushes in from the adjoining room with a look of consternation. He has forgotten until this very moment that tonight is the biggest party of the year, thrown by his best friend. "Can you please take me right now, Mom?" Before I can answer, the doorbell rings. It's Cathy, my hairdresser. Right behind her is a woman I've never seen before, who grabs me by the arm and gushes: "Oh, Cybill, I can't wait for your book to come out. My marriage is falling apart, my kids are driving me crazy, and I'm premenopausal too." I take one look around me—at my pleading son, my ringing cell phone, the accoutrements of my soon-to-be onstage self strewn all over the floor, and my only thought is *But clearly I'm writing more of a How-Not-to book.*

8:20 P.M.—"Mmmraahhh. Mmmmmmmrraaahhhh." I'm vocalizing. While Cathy teases my hair, I console Clementine on the cell phone about the state of Petunia's kidneys, and the stage manager pops in with the ten-minute warning while I try to remember the lyrics to "The Lady Is a Tramp."

8:30 P.M.—"Please, Mom, can't you take me now," Zach implores as I slop on some makeup and throw on my clothes.

"I love you," I say, trying to remember the lyrics to "One Monkey Don't Stop No Show," "but Mom has to work now and I can't go anywhere except onstage in about thirty-eight seconds."

8:33 P.M.—Outside the door of the Cinegrill, the stage manager hands me my microphone as I slip into my shoes. I've mollified Zach. He's upstairs doing his homework. Petunia's kidneys have resumed functioning. And Clementine and Ariel are on the way. The band jumps into the intro of "That Old Black Magic" as the announcer intones, "And now, ladies and gentlemen, please welcome . . . direct from polishing her star on Hollywood Boulevard . . . Cybill Shepherd."

CHAPTER ONE

"Who's the Fairest of Them All?"

PEOPLE WHO HAVE NEVER LIVED THROUGH an earthquake assume that one of its salient features is noise—the sounds of splintering glass, the symphony of physical destruction, the uncanny moaning of buildings as steel and wood and concrete are strained to some implausible degree. But that's quickly over. Far more shocking is the eerie quietude: the power failure that eliminates the humming of air-conditioning and refrigerators, the absence of music, the traffic that has come to a standstill. It's as if a mute button has been pushed on the world. That's what it's like when a television series ends. The lights go out, the people scatter, the magic has died. And the *Cybill* show did not go gently. I did not go gently.

Over a thirty-year career, I had died before—cacophonous, public, psychically bloody deaths engineered at the box office and at the hands of critics—but this demise was singularly painful. I'd given my name and much of my identity to the series, blurring the line between real life and fiction, much more than is customary in television. (*Murphy Brown* was not called *Candice*, and the character didn't grow up with a wooden dummy for a brother.) Every door on our CBS soundstage had a plaque with CYBILL inscribed inside a blue chalk star, just like the one used under the opening title that pans across the Hollywood Walk of Fame. *Gunsmoke* was produced on that stage for eighteen years, but there was no trace of that iconic piece of American television history in the wings. As I drove off the lot for the last time, I knew how quickly my presence would evaporate, how soon the studio maintenance department would remove those plaques and the billboard-size CYBILL on the side of the stage.

The eulogies were not kind. While the real reasons for the show's demise were never made public, I was accused of professional paranoia and megalomania, of being, as Lady Caroline Lamb famously said of Lord Byron, "mad, bad and dangerous to know." I was labeled a jealous egomaniac, a self-promoting bitch, and a few other well-chosen words whose invocation would have gotten my mouth washed out with Camay in my Memphis childhood. I preserved all the poison-pen notices as a record, hard evidence of what I had survived and the proof that I wasn't paranoid. I had clearly made people exceedingly angry, committed some unpardonable transgression. It was not the first time.

What got me in trouble, what has always gotten me in trouble, was disobedience. On the *Cybill* show, I had been 57 different kinds of disobedient. From the beginning, my strategy was to challenge—always with humor—the conventional wisdom about "appropriate" subjects for television audiences. I was the first baby boomer to have a prime-time hot flash, and we skewered the injustice of a culture that pretends women over forty are invisible. I persuaded the writers to incorporate ideas from my own odyssey of discovery, like cultivating a reverence for three symbolic stages of a woman's life: maiden, mother, and crone. (Okay, okay, there's a brief cheerleader phase in there that can't be ignored.) I had the temerity to become a grandmother on American television, one experience not replicated in real life, but when my character cooed to her TV daughter, "And you even got married first!" it was a mocking reference to my own pregnancies before marriage. When my character's two ex-husbands happened to be in the living room just as her date showed up on the doorstep, art was mirroring my life, as it was in an episode about male impotence (delicately referred to on the show as "failing to perform").

Strange to think that these themes were considered radical by network executives and reviewers, but women who represent the cultural gamut of sizes and ages aren't too welcome in any media. After nearly a decade of murmuring "I'm worth it" for L'Oréal, I was fired because my hair got too old—approximately as old as I was. It's okay for Robert Mitchum to get up early in the morning and look like Robert Mitchum, but it was not okay for me to wake up in the morning and look like Robert Mitchum. Fans are always asking why Bruce Willis and I don't reprise our *Moonlighting* roles for the big screen. The answer is: studio executives would consider me too old for him now.

With few exceptions, American television has become the Bermuda Triangle for females over forty. There was a wide variety of middle-aged women on the air in 1998, and they were all gone by 1999. Not only *Cybill*, but *Murphy Brown*, *Ellen*, *Roseanne*, *Grace Under Fire*, and *Dr. Quinn, Medicine Woman* all disappeared the same year. It's true that these shows had been around for a while and may have run their course, so this chorus of swan songs takes on a deeper significance when we see the replacements: *Felicity*, *Dharma & Greg*, *Moesha*, *Ally McBeal*, *Sabrina the Teenage Witch*, *Buffy the Vampire Slayer*, and those very skinny *Friends*. No one over thirty need apply.

But I had defied convention beyond my approach to *Cybill*'s subject matter. From the start, I let it be known that I wanted an ensemble cast, that everybody's part should be great. I meant me too. I wanted the star of this show to have funny dialogue, clever story lines, and interesting dilemmas, without dumbing or dulling down the other characters. I insisted on having the grown-up female friendship that was the centerpiece of the show, a relationship with a sidekick rich in outrageous comic potential perhaps last tapped when Lucy Ricardo got Ethel Mertz to work in the candy factory. But that show was called *I Love Lucy*, not *Lucy and Ethel*. When I acted as an advocate for my character, trying to take the show in certain directions and expressing concern that the humor had become predictable, my efforts were viewed as territorial, the demands of an overblown ego afraid of being overshadowed. Three of my producers left, all rancorously: one said he had failed to save me from myself; another called me insensitive, bordering on anti-Semitic (rather ignoring that his replacement was Jewish and that I have two half-Jewish children); the third was dragged from my presence screaming "I'm a better person than you are." The studio producing my show cut me off at the knees the minute I was off camera, arrogating my authority as executive producer. And my costar, hand-picked for the role and richly rewarded for her good work with money and accolades, walked out on the re-hearsal of the last episode.

It was a clusterfuck of a year. Ten days after filming the last episode of *Cybill*, I found myself in the hospi-tal with a gut-wrenching pain. A doctor I'd never seen before was telling me that I needed emergency ab-dominal surgery and that the scar wouldn't be pretty. My intestines, it turned out, were twisted into some-thing resembling fusilli marinara, and I can't help making metaphysical metaphors about the gut being the site of intuition, about literally going under the knife at the same time that I was being cut and killed off on CBS. As it happened, my worst turncoat was much closer at hand, and a few months later, with stunning surgical precision (last metaphor, I promise) I was eviscerated by the man I thought would be shar-ing my dotage and my denture cup at the Old Actors' Home. He was my lover, my friend, my colleague, and my supposed life partner. But he concluded his busi-ness with me, after making sure he was paid, and an-nounced that our relationship was over. In the blink of a Saturday afternoon, he was gone.

THE LONGEST, DEEPEST STREAK OF DISOBEDI-ence in my life has been about sex. Although the strictures of southern womanhood were honed to a fine edge in my family and I followed some of them flawlessly, I never observed the sexual canons. I did exactly as I pleased, and what pleased me was sex—early with a man I naively thought would be the love of my life, later with a dispensable succession of partners. Sex became politicized and endorsed by my generation, made safe with the advent of the Pill, even though such behavior was still a moral issue for lots of people, including my parents. I was a very, very bad girl, living out the epiphany of the 1970s for women: that sex and love aren't necessarily the same thing.

I don't know if I've accrued more than my fair share of lost loves, but I'm something of a haunted person from the damage. Many times I was confused about the men I slept with, not knowing for sure whether I was genuinely attracted to them, or if the impetus was their attraction to me. I had to be kicked in the head by a few mules; now I've given up riding. In one of life's little full circles, I have become a creature of the sexually retrograde 1990s, just as I was of the sexually voracious 1960s. Society has been reindoctrinated to idealize monogamy and all the other virtues our mothers preached, but these days I'm sleeping alone. Sometimes I wake up in the middle of the night, put on blue eye shadow, and try to learn country line dancing in front of the TV. At least there are other people on the video.

Not until now have I realized how supremely important it was for me to confront and embrace my lifelong sense of profound loneliness, to stop making choices based on avoiding that demon. There's loneliness in being the child of parents whose own problems divert their attention, as mine did. Now that a grown daughter has already left the nest and her younger siblings have their wings spread, I'm facing down the devil once again, wondering what will be next? Is it okay for a woman to be alone? Is monogamy necessary? Will I only feel safe with a partner if there's a clearly delineated "yours," "mine," and "ours"? Can I trust someone who doesn't have as much to lose as I do? And who would that person be?

Three decades ago I fell in love with a married man who turned his life inside out because of me. He would be one of the most significant people in my life, a mentor and lifelong friend, but I was deemed a "home wrecker," someone who showed up unbidden with self-aggrandizing motives that bordered on the immoral and violated cultural bylaws. Forever after, it seemed, I was slated to be the bad girl. People said, "She has no right to_____," and filled in the blank. I decided I had to trust myself, which has led to some ungainly ups and downs. I've had two failed marriages and a few real-life soap operas. There are people in Hollywood who won't return my calls or run screaming from the room at the mention of my name. I've been in a few films that could serve as paradigms of the form, and more than I care to count of the straight-to-video kind.

I can't escape the conviction that fate has something to do with appearance, with the perception of personality or merit based on veneer. I earned my living on my looks for a long time, and it taught me that the accident of beauty incurs resentment—why should something that requires no effort or skill be rewarded? People seldom let their envy show so blatantly as a teaching assistant in an English class who once gave me a C for a poem that her supervisor later upgraded to an A+. At eighteen my looks were as close to perfect as they would ever be, but I was deeply insecure because I knew that appearance constituted my sole value, and eighteen is ephemeral.

Sometimes I wore my looks like a mantle with a certain degree of discomfort. People, especially men people, happily inconvenience themselves for a woman so marked, but she'll pay one way or another. I always knew that the power I gleaned from beauty dwarfed any other kind of achievement. No matter how hard I worked, I was credited only for the one thing that was effortless. The looks I was born with meant that I never lacked sexual partners but also meant that I could rarely discern who really cared about me. I learned from Yeats: "Only God, my dear, could love you for yourself alone and not your yellow hair."

The vain, murderously envious queen in *Snow White* poisons the young beauty but still doesn't feel safe when told that her rival is dead. She continues to look in the mirror, asking, "Who's the fairest of them all?" I grew up with this fairy tale and with the presumption of female envy. My mother absorbed this common cultural belief and passed it on to me, but I'd like to think that I've protected my daughters from it. When I look at my eldest now, I know absolutely who the fresh young beauty is, without begrudging her the role. I've already played it, and I'd prefer not to play the evil queen, in life anyway.

THERE'S A DIXIE CHICKS SONG WITH A WISE and placating lyric that goes "You gotta make big mistakes." I've made my share, and I ask for no jeremiads. I've been blessed with success in public life. Early on I fed readily and greedily off the seductive culture of narcissism and celebrity worship that abandons and replaces its acolytes at warp speed. Sometimes I've failed to hold myself accountable. Now I'm looking at my own trajectory, hoping to discern Cybill the Good and Cybill the Bad, trying to understand in order to be understood. I want to figure out how I became one of the Furies—me, the same person voted Most Cooperative at Camp Pickwick in 1959.

Some people have asked why I'd subject myself to the scrutiny of public confession when there are so many reasons not to: it's painful, I'm too young, I will be harshly judged. But events of the last year, symbolized by the not-so-pretty scar that means I've worn my last bikini, have forced me to realize that there are no guarantees about our time on the planet. Last year I went on *Good Morning America*, discussing menopause and a recently published list of sex symbols over the age of fifty. Just shy of my fiftieth birthday at the time, I didn't qualify, but if I'm not on the list next year, I'm coming after them. (Hell, if Judge Judy can make the cut, I'd better be included.) Just before we went "live" with the interview, Diane Sawyer leaned over to me and said, "If you had to choose one song to sum up your whole life, what would it be?" I frantically mused for just an instant before the song popped into my mind: "For all we know, this may only be a dream; We come and go, like a ripple in a stream . . ."

So I'd like to tell my story now. I've actually been doing autobiography in front of the public for a long time, but the standards of memoir are daunting.

Memory is revisionist and selective by nature, and it is tempting to edit out the nasty, unflattering, what-was-I-thinking parts. "Tell it all, Mom," my elder daughter advised me. (Hell, no, I'd end up in jail.) I've given sobriquet to a few key players who don't deserve to have their names spelled right. This is how I remember it. And if my mother objects to any reminiscence in these pages . . . it didn't happen.

CHAPTER TWO

"Stay Puuuuure Vanilla"

THERE IS AN IMAGE ENGRAVED IN MY MEMORY vivid enough to evoke a smell (the red vinyl of a well-used armchair) and a sound (the flick of a cigarette holder against a metal ashtray): it's the image of a twelve-year-old me, gangly and no longer a towhead, much to the chagrin of my mother, who seemed to greet the natural darkening of my blonde hair as a dereliction of filial duty. Also to her dismay, I was utterly contemptuous of most girlish playthings but fanatically preoccupied with horses. The school librarian looked squint-eyed at me for years, suspecting I'd stolen a copy of *Olympic Horseman* (I had), and I saved up the nickels allocated for orange Creamsicles to buy miniature plastic horses and Black Stallion books at the Poplar Plaza Shopping Center. At times I morphed into equine behavior myself, cantering around the house with a jump rope in my mouth and a bath mat belted on as a saddle. I would make a steeplechase out of the hedges separating the yards on our street and neigh in response to questions. But owning a horse was an extravagance far beyond the middle-class means of my parents, for whom canned asparagus constituted a luxury. The necessary deep pockets were worn by my grandfather.

We called him Da-Dee (accent on the second syllable), and my grandmother was always Moma, resistant to the notion of being "Grandma" and relegating her own daughter to the more formal "Mother." Outside of the family, they were Cy and Tommy, both nick-named for their fathers. Norville Shapleigh "Cy" Shobe, the son of Missouri poultry farmers, was an electronics wizard, just a boy when he made front-page news in Kansas City by assembling the first homemade radio in the state—strangers from half a dozen counties drove right up to the porch in four-wheeled surreys to hear the raspy wonder of it. When the family moved to Arkansas, he fell in love with fifteen-year-old Gladys "Tommy" Toler, whose father owned a dry goods store, and married her within the year. (At the time, the term *child bride* was more custom than pejorative.) To the newlyweds, Memphis was The City, where the delta was said to begin in the gilded lobby of the Peabody Hotel, and it was the only place for a young man with prospects.

My grandfather was named for the hardware store where his father earned the money for the chicken farm, and it was with a letter of introduction from Mr. Shapleigh that he got a job interview in Memphis at Orgil Brothers Hardware, agreeing to be a salesman only if they would agree to sell radios. From there he started his own business distributing wholesale appliances, and it provided well: in 1950, the year I was born, Shobe, Inc., grossed $5 million, a fortune half a century ago. (The company logo, a rooster boasting "We're crowin' because we're growin'," was immortalized in various shades of red stained glass on the porch door of my grandparents' house.) It was this honeypot that could yield the horse and riding lessons I wanted. "You go on into the sitting room," Moma told me in a conspiratorial whisper, "and love up on Da-Dee's neck. He'll give you anything you want."

My grandfather was a lank and looming man, the angular contours of his body seeking out the familiar dents and curves of the red easy chair that served as his sanctum sanctorum in the second-floor study. His cherished pastimes were shooting and flying, and he sat beneath a gun rack and a pilots' flight map of the United States. There were hints of tobacco and chicoried coffee in his clothes as I climbed onto his lap, ludicrously big for such an assignment, and nuzzled against his neck with my request. At first he responded with a low growl, more theatrical than alarming, to my "pretty please with sugar on top," and his right hand tapped ashes off the Camel in its crystalline holder. Then the tiny pings stopped, and his muscular hands tightened around my skinny arms. He wouldn't answer, and he wouldn't let go. He held me down on his lap, his body stiffening. In some inchoate way, I knew to run from such an encounter, although I didn't recognize that it represented an exchange of money for feminine charms and wouldn't know until much later what such a transaction was called. All thoughts of a horse vaporized as I managed to wriggle out of his grasp. I ran from the room, his muffled laughter mocking my retreat.

Love up on Da-Dee's neck. More than any other fillip of memory, those words summon up the paramount message and mandate of my childhood: I was pretty, and my looks were a kind of currency. Nobody would care what I did, what I said, what I read, but beauty had magical powers, a kind of legerdemain especially effective with men. It was like being taught double-entry bookkeeping. At that moment I was to hug my grandfather not because it was good to express affection but because I had blonde and blue-eyed assets that might get me a horse.

Rather ironic, considering that I was not even supposed to be a girl. My mother had miscarried twice in the four years since my sister was born (christened Gladys, for Moma, but called Terry). Her unexpected pregnancy was ascribed with a sacred duty to provide my father with a son, but it was deemed a washout the moment the doctor peered at me and said, "It's a girl." (When Mother did produce a male heir four years later, she triumphed in a rare practical joke on my father, bringing my brother, Bill, home from the hospital with a pink ribbon Scotch-taped to his bald head—a small "up yours" to the intimation that boys were better than girls.)

Perhaps I sensed in vitro that my gender would come as a major disappointment to my family. I was in no hurry to enter the world and literally backed in, rear first (never the smallest part of my anatomy). "You were easy to deal with," Mother told me, "until you were born." She had gone to the Methodist Hospital when her water broke, naturally expecting contractions to start. When nothing much happened, she summoned my father from the clouds of cigar smoke in the waiting room and, in true iron butterfly spirit, went to have her hair washed and set at Gould's Beauty Parlor. She had just ordered mint tea and selected a pleasing tangerine frost for her nails when my position in the womb, called a frank breech, became apparent and progressed to a harrowing labor, for which Mother has yet to forgive me. I was born with a birth defect, a nerve tumor on the back of my neck that had to be removed. (Ironic that someone who would earn a living projecting an image of female flawlessness would get the first of a lifetime of scars before even leaving the hospital.) I remained "Girl Shepherd" for several days while my family debated what to call this female child, finally justifying my presence by combining the names of my grandfather (Cy) and father (Bill).

Well before I could have articulated it, I was instinctively aware of my assignment in the family: to be perfect. If I couldn't be a boy, at least I could be the über-female: pert, polite, charming, compliant, and above all, lovely to look at. (It was implicit that my sister was excused from this commission, being bigger, brawnier, and brunette.) Certainly I was not to say or do anything controversial or unladylike. "Siboney," my grandmother would intone, making a pet name out of the unofficial national anthem of Cuba where my grandparents often vacationed. "Don't go too far to the left or too far to the right. Stay in the middle of the road. Stay puuuuure vanilla." I wore white cotton gloves with smocked floral dresses. Against my vehe-

ment protests, my hair was tortured into a frightening
mass of deep-fried curls, which was considered more
feminine than my straight hair with the recalcitrant
wave in back. My godmother, Marie Hay, asked me to
select my silver pattern ("Chantilly") when I was ten,
and I learned to dance by standing on my father's
black and white wing tips, swaying to "Just the Way
You Look Tonight" while my mother primped for an
evening out. There was a limited choice of destinies
for a girl like me, with the distinct suggestion that life's
ultimate achievement was to be anointed the Maid of
Cotton, fetching symbol of Memphis's most important industry, or (spoken in reverential hushed tones)
Miss America, a possibility that might have justified
being born female.

All of which conflicted with my natural inclina-
tions. I jumped from the highest branch of trees, hiked
the old Shiloh military trail, and used a key worn on a
lanyard around the neck to tighten metal skates,
which left me with perennially bleeding elbows and
knees. I declined to brush my hair until compelled to
do so, and wore the same pair of tattered overalls until
they disappeared from my closet (my mother quietly
consigned them to incineration). To avoid getting
dressed, I streaked naked next door and sat on the
neighbors' porch swing until my mother came and got
me. Once I tried to please my mother by assembling
what I thought to be a decorous outfit: a pink dress
with puffed sleeves and my favorite red sneakers.
"Look, Shep," she called to my father, as if I had
placed a lampshade on my head, "she picked this out
herself." My grandfather would grasp my hands with
unedited distaste for my gnawed cuticles, saying, "You

can always tell a lady by her nails." I rejected all dolls, especially the busty new Barbies coveted by my prepubescent crowd, all of us still wearing Fruit Of The Loom T-shirts over flat chests, and when my brother got electric trains (derisively telling me, "That's for boys"), I sulked for weeks and contemplated various means of derailment. (He also got a cross-country turnpike set, a Rin Tin Tin badge, and a Fort Apache. I got talcum powder and a bath mitt.)

The tomboy temperament that vexed my mother helped forge a bond with my father, even after my brother came along. He endorsed my interest in sports, didn't think it was weird to toss a football with me on the front lawn, gave me a baseball glove, and shared the sacrament of rubbing the leather with oil and shaping it by letting it spend the night cupping a ball. He even exulted when I beat the crap out of a bully named Chris Crump (as much crap as a whiffle bat could extract) for holding my little brother's hand in an anthill. In those years when I was a surrogate son, my father let me accompany him on Saturdays to the warehouse he ran for Da-Dee, when it was quiet enough to roll a secretary's swivel chair up and down the aisles. He taught me to swim by buckling on an orange Mae West and dropping me off the end of the pier at my grandparents' summer home.

For the great French writer Marcel Proust, the door of memory was opened by the taste of a madeleine cookie. For me, it's Dr Pepper: one sip, and I am returned to that summer house on a slender tributary of the Tennessee River in Alabama called Shoals Creek. It was built in the 1930s as a hunting lodge on a remote promontory near a forest of cedar, pine, and burr oak, but the original owner felt too isolated and sold the five-acre property to my grandfather for the 1950 bargain price of $35,000. As a toddler who couldn't pronounce the letter *l*, I called it the "yake house," and the moniker stuck with the whole family. On the four-hour drive from Memphis, we stopped at filling stations with green glass jars of sour pickles for sale by the cash register. (I could make a pickle last all day. The goal was to suck out the insides but maintain the outer shell so you could blow it up like a balloon, make it breathe. I'd find the jettisoned ends of pickles under my sister's bed.) Da-Dee arrived in a style more befitting the lord of the manor, landing his own twin-engine Beechcraft Bonanza on an airstrip across the creek and announcing his presence by buzzing the house from the air so that Moma would be waiting on the tarmac when he touched down.

In the early summer mornings, before the humidity would slap down like a biblical plague, Da-Dee and I got up before the others to sit in penumbral shadow on the long screened porch and watch the choppy surface of the water become streaked with first light, which looked like thousands of glittering broken mirrors, so bright that we had to squint. We'd wad up some day-old bread, stick the gummy ball on a hook and line at the end of a cane fishing pole, then plop into the reclining chairs on the pier and wait for the bite of catfish and bream and crappie (a delicacy not yet appreciated by chic chefs). I was the only one in the family with enough guts to eat calves brains and eggs with Da-Dee. There was a huge black cauldron in a tarp-covered clearing near the house for deep-frying fish and hush puppies, the crisp puffs of cornmeal meant to placate dogs driven mad by cooking smells but appropriated by smart humans. Moma kept baby goats, which ate up the shrubbery, and peacocks whose shrill reveille I learned to imitate with ear-splitting accuracy, and hens that roosted in the trees at night, but these were more pets than livestock. Dinner was often an anonymous quail or duck shot by Da-Dee (there were usually a few vanquished carcasses hanging in the kitchen), and we never sat down to a summer meal that didn't include tomatoes, often fried green tomatoes, even at breakfast. I took the red paisley bandannas that served as napkins and made streamers for my bike or slings for a fake broken arm.

It was there at Shoals Creek that my grandfather seemed most content, only vaguely morose. He would lapse into a private reverie, occasionally broken with an enigmatic aphorism ("Everythang's gonna be allll right") said as much to himself as to anyone else. I never considered his taciturn manner an indication of a dissatisfied soul—he had every conceivable creature comfort and was coddled by the sort of wife who put the cuff links in his shirts every day. Years later my father told me that he imagined the wistful cast in Da-Dee's eye was a woman named Daisy, ensconced in a downtown Memphis apartment with my grandfather's name on the lease. When Moma found prima facie evidence of the affair, she sent his suitcase to the Peabody Hotel, then thought better of it. I heard that she threatened to study taxidermy and mount the stuffed and formaldehyded bodies of Da-Dee and his mistress alongside the deer head over the massive stone fireplace at the yake house. Daisy disappeared, as did a certain kick-ass vigor in my grandfather's spirit. He mentioned her name in the narcotic musings of his deathbed, when I guess he felt he had nothing left to lose or hide.

Moma was not about to abdicate from the perquisites of an indulgent marriage, exemplified by more than a hundred pairs of shoes filling three closets—a tottering chronicle of fashion victimization that ranged from Duchess-of-Windsor bejeweled to Chiquita-banana tacky. Years later I learned about one source of her shoe fetish: back home for a visit, I was exploring the Memphis Yacht Club, the hyperbolic term for what was then a series of wooden boathouses strung together with steel cable and wired with yellow lights to keep the bugs away. I was shocked to see a sailboat tacking back and forth across the Mississippi River. Sailing on the Mississippi? What kind of nutcase would try that? There's a constant traffic of enormous barges, several city blocks long, that move huge amounts of water out of their way, and it takes these behemoths thirty minutes to stop, often sucking smaller vessels into their wake like helpless anchovies. The current runs strong only one way over treacherous whirlpools, and the depths of the muddy water can be deceptive. So it was axiomatic that nobody would try to navigate the river without at least one engine. The mad sailor turned out to be a devilishly handsome silver fox named Smith. When I reported our meeting to Moma, she got a dreamy look in her eyes and said, "Oh, that's Smitty from the Julius Lewis Department Store. I must have bought fifty pairs of shoes from that man."

Most of her wardrobe came, apparently without erotic subtext, from The Helen Shop: sherbet-colored chiffon sheaths for charity balls, pearl-buttoned cashmere cardigans, scarves to match every outfit, a prized chinchilla stole—all supported by a long-line girdle that redistributed a thickish waist from bust line to just above the knees. There was one set of noises when she was putting it on and another when she was desperately pulling it off, the indicia of zippers and garters pressed into flesh like thumbprints in yeast dough. In one of her closets were two tan leather suitcases with yellow knit bows on the handles, kept packed at all times in case Da-Dee had an urge to fly off for a "rendezvous," one of the parties held by the Sportsmen Pilots Association all over the country, with buffet tables set up right in the hangar. I got taken along once as a teenager, and the gin and tonics started before the propellers stopped spinning.

Like me, Moma had been something of a jock, a predilection uncommon to her generation, until a heart attack in her forties curtailed all sports but golf. I liked to play with her trophies from country club tournaments, topped with tiny gold-plated figurines of sturdy women swinging drivers over their heads. Ladies' Day at the clubhouse was the only time I saw my grandmother in pants, the kind of clothes I appreciated. She hated the female liturgy of the beauty parlor, preferring her own Aqua Net, and claimed she owed her baby pink complexion to a nightly smear of Lady Esther cold cream—once a week she left it on all day long, walking around the house with a greasy mask. Years before, according to the fashion of the times, she had plucked out her eyebrows and had to draw them back on. I would watch her apply the Max Factor brownish-black eyebrow pencil as we sang a duet of "Jesus Loves Me, This I Know," with me doing the harmony part. Moma loved music more than anything, and growing up she taught herself to play the church organ. I never visited her house that she didn't sit down either at her organ or her piano to accompany us kids singing the gospel hymns of her childhood. A few years after my grandmother's death, my mother came across a note scrawled on a yellow legal pad concerning Moma's only regret: that she hadn't "followed up and done something with her music." She was always urging me to do what she called those "sweet songs" like "Michael Row the Boat Ashore," and at her insistence I sang it as my talent portion of the Miss Teenage Memphis Pageant.

Moma grew up in the small rural town of Carlyle, Arkansas. The churchyard was kept at full occupancy by the influenza epidemic of 1918, which claimed her mother when Moma was only seven. Startled by an unusual thump coming from the parlor where the body was laid out, she refused to accept that the window had slammed shut, believing that the coffin had been tumbled off a table by ghosts, and engendering a fear of spectral spirits that was not completely dissipated in adulthood. The care of three younger siblings fell to this child, with devastating consequences: baby sister Edith crawled too near a fireplace, and her leg was so severely burned that it was amputated above the knee. As a child I was fascinated by her prosthesis and was always trying to get a peek of it or her without it. But Great-Aunt Edith never let her false leg keep her down. She became a graceful dancer, married Saul Byarly, who printed the *Arkansas Gazette*, and had four impressively achieving children: an airline pilot, a doctor, a lawyer, and a chief nurse in cardiovascular surgery.

As adolescent lady of the house, Moma enjoyed certain benefits along with the burdens, partnering her widowed father at every rural shindig. When her position was subsumed by a stepmother, she began a rebellion of such ornery defiance that she once ate an entire shipment of green bananas meant for the store and was sent to live in a Little Rock boardinghouse owned by a family friend. With only one line left on her dance card at the DeMoolay Young Men's Organization, she caught the eye of a hulking blond boy with elephantine ears and a killer smile, two years older and ready for a wife. Perhaps she saw marriage to a clever and ambitious fly-boy as her ticket to ride. Moma and Da-Dee crisscrossed every square mile of the delta in his plane, which was red canvas covered with two open-air cockpits. Having baby Patricia Cornelia Shobe didn't much crimp their style; my mother was often left on the farm with grandparents who doted on her, waiting for her parents to swoop down in a cleared field and pick her up. I have a photograph of Patty, Tommy, and Cy when my mother was a toddler; they look like the American dream, an enviable portrait worthy of a cereal box or a postage stamp.

The custodial grandmother, Clara Shobe, was known as Ma-Maw. Every Sunday morning she chose the plumpest chicken in the yard, casually wringing its neck for dinner, and the storm cellar was lined with Mason jars of her bread-and-butter pickles and Prohibition "home brew." My grandfather, the electronics wizard, made sure they had the first telephone in those parts and installed a gas range, but Ma-Maw preferred the old woodstove and wouldn't let him remove it. With their only son gone, the older couple adopted a series of orphans who helped satisfy my mother's endless yearning for siblings. On summer nights, she caught lightning bugs in a canning jar and put their illuminated tails on the boys' model planes.

Patty Shobe was not destined for animal husbandry but for husbandry of another kind. In 1943, she was engaged to an air force bombardier who was the scion of a prominent Memphis banking family. Like all the young ladies in the area, she dug a pretty dress out of the cedar closet and went to help entertain the servicemen at the Millington Naval Air Station, where her father was serving as head flight instructor. A handsome young cadet saw her swaying to Glenn Miller and asked her to dance. He was William Jennings Shepherd from Buckingham Courthouse, Virginia. (The town took the name of its most prestigious edifice, which was designed by Thomas Jefferson, but was so small that it reported only two surnames to the census: Spencer and Shepherd.)

"Do you know Cy Shobe?" Patty asked her dance partner. "He's my father."

"Oh, c'mon," Shep answered. "I've had five girls tell me that tonight." Apparently my grandfather's name was invoked to ensure proper behavior from any man dancing with his "daughter."

Bill Shepherd's mother and grandmother had died on the same day, both from cervical cancer, surely evoking disturbing feelings about female fragility and creating a powerful urge for someone to ply the womanly arts in his life, to do the caretaking. He proposed to Patty on their third date, saying he urgently needed an answer before being assigned overseas. When she accepted, the two of them made an appointment to see her former fiancé's father at the bank, carrying a Dear John letter to be forwarded. Her guilt at writing "I'm sorry I've fallen in love with someone else" was compounded when she was told the bombardier had just been shot down over Germany and was a prisoner of war. My father never did get shipped out; the POW returned a war hero and married a childhood friend of Mother's. More than fifty years later, this woman sometimes encounters my mother in Memphis and sighs, "You know, Patty, he's still in love with you."

It was simply taken for granted that my father would go to work at Shobe, Inc. (his only experience had been on a high school football field and in the cockpit of a pilot trainer), but that opportunity dissolved into a classic scenario of the son-in-law who feels gotten for cheap. Dinnertime at my house was often punctuated by his tirades about Shobe stinginess, despite his ascension from warehouse stock boy to executive vice president. "Nobody's told the son of a bitch that the slaves were freed a hundred years ago," he railed. "How's it fair that he lives so high on the hog while we eat chitlins?"

My parents must have been salivating when they went to Little Rock to help settle the estate of Da-Dee's Aunt Diloma, one of the first women in Arkansas to work for the phone company. Jilted by her fiancé, she lived with Dickensian eccentricity: she continued in her job for half a century, a stylish woman in cinch-waisted suits and a Gibson-girl pompadour (her fifty-year employee pin is still hanging from my mother's charm bracelet), but she talked to cows and secreted money in mattresses and walls. Da-Dee got most of the cash, plus a fortune in AT&T stock, hidden in burlap tobacco sacks, and my parents hoped some of the windfall might trickle down to them. The Shobes denied themselves little but acted as if gifts to their only child and grandchildren were debts to be grudgingly paid. Maybe they couldn't forget that in Memphis, unless your money came from King Cotton, you weren't rich, just nouveau. Maybe the Depression mentality endemic to their generation had ripened into a canon about the perversity of the universe, which holds that good luck is transient and bad times last forever. Maybe it was just a pissing contest between my father and grandfather. But the Shobes had little talent for sharing.

Most of my childhood was spent in a one-story brick house on Highland Park Place (you could stand at the front door and see straight through to the backyard) with a fake fireplace mantel, plastic violets in a vase, and a mechanical bird that sang in a cage (a gift from my grandmother). One of the few genuine furnishings was a leather-top table that became a disaster of watermarks from cocktail glasses. My mother pasted S&H green stamps into books and redeemed them at the catalog store on Union Street for a prized lamp with a silk shade. I took a cold bath on nights when my sister's rank as firstborn gave her priority and there wasn't enough hot water to fill the tub a second time. Neither was there money for the piano lessons I wanted, much less the instrument itself. So I borrowed my grandmother's old ukulele and songbook I found in her attic and taught myself everything from "In the Evening by the Moonlight" to "Ja-Da." Whenever my parents had guests, they insisted I entertain. When I finished my songs everyone always seemed slightly underwhelmed. This definitely eroded my confidence, but nothing, it seemed, would ever stop me from singing: It was something I just had to do, like walking or breathing.

My grandparents, by sharp contrast, had a piano and organ in each of their three homes (Memphis, Shoals Creek, and Fort Lauderdale), including one painted Moma's favorite cherry red. (My mother detested the color, and after my grandmother's death, I was given the red organ on the condition that I have it refinished.) When I was ten, we got a tabletop keyboard with a fake wood veneer and a songbook showing how to push preset "chord" buttons. The spine of the book was permanently opened to the two melodies that got played ten times a day: "On Top of Old Smokey" for Terry, "Liebenstraum" for me. (When I first saw the title of the song, I thought it was an ode to Liederkranz, the stinky cheese my mother loved but my father banned from the house.)

Less than a mile but light-years away was my grandparents' elegant three-story Tudor house on East Drive, with an S for Shobe on the awnings, harlequin print drapes at the windows, jewel-toned Oriental carpets, and crystal chandeliers. The silverware was gold-plated, and the furniture was made of rich woods, rather too grandly ornate and ostentatious for my tastes (then or now) but substantial in a way that represented money. Visiting was entry to Valhalla, seductive but tenuous. They financed what they considered good for business or social standing, like membership for my family at the Chickasaw Country Club, even though the monthly dues took food off our table. As a child, I gorged on several grilled cheese sandwiches a day at the poolside café and an astonishing tomato ice cream in the dining room, and I stood under the shower in the ladies' locker room for an hour at a time, never running out of hot water as I did at home.

The family business being appliances, my grandparents bragged that they had a television in every room, even the bathroom (competing in entertainment value with a book called *Jokes for the John* that lived on top of the wicker hamper). My parents did achieve some permanent prestige on Highland Park Place with the first TV on our block (perpetually tuned to wrestling or *Dragnet*) and the first air conditioner (installed in my parents' bedroom, where all of us gathered when the August heat sucked the breath out of our own rooms). We participated in the careless abundance of my grandparents' lives, like the wondrous fruit ambrosia with marshmallows, coconut, and pecans, or the three kinds of turkey dressing and cavalcade of pies at Thanksgiving.

Perhaps it was only the disparity with my grandparents' groaning table, but I never felt that there was enough to eat at home, with only rare trips to those exotic pleasure palaces: the Joy Young Chop Suey restaurant and Pappy's Lobster Shack. What we never ran out of was pickles, pork rinds, and canned Vienna sausages, and we ate a lot of "falling off the stool" eggs (soft-boiled and mashed with butter), so named because my brother fell backward off the stool the first time Mother made them. About once a month my grandmother would take me to the "curb market," where local farmers brought their produce to town.

She'd buy a big bag of wild greens called "polk salad," which she described as a spring tonic (the digestive equivalent of spring cleaning), and we got thinly sliced ham sandwiches slathered with mayonnaise from a large man with the improbable name of Mr. Ham.

My mother had a taste for sophisticated foods like artichokes that weren't popular in the South, but these were so expensive that she examined our plates for microscopic edible morsels possibly overlooked. ("You haven't cleaned that leaf," she'd say. "Do you know how much it cost?") I scrounged food with the thrift and cunning of the Artful Dodger, stealing from my brother's dish when he looked the other way and licking the pots and pans before washing them.

Half a mile away, in the home of my best friend Jane Howard, there was a ubiquitous earthenware crock of homemade pimiento cheese, and okra stewed with tomatoes, and endless rashers of bacon for breakfast—only part of the salvation she provided in my life. Jane and I bonded in the fifth grade when, as teacher's pet, she was given the honored responsibility of collecting the girls' purses after lunch, to be stowed in a closet during recess—a pile of child-size pastel plastics and black patent leather. She needed an assistant and chose me. Very soon we discovered our mutual passion for reading everything from the Nancy Drew mysteries to Emily Brontë's *Wuthering Heights*.

Jane and I defied the carefully delineated job description for southern female adolescence. "Those girls have too much fun," a neighbor observed to my mother. (Jane continued this pattern with my children, whom she taught to burp on cue, her theory being that there are some things in life you just need to know.) I was awed by her ability to shoplift licorice by stuffing a huge wad of it in her mouth, and when she failed to grasp the concept of grapefruit segmenting in home ec., she glued her botched slices back together, to the outrage of Mrs. Kernodel. We played soldiers in the musty third-floor attic of my grandparents' house with German military memorabilia—some of the men who trained under Da-Dee must have brought the souvenirs back at the end of the war. We joined the Brownies, thinking that we were going to whittle and tie knots and light campfires, but the troop leader thought it more valuable to learn proper place settings, and her idea of an interesting craft project was waterproofing paper bags from the Piggly-Wiggly grocery with shellac so we could sit on the ground without sullying our uniforms.

I got admonished and ousted by parents and teachers for a lot of Jane-inspired misconduct (the only time I got sent to the principal's office was after Jane double-dog-dared me to slide down the school banister), but she often got away clean and had an enviable ability to defy grown-up rules and constraints without seeming insolent. My mother once tried to enlist her help in clearing the detritus of an evening at home— the empty bottles of Wild Turkey left like deflowered vases on the windowsill, the stale stubs of cigarettes heaped so high in ceramic ashtrays that they'd spill on the way to the trash can. "I'm sorry, Mrs. Shepherd," Jane said, "but I didn't make this mess and I'm not cleaning it up."

At eleven o'clock every day, my mother had a Coca-Cola, which I sometimes prepared to her specifications: the ice-cold soda had to be poured like beer down the side of a tall glass to preserve every bit of carbonation. There were slightly different regulations for cocktails: I was taught to select the right highball glass (squat but not too squat), measure out a jigger of Scotch and fill the glass with ice, leaving just a little room for water. I never saw Mother drink a beer, but once when I knocked someone else's beer off a tray, my mother said, "That's the best thing you can spill because the smell doesn't stay in the carpet." (I still say that but have no idea if it's true.)

In my family, the happy hour began before noon on weekends with Bloody Marys, by sundown on the average weekday. Drinking was a subject of unabashed levity, without menacing undercurrents. There was a gag clock at the lake house bearing the epigram NO DRINKS BEFORE 5, the punch line being fives at every point on the dial, and cocktail napkins imprinted with whimsical instructions on "How to Recover from a Hangover." Da-Dee had a full bar in the room back behind his office, a dimly lit tabernacle to the manly creeds of liquor and cocksmanship, with a plaque praising "men who come together and find contentment before capacity." I liked to sneak up onto the tall bar stools and touch the beer mugs that had naked ladies as handles.

Da-Dee's drinking followed a predictable and not very alarming pattern, winding down to sullen solitude. Moma just tried to keep up with him. One night at the lake house when I awakened to hear virulent cursing, my sister informed me it was a bogeyman from the bottom of the lake (she had recently been impressed by readings about the Loch Ness monster).

But the disturbance was just Moma, roaring drunk
and attempting to move a sofa upstairs by herself. She
gave up drinking for twenty years, then started taking
"just a sip" of wine, ending up with a twelve-ounce
tumbler and turning the basement into a wine cellar,
the ceiling covered with clusters of plastic grapes and
stocked solely with her favorite Blue Nun.

It was said, in a jocular tone, that my father could
find his way driving home by feeling for the curb with
his foot. One Thanksgiving he passed out in the front
vestibule, the door wedged open by his inert body until a chilly draft alerted the household. My brother
grabbed his arms, my sister and I his ankles, dragging
him far enough inside to close the door, then we
turned out the lights and ignored the phone, pretending that no one was home. During their parties I huddled in bed under an inadequate bunting of
protection provided by my nubby white chenille
spread. With cotton balls stuffed in my ears, I sang to
drown out the raucous laughter from downstairs.

One morning I awoke to find a huge oval crater in
the wall outside my parents' bedroom. My mother
had locked my father out, and in his attempt to force
the door open, he ricocheted backward, pushing his
body through the opposite wall. The hole was plas-
tered and painted over the next day, but we all knew it
was there, like pentimento on an artists' reused canvas. My legacy from this incident is a recurring nightmare: I run from door to never-ending door of the
house where I grew up, frantically making sure
they're all locked, but there's always one I don't get to
before someone or something gets in, and I wake up
screaming.

Men of my father's generation never heard the expression "What part of 'no' didn't you understand?" As an adult, I have come to know that there is a place between consenting partners where "no" can be erotic, and that sexual fantasies don't have to be politically correct. The sounds of sex are confusing to a child, who can't distinguish between pleasure and pain. Once when I tried to come between my parents, my father flung me out of his way and then roared "The hell with both of you" as he lurched from the room. And I still can't explain or forget the time I walked into my parents' bedroom and found my mother weeping while my father and grandfather stood near the end of her bed, laughing.

Without warning, the loving man who coached my softball team and taught me to dance and painted my rusty bicycle bright red like new would disappear, and I knew instinctively to stay away from the drunken impostor who took his place. Logically, I thought, if the poison that made him act crazy wasn't in the house, my real father would prevail, so one night I took all the bottles from the bar and stashed them creatively— beneath sofa cushions and inside the zippered stuffed animal that was the "pajama buddy" on my bed. He found the bottle I'd stowed under the sink and mumbled something about being lucky that he hadn't drunk the drain cleaner in the "new" liquor cabinet.

The morning after one of these episodes, my father would come down to the kitchen with amnesia, smooth-shaven over a gray pallor. He'd skulk up behind my mother, encircling her waist with his arm, and give her neck a quick kiss. She'd elbow him away, her voice taking on a noticeably defeated tone as she got breakfast ready, making the choice between Kellogg's Frosted Flakes and Rice Krispies sound like a matter of critical attention. My father poured his own coffee and settled behind the newspaper, pretending not to notice the punitive silent treatment.

As if by consensus, my siblings and I ignored the frisson between my parents and never discussed the family drinking patterns, except that we referred to Moma and Da-Dee's Florida condominium as Fort Liquordale. Sometimes my grandparents, for the moment lucid and sober themselves, herded us into their white Cadillac, its leather seats the color of coffee ice cream, and gave safe harbor. Moma would put us in a guest bedroom and bring us thin-sliced raw potatoes and radishes in ice water while we watched *What's My Line*. Our tacit contract matched the adults' denial: if we didn't name the problem, maybe it wasn't true, or would just go away, and it wasn't really polite to mention it anyway. Southern etiquette requires no validation of unpleasantness, the kind of social myopia related in a quirky story called "My Mother's Dead Squirrel" (everyone ignores the stiffened creature on the sofa out of a sense of good manners).

Our family turmoil seemed to go unobserved in the other houses on Highland Park Place. The chief of police, who lived across the street, just called his customary "Morning, Shep" to my father as they both left for work. I was a little blonde ornament high in many trees on our block; sometimes climbing a neighbor's elm was the safest harbor from my parents' warfare.

I did not ascribe any special significance to the delivery of new twin beds for my parents, just like the ones Lucy and Ricky Ricardo had. It was unthinkable that a marriage (theirs or anybody's except Elizabeth Taylor's) could be vulnerable. Parents weren't supposed to be happy or unhappy, satisfied or not, and the word *dysfunctional* was not part of the common parlance. Their old double bed was moved into the room that my sister and I shared, and it was thrilling, at the age of four, to leave my baby bed, to finger the fat puffs of faded blue quilting on the big new headboard. I was already under the covers when Terry turned in for the night, and I reached out to cuddle against her, but she kicked me away and pummeled me with her fists, yelling, "Leave me alone." Hugging a few inches of mattress edge, I whimpered all night.

When my father saw my bruised shins and redrimmed eyes, he made Terry bend over, hands to ankles, and walloped her with his belt. She incurred a similar punishment every time she chased me around the house and attacked me, which was often because I regularly provoked her (awfully dumb, since she was older, bigger, stronger, and faster). I hid over a floor furnace in the hallway outside the den every time she was punished, talking to my plastic horses while my sister yelped, determined to avoid such punishment myself. I, Miss Perfect, rarely got whipped: my most egregious sins were repeatedly scribbling in crayon on the living room wall and taunting my brother to bite me, then telling on him when he did. The spankings came to an end when I stopped crying.

My sister had every right to be jealous over my designation as "the pretty one" in the family, but I was hardly her only target—she once took a hammer to the TV because the picture kept rolling across the screen. I wonder if her aggression wasn't the inevitable result when kids are asked to be the container for family turbulence. My brother and I were close playmates until he reached puberty and made an early emotional defection from the family. All our attempts at building bridges seemed to fail. For a while we went for counseling together, and at one session the therapist suggested, "Draw an imaginary line around yourself showing how close you want people to get." When I made a circle about fifteen inches away from my body, my brother looked stricken. "I don't know why you'd shut me out like that," he said.

I've never stopped mourning how my sister and brother were lost to me at an early age, in ways that have been difficult to recoup even with adult understanding—a wound that wouldn't be cauterized. I knew I was loved by our parents, perhaps loved better than Terry or Bill because I tried so hard to be perfect. But our sibling relationships were defined and limited by our mutual needs to survive and to contain the secrets of our fragmented lives. When there's so much anarchy, so much hidden in a family, the natural ability to bond and establish meaningful connections is broken because it's every man for himself.

And yet each Sunday we answered the carillon bells of a city that was reputed to have more churches than gas stations. We washed our tearstained faces and put on clothes that smelled of Niagara starch, to sit in sanctified silence at Holy Communion Episcopal Church. I sang in the choir, a perfect perch for looking at my family in a front pew, miserable but spit-shined behind a Donna Reed facade. Whatever tempest had been weathered at home, I would feel renewed and forgiven after church, caught up in the exotic, quasi-erotic imagery of eating the body and drinking the blood of Jesus Christ. The Holy Communion itself, that most blessed of sacraments, seemed to speak directly to me: "Almighty God from whom no secrets are hid, cleanse the thoughts of our hearts." I made Faustian bargains in silent prayers: *I'll be good, just please make Terry stop hitting me, please make Mother and Dad stop fighting, please make everybody stop drinking. I'll be good, I'll be so, so good.*

Of course, I was almost a teenager, and good was out of the question.

CHAPTER THREE

"Going All the Way"

IF THERE'S A LIE TO BE TOLD ABOUT SEX, I'VE told it, although never to get a job or to get even, mostly to have more sex. I suspect I've spent a lifetime trying to rewrite my mother's chary lessons on the subject. When I was ten, I interrupted her in the bathroom as she lathered her legs for shaving, one foot poised on the edge of the tub, and seized the occasion to ask where babies came from. Screwing up her face with displeasure, she said, "The man takes his thing and puts it in there," pointing somewhere in the vicinity of the shaving cream, making it clear that she found the whole matter repugnant and had no intention of elaborating.

In the night table next to my mother's bed, I found a copy of *Lady Chatterley's Lover* and thrilled to see words never uttered in polite southern society (although "John Thomas" was lost on me). Jane helped to supplement our carnal knowledge by filching her family's pictorial edition of *Gone With the Wind*, which contained many heaving bosoms and taught us that sex was about a thrashing Scarlett O'Hara being carried to a scene of conjugal rape. Only slightly more descriptive was the compulsory sex education given in the same school basement where I'd gone to kindergarten. Tedious anatomical drawings were shown on an 8-millimeter projector: a triangular patch of womb, spots with kite tails swimming along tubes. Sperm and eggs were anthropomorphized with the same male and female traits assigned to southern men and women: the sperm described as aggressive, the eggs as almost demure. There was no discussion of pleasure, certainly no mention of female orgasm or of a moral compass offered beyond the oxymoronic: don't do it before you get married, and don't be a cock teaser.

I hadn't a clue why there was blood on my underpants at camp the summer I was eleven—Mother had skipped that subject altogether. I imagined it as a stigmata, a penance for willful tomboyishness, or perhaps evidence of a rare and incurable gastrointestinal disorder. I padded myself with toilet paper until a teenaged counselor discovered I was the source of the cabin's TP shortage and provided a long overdue biology lesson. When I summoned up the courage to report my new status as a woman to my mother, she shook her head in commiseration, muttering something about "the curse." In the school bathroom, I would stand frozen in the stall, working up the courage to walk nonchalantly to the wastebasket with my wrapped-up sanitary napkin. I cannot overestimate the significance of the invention of flushable tampons.

Before menstruation, I was physical and athletic

and strong. I could run, jump, climb higher than any boy. I earned Shark Club membership at camp (for swimming the most laps) and wrestled with the lifeguards at the pool in unbridled horseplay. Suddenly I had no choice but to act like a lady, which seemed like a dangerous narrowing of perspectives. Whatever lessons in personal deportment were not covered at home I learned in charm school at the country club, a virtual petri dish of southern womanhood. I sat with the other daughters of members in collapsible bridge chairs, practicing how to cross my legs at the ankles, balancing books on my head to achieve the proper floating, ladylike gait: shoulders back, chest out, chin up. Occasionally we'd test-drive our newly honed skills at coed dance classes: giggly girls with bad home perms and pimply boys with castrati voices, slouching awkwardly and improbably through the bossa nova, the Lili Marlene, the bunny hop, balling the jack.

My body seemed to change before my eyes. One year my breasts were embarrassingly too big and the next year they weren't big enough. Advertisements were touting the wonders of Cross-Your-Heart bras and 18 Hour panty girdles. It was definitely not considered ladylike to have a butt that jiggled under my clothes, and it was particularly mortifying to be observed by Da-Dee, who leered at my new shape and said, "Cybill, you're getting yourself a T-heinie." When he announced his intention to give me a twenty-gauge shotgun for my twelfth birthday and take me to the Memphis Gun Club to shoot trap and skeet, my mother considered it a royal edict and high honor. I was thrilled at the prospect of having my own gun, but it was impossible to explain the uneasiness I felt in my grandfather's presence, and I pressed myself against the passenger door when I rode with him to target practice.

Mother may have taken a pass on sex education, but her imparted wisdom about beauty was exacting. "Honey, you've got to suffer to be beautiful," she'd say as she drove me to Lowenstein's department store for underwire bras, depositing me in a draped dressing room and smoking a cigarette with the bored saleswoman while I stuffed reluctant breasts into unforgiving elastic. My mother wrapped her freshly coiffed hair in toilet paper at bedtime, but I slept with fat brush rollers digging into my scalp. On several occasions, I found my sister sound asleep, wearing the pale pink plastic hood of a bonnet-style hair dryer, attached to a heat-conducting hose. I once awoke to the smell of something burning and shook Terry to tell her that her bonnet was melting.

Even as I understood that beauty was armored protection in my family, a cosseted thing that guaranteed my status as the perfect child, I seemed determined to imperil it with some regularity. I never saw the rusty filament of barbed wire sticking out of the vine-covered fence I was trying to scale on my aunt Gwen's farm and didn't notice the blood pouring down the front of my new white vinyl snap-up jacket, only the pale look of horror on my mother's face when she saw the triangle of flesh dangling from my upper lip. It was my great good fortune that the doctor on call in the emergency room of the local county hospital refused to sew me up, recognizing that a plastic surgeon's hands were called for. I lay on the backseat of our station wagon with an ice pack until we got to Memphis and Dr. Lee Haines, who put over two hundred stitches into an area half the size of a dime. I went home with a huge dark lump crisscrossed with black thread, and when I cried as I looked in the mirror, the tears washed over the shiny, gooey salve, carrying a foul medicinal taste into my mouth. But my own horrified reflection was no worse than the revulsion I saw on the faces of my parents and grandparents. I hid when the doorbell rang, sure that the neighbors were asking, "Whatever happened to that pretty girl?" It took three years for the scar to heal, leaving a faint triangular line below my nostrils, but I learned an important lesson about the transience of beauty: in the blink of an eye, my unique family position was jeopardized. Disfigurement was not lovable. And I would never be perfect again.

I singed off my eyelashes and eyebrows when I tried to light the gas grill of our backyard barbecue, but I dutifully rubbed them with petroleum jelly, a therapy I'd used on horses to help their hair grow in over scars. When my lashes came back longer and thicker, Mother stopped just short of recommending conflagration as a beauty treatment to her friends. In her continuing obsession with my hair color, she marveled at a new product called Summer Blonde.

"This is great," she said in a hushed tone as she hurried me into the bathroom with the box of magical elixir. "All you do is spray it on, and we don't have to worry about your hair getting darker ever again."

My whole life I had encountered disbelief when I insisted that my hair color was natural. Now I would have to lie. "What am I going to say when people ask if I dye my hair?" I fretted.

"This is not dye," she insisted. "It's a lightener, just like sitting in the sun." With maternal endorsement for the white lie, I dutifully sprayed on what I discovered, only years later when the FDA became more rigorous about labeling, to be peroxide.

Shopping with my mother usually involved the Casual Corner on Union Avenue, then lunch at the Pig 'n Whistle Bar-B-Q, where she'd gone as a girl. The implicit uniform of junior high consisted of a white oxford cloth blouse, circle pin at the rounded collar, cabled cardigan sweater with matching knee-socks, and plaid wraparound skirt. The outfit had to include black and white saddle shoes or Bass Weejuns (I favored tassels over penny loafers, since I could never squeeze the coins in the allotted slots). We were fashion lemmings so early in the game, but occasionally I was downright rebellious. Once I got sent home from school for wearing culottes, which were deemed too closely related to pants. The assistant principal called my mother to say, "Please come pick up your daughter and have her return in a skirt." Mother thought it was ridiculous and took me out for barbecue.

She didn't know she was quoting Dorothy Parker when she said, "Men seldom make passes at girls who wear glasses," but I knew there were no Barbie dolls with spectacles. I was fifteen when I failed the eye exam for my driver's permit, and my mother, refusing to believe the results, got a family friend who was an eye doctor to write a note certifying that I did not need glasses to drive. This explanation did not impress the civil servant at the Tennessee Highway Patrol, nor did my failing the eye exam a second time. I was finally permitted to consult an optometrist for the glasses I so

obviously required—I'd been squinting at black-
boards, movie screens, and my competition on the
basketball court for years. Mother sat next to me while
I was fitted with owlish round black frames, a stoic
look of loss and resignation on her face, the reflection
of the perfect daughter created in her image once
again marred. When I reported passing the eye exam
on my third try, she said "Fine" in a dull tone that implied nothing fine at all.

The commandments of beauty seemed even more
stringent than those of the church, but I didn't have to
wait for the hereafter to reap the rewards. Despite my
glasses, the boys did make passes. And I was a born receiver.

I CAN TAKE A TRIP DOWN MEMORY LANE JUST BY
walking past the men's cologne counter of any department store. English Leather—that's Mike. Canoe—
that's Sam. Jade East—that's Lawrence. British
Sterling . . .

I did not vomit from my first kiss, but I spit into the
sink for a good five minutes and then used half a tube
of Crest. I was fourteen and it was at night on my front
porch, after a Memphis Chicks minor league baseball
game. I had gotten tired of watching the make-out
scene from the sidelines and vowed to get it over with.

You might think I'd been vaccinated against drinking from the examples at home, but when I was fifteen
I went along with the group that trawled Joe's Liquors
looking for someone who could be bribed into buying
us quarts of Miller Black Label. An old man leaning
against the store's gyrating *Sputnik*-shaped neon sign

was easily persuaded, and my few ounces of the pur-
loined stuff, guzzled out of the bottle in a brown paper
bag, created a quick buzz. I found myself dancing to
"When a Man Loves a Woman" and nuzzling against
the sweet-smelling neck of a nineteen-year-old boy
with a doughy little cleft where his chin should be,
Mick Jagger lips, and bleached blond hair cut in a
long mop. When Mike picked me up for a movie date
a few days later, he displayed excellent credentials for
a first boyfriend: my parents hated him on sight.

My tradition of sex and lies began when I started
sneaking out to see Mike using Jane as an alibi. Jane
owed me big time since I had saved her from drown-
ing at Shoals Creek—she had jumped off the pier to
chase a toy football that my brother threw downriver,
got tired fighting the current, and was about to go under when I got to her with a life preserver. But she did
not appreciate her role as a beard, nor the fact that I
bailed on her if there was a chance of seeing Mike.
We had to find other venues when he left a racy, un-
sealed note for me on Jane's front porch, and her father got to it first. We steamed up the windows of his
MGB all around town, arms and legs splayed in ungainly positions when a policeman interrupted our
foreplay with a flashlight's beam. But our preferred
sanctuary was behind my grandparents' house when
they were out of town: once past the porte cochere, we
were hidden from the street, safe from discovery.

I was absolutely stunned by the intense pleasure of
kissing and caressing, a visceral experience I had no
right to expect, given my mother's counsel. After six
months of exquisite teasing, we'd done everything but
"go all the way." On a clear cold night I walked out on

our front lawn, across the grass that was crunchy with frost, gazed at the starry night sky, and negotiated with God in what has come to be known as Clintonian logic. "It's not intercourse," I offered, "it's just outercourse. And I won't do it anymore." Then I went inside, looked at the photograph of Mike I kept hidden under the library card in my wallet, and thought: *Who am I kidding?* I stuffed rollers into a hairnet, placed it on my pillow, and arranged a lump of clothes under the blanket in a vaguely human shape. I climbed out the window and found Mike's car around the corner.

I felt oddly detached from my first time, as if it were more a rite of initiation to be crossed off a list than a sexual epiphany, but Mike had warned me that it would get so much better. As I climbed back through the window of my bedroom, the ceiling light suddenly switched on, illuminating my father's face. Wordlessly, he walked down the hall to the laundry room where he kept his toolbox, his silence more frightening than the usual bluster of his anger. My throat seemed closed tight, but I managed to mumble, "What are you doing?"

"Nailing the windows shut," he said.

"But what if there's a fire?" I asked, watching helplessly. "I won't be able to get out."

He never looked back at me as he took out a ball peen hammer and answered, "That's not the fire I'm worried about."

It was too late to safeguard my virtue. Mike and I were already scouting locations for the next time, and the next, and the next, exploring the various versions of lovers' lane in town. I walked out the front door to meet him now, sanguine behind a careful latticework of lies. A subtle change occurred at home: once I became a sexual creature, nobody in my family seemed to like me anymore. My father sensibly realized he could not act as full-time sentry, but he glowered across the dinner table and spoke to me in staccato bursts, as if conversation was expensive. I knew from the rearrangements in my bureau drawers that my mother was looking through my papers, finding letters from Mike, but she referred to my behavior only obliquely, with thinly veiled references to men who don't buy cows when the milk is free. I kept up my own part in the pretense, wearing Mike's school ring on a chain hidden under my blouse when I was home and putting it on my finger at school, the fraying bits of white surgical tape wrapped around the band to make it fit.

The most safety and seclusion was in a new development off Walnut Grove Road, where the streets were paved but the houses not yet built. When the weather turned warm, we spent every weekend at the drive-in movie, facilitated by Mike's new Nash Rambler with collapsible seats. We were hardly the only teenagers grabbing illicit Saturday night sex—by daylight, the grounds of the drive-in were littered with more discarded condoms than popcorn kernels. Emboldened by lust, we planned on adding a Wednesday night and a real bed to our repertoire, since that was when Mike's parents and younger brother went to Bible meetings. Watching from a safe distance as the family car pulled out of the driveway, we left the Rambler down the block and crept into the house like burglars. We'd barely undressed when there was the unmistakable sound of a key in the front door and a young boy's voice saying that he did so have a stomachache. Grabbing our clothes, we whispered a frantic escape plan, which entailed my climbing out a chest-high window, running half-naked across the vacant lot behind the house, and waiting behind a magnolia tree until Mike retrieved me.

Longing for a place where we couldn't get caught and wouldn't be arrested, we saved up for a room at the Rebel Motel on Lamar Avenue, the highway south toward Mississippi. There was a flashing confederate soldier's cap over the VACANCY sign as we pulled into the parking lot. Although we were unlikely to see or be seen by anyone familiar, I was technically jailbait and ducked beneath the dashboard while Mike paid nineteen dollars for a room with cinder block walls painted the color of iceberg lettuce. I refused to touch the frayed graying towels. Only the magnitude of pent-up teenaged hormones could overcome the bed, made with matching gray sheets over a mattress that smelled of mildew and collapsed in the middle like a taco. But the privacy and lack of interruption overcame the lack of aesthetics. This was the real first time. It was daylight when we arrived, and I was shocked to see that it was dark when we left.

Mike was slightly schizophrenic about birth control: he was always prepared with condoms but delayed using one until the last possible moment, relying on the notoriously imprecise method of withdrawal, which I naively accepted. I went through craven watchful waiting for my period every month. One day late, and I couldn't eat or sleep. Three days late, and I was stumbling in a trance through the green-tiled halls of the school, chastising God for combining the pleasures of the flesh with the only occasional need to reproduce. Five days late, and I was swearing off sex forever, convinced that my life was over. At the first twinge of cramps I'd start to breathe easier, and with the first sign of blood, I dropped to my knees in prayer. Hallelujah! Pregnancy anxiety forever changed my attitude about menstruation—never again "the curse" that my mother described but reason to rejoice.

When I told Mother that my periods were irregular, she made an appointment for me with her doctor, a family friend who used to hunt squirrel and invite us over for stew. Nate Atherton was as wide as he was tall, with a narrow circumference of hair that made him look like a tonsured monk, but he was kind and avuncular as he questioned me, obviously aware that I was sexually active.

"Do you have a boyfriend?" he asked. Unable to meet his eyes, I mumbled yes. "Are you in love?" he asked. Again I said yes, and assured him that we planned to get married one day. He wrote something illegible on a prescription pad, and I blithely handed it to the same pharmacist who'd given me penicillin when I was five, cough medicine for innumerable childhood viruses, Jean Naté for many Mother's Days. I almost choked when I looked in the bag and saw a pink plastic container with thirty tiny pills on a round dial. Speaking in a hoarse whisper of excitement, I called Mike and said, "I think this is birth control!" We drove to the other side of town, and I cowered in the car while he confirmed that I had been given the miraculous Pill from a druggist I felt certain wouldn't be bumping into my father at the hardware store.

I still marvel at the doctor's act of compassion: he knew I would discover that I'd been given a way to escape unwanted pregnancy but avoided any direct conversation about it, saving me from a confrontation with my mother and allowing her to continue being an ostrich. Twenty-five years later I asked my mother, "Did you know that Dr. Atherton gave me birth control pills when I was sixteen?"

"No!" she said, but allowed as to how it was probably a good idea.

THAT SUMMER, MY PARENTS AND GRANDPARENTS were going to an appliance convention (the Philco Hawaiian Holiday), and their invitation for me to come along was camouflage for a plot to drive a wedge between Mike and me. Even though the plan was pathetically transparent, I figured true love could survive a vacation, and I could hardly pass up a trip to Honolulu—I'd never been north of the Mason-Dixon line. As we stepped off the plane, we were greeted by glorious women with burnished skin who placed leis of fragrant white plumeria around our necks, and by an attractive young mainlander introduced as Joseph Graham Davis, a Columbia Law student who'd taken a summer job with the travel agency that arranged our trip. He called himself Gray, a patrician name to match his preppy clothes (cotton T-shirt tucked into khakis) and prodigal swath of Kennedy hair. He offered to show me around the island, and with the sense of urgency and speeded-up time of a vacation, it didn't take long to progress from whiskey sours on the deck of an oceanfront bar to passionate necking on

Waikiki Beach. That evening when we returned to the hotel, my father was pacing the lobby with a security guard, a walkie-talkie belching static as he conferred with colleagues around the property. My parents took one look at my disheveled clothes, my shoes and pockets filled with sand, and decreed that I was to remain within spitting distance for the rest of the trip.

I managed to slip Gray my address as I was boarding the plane home, and we exchanged long, philosophical letters about our ambitions and goals (his were written on a yellow legal pad so the lawyers at the New York firm where he was clerking would think he was hard at work). Our relationship probably should have remained epistolary: when I went to New York almost two years later, I was thrilled at seeing him again—a built-in boyfriend. We drove to his parents' empty house in Westchester County and climbed into their bed, in an old-fashioned frame high off the floor, but our fondling was interrupted by his parents' unexpected return—a classic scenario in my sex life. I dived under the bed just before his mother came into the room and could see her pink pumps from my hiding place, barely breathing until her bathroom needs gave me a window of escape. A few days later we tried again at the family beach house on the Jersey shore, deserted for the winter, but we both sensed that we were trying too hard and ended up in bunk beds. Driving back to New York in silence was a glaring contrast to our lively conversations before attempting to be sexual. Gray Davis always drove twenty miles faster than the speed limit and was still always two hours late. I would guess that he's stopped speeding and is more punctual now that he is the governor of California.

The trip to Hawaii did derail my romance with Mike, to the delight of my parents. It's a bittersweet moment, the recognition that a first love is just that. The person who evoked such hunger and longing and indiscretion isn't going to walk into the future with you. There will be others with voices like tupelo honey, whose touch will make your palms damp. I broke up with Mike (on the telephone—remarkably easy) and moved on.

Sam wore Canoe. He dressed in preppy blazers from Brooks Brothers and was a founding member of a young men's social club called the Midnight Revelers, famous for their parties. He was one of the lifeguards I had periodically dunked at Chickasaw Country Club and was considered so socially acceptable by my parents that I was granted permission to visit him that fall for homecoming weekend at the University of Tennessee in Knoxville, on the edge of the Smoky Mountains. The campus seemed to glow with an unearthly light from the preponderance of clothing in the school colors: Day-Glo orange and white. Just before the football game, Sam gave me a corsage, a huge white mum trailing orange and white ribbons, and as I sat in the stadium, baking in the noonday sun, I kept sticking my face in the flower, inhaling the mushy coolness. We were so highly chaperoned that the only time we got to touch was when we were dancing. The proctor in Sam's dorm wrote to my mother expressing her delight in such a well-mannered guest.

When Sam came home to Memphis for weekends and holidays, there were no chaperones, and we borrowed his grandmother's basement—the ultimate den of iniquity, with a fireplace, pool table, TV, wet bar,

My mother
and her
parents:
They'd come a
long way from
the chicken
farm.

My parents,
William
Jennings
Shepherd III
and Patty
Cornelia
Shobe, the
best jitter-
buggers in
Memphis.

Two years old, natural blonde. Ten years old, still a natural
blonde. Fourteen years old, soon to be a not-so-natural blonde.

Christmas morning with my sister and brother: Yeah, I'm smiling, but what I really wanted was my brother's gun and holster.

BELOW: Fall, 1969—In this photo, my parents are still a couple, but moments later I found out they wouldn't be for long.

ABOVE, LEFT TO RIGHT:
Singing and not winning Miss
Teenage America; winning Model
of the Year.

BELOW: Winning Miss
Teenage Memphis.

Of all the covers I'd done, this one caught the eye of the director
Peter Bogdanovich. He was impressed by what he called my
"fresh, sexual threat."

"Oh, quit prissin'. I don't think you did it right anyway."
—Jeff Bridges and I on the set of *The Last Picture Show*, 1970.

(Photofest)

In 1991, Jeff Bridges and I were reunited for *Texasville*, the sequel to *The Last Picture Show*. I finally made it as homecoming queen.

People in Hollywood perceived us as bragging to the world, "We're Peter and Cybill and you're not."

BELOW: Peter, my first director and acting coach, on the set of *The Last Picture Show*. (Everett Collection, Inc.)

On the beach shooting *The Heartbreak Kid* in 1972: Charles Grodin was brilliant in this movie. At the time of the shooting, however, I found him unfunny and unattractive. It took me fifteen years to change my opinion. (Photofest)

Despite Burt's hyperventilating and my slamming doors on fingers, we actually had a blast shooting *At Long Last Love* in 1974. (Photofest)

With Robert DeNiro on the set of *Taxi Driver*.
What I was thinking: "Bobby, I'm sorry I didn't give you a tumble."
What he was thinking: "You can't imagine what you missed."
(Photofest)
BELOW: *Playboy*, eat your heart out.

and a plush velveteen sofa. Grandma rarely left the second floor of her weathered white-brick house, sometimes yelling downstairs, "Y'all okay down there?" Sam would holler, "Doin' Jim Dandy," with a surfeit of enthusiasm and peel off my clothing to the accompaniment of Ella Fitzgerald and Sinatra LPs. Unlike my girlfriends, who were fooling around to the Four Tops and the Temptations, I was wooed with the music of my parents.

Sam recognized that the way to my heart was through my stomach. I can still taste the pompano almondine and three kinds of oysters (bienville, casino, and Rockefeller) at Justine's, the most exclusive restaurant in Memphis, in an antebellum mansion with a rose garden (even my grandparents had only been there a few times). I worshiped at the altar of the killer pecan pie Sam's mother made from a recipe on the bottle of dark Karo syrup. On Valentine's Day he left the industrial-size Whitman's Sampler at my door, along with a giant wooden heart inscribed "I love you" on the front lawn, pounded into the frozen earth on a garden spike. But I was restless and bored with college-boy sex. I'd be graduating from high school in a few months, and despite the number of ways I found to write "Mrs." in front of Sam's name on my loose-leaf notebook, I was pretty sure that his circumscribed image of our life together would grate. Fat tears slid down his cheeks and his face fissured as we sat in his Mustang on a chilly autumn day, but he wasn't fooled for an instant as I lied that I'd been chatting with God about the sin of sex before marriage. A month or so after our breakup, I was kissing a new beau good night at my front door. Turning to go inside the house, I looked through to the backyard to see Sam watching, wearing his Revelers tuxedo and scowling like Heath- cliff.

Lawrence wore Jade East. He went to Florida State, played golf like a pro, and drove a pale blue Thunder- bird, which we would park on the far side of Galloway Golf Course. He was more . . . esoteric in his amorous tastes. "I'll show you what I like," he said during what I assumed to be a moment of high arousal. He undid the button at the wrist of his shirt and rolled his sleeve back slowly, all the way above the elbow. Then he said, "Just stroke my arm." I was thinking: *This guy is really weird. He doesn't want to do anything.* And I did it wrong, first too hard, then too soft, so he said, "Let me show you how." From the vantage point of several experienced decades, the arm-stroking thing now seems fabulously sophisticated, not to mention the ul- timate safe sex. And I came to think that a golf course is a rather erotic place, as long as you don't get ar- rested.

SEX WAS TOO EARLY AND TOO URGENT IN MY life, and I wonder how my sexual energy might have been deferred or given another outlet. When I was growing up, there was no Joycelyn Elders to encour- age masturbation rather than motel rooms. Academia might have sufficed as distraction, but it was given scant regard for girls in my family. The $150 scholar- ship I was offered to attend a private high school didn't cover the cost of tuition, and my grandparents wouldn't put up the additional money. Our house- hold was big on Collier Junior Classics and Reader's

Digest Condensed Books. I read everything in the bookcase ("That girl always has her head in a book," my mother said, and she didn't mean it as a compliment). I even trained myself to read in the car without getting sick. The first time I went to the Highland Avenue branch of the Memphis Public Library, I was overwhelmed. "You mean I can take out as many books as I want?" I asked. I couldn't understand why I got punished for bad behavior by having to bend over and get walloped with a belt, while my friend Martha got punished by having to memorize "The Raven."

As adolescent virgins, my friends and I had gabbed without much information about "going all the way," but I stopped talking about sex when I started doing it, and lying about it extended to my best friends. I knew with an unshakable certainty that none of my crowd— all good southern girls—were experiencing what I was, and it was inconceivable to share the intimacies. Even within my troika of Jane, Patty, and Martha, our gossip about social pairings had tacit boundaries beyond which we didn't venture, resorting to a discreet policy of "don't ask, don't tell." Later I would find out that I was indeed way ahead of the pack.

Certainly Delta Alpha Delta was virginal. High school sororities constituted a cherished Memphis heritage with a fixed protocol that brooked no deviation. During rush week, prospective pledges wearing themed name tags (in the shape of bongo drums, perhaps, or Nefertiti's head) were invited to partake of cucumber sandwiches and Rotel dip (made with a can of Rotel brand spicy chiles and tomatoes melted with Velveeta cheese) at the homes of older "sisters." On the weekend that votes were tallied, each girl would wait, hoping for an invitation to join, which was announced by a caravan of cars pulling up to her house, with crepe paper streamers and blaring horns. (Each sorority had a distinctive honk, recognizable from blocks away.) I didn't just join D.A.D.; I became the class president in my senior year and immersed myself in its genteel traditions of charity work and partying. We formed a white girls' version of a Motown group, performing at hospitals and nursing homes. To raise money for the parties, we sponsored pancake suppers and car washes, and once a month I'd rise at 5 A.M., drive to the Krispy Kreme, and pick up sixty dozen (or perhaps sixty thousand) doughnuts that we'd sell.

Despite these mannerly rituals, my waterloo in high school was the "charm notebook" required for phys. ed. I can only imagine what hyperkinetic gym teacher of an earlier era, perhaps damaged by overexposure to *Gone With the Wind*, conceived of such a curiosity, quaint even by 1960s standards. We were supposed to put together information about clothes, hair, makeup, and other womanly wiles. Surely this was an assignment for which I'd been in training since the crib, but I thought it was asinine and made an obviously slapdash effort, sloppily gluing pages from *Glamour*, *Mademoiselle*, and *Seventeen* on construction paper. I earned an F. (No small irony that in less than three years I would be on the covers of these magazines.) I'd played on the church softball and basketball teams and set a district record in the long jump (formerly called the broad jump, until the term was deemed politically incorrect). A contender for best female athlete, I failed gym.

My father was outraged and showed up at school to

defend me, certain that he'd just "fix" things with the bottomless tool kit of parenthood. I was filled with a smug pride as he strode into the gymnasium to see the evil Mrs. Hotchkiss, keeping close to the wall as his wing tips clacked against the wood floor. They vanished into offices behind the girls' locker room, too far for me to hear. As my father stormed away from his failed mission, he caught my eye and said, "Sorry, Cy, I couldn't get her to change her mind." With a failing grade, I was kicked off the cheerleading squad—the ultimate disgrace—and the next semester, when all of my friends were learning to type, I had to repeat gym. I was still half a credit short at graduation, a deficit magnanimously overlooked by the authorities. In another recurrent dream of my adulthood, I am capped and gowned, marching into the auditorium to the strains of "Pomp and Circumstance," only to be yanked back to sit with the kindergarten class while a toothless Mrs. Hotchkiss, looking remarkably like the Wicked Witch of the West, chants, "I'll get you, my pretty."

CHAPTER FOUR

"And the Winner Is . . ."

$\mathcal{M}$OMA CALLED SOMEONE WITH A BIG EGO "such a much." I was certainly supposed to spend time and energy on my appearance, heeding my mother's remonstrance that women must suffer to be beautiful, but I wasn't supposed to act prideful about the results. This confusing message left me with only disdain or indifference about the beauty pageants that were endemic to the culture in 1966 (it seemed as if there was a Miss Magnolia Blossom or Miss Local Carburetor Shop being lauded in the papers every other week). I considered beauty pageants dorky and myself anti-establishment: failing gym, cheating in Latin, smoking Prince Edward cigars with Jane, and sneaking out for sex. Ignoring my disinclination to enter such a contest, my cousin Tom Byarly (son of Great Aunt Edith, who crawled into the fireplace) decided that I was the perfect candidate for Miss Teenage Memphis and kept sticking that application under my nose, saying, "Just sign it." With no real enthusiasm, I signed.

Every aspect of the contest was scrupulously regulated. Instructions for a written test, to be administered at the local Sears Garden Center, were a source of unwitting humor: "There is no way to prepare for this test. . . . Dress is optional, but try to look your best. . . . You are encouraged to socialize with other girls while enjoying free Dr Pepper." I answered questions such as "How would you achieve world peace?" without a trace of irony.

Each girl was allotted two minutes for a talent routine that was taped early in the week—I sang "Michael, Row the Boat Ashore" while playing the bass ukulele. ("Get into costume immediately, then relax.") The finals were to be broadcast live on WHBQ, the local ABC-TV station. ("Be yourself" and "Use all available knowledge about good grooming.") I was a nervous wreck that day but declined Mother's offer of a mild sedative (she said everybody took them). I dressed in the gold and white formal we had selected and then I submitted to the hairdresser, who managed to achieve the perfect flip that had always eluded me.

I heard George Klein, the master of ceremonies, announce, "And the winner is . . . ," but when he said my name, I looked around for a moment to make certain there wasn't anyone else named Cybill Shepherd in the group. My parents bolted out of their metal folding chairs in the TV studio, beaming broad smiles and clapping wildly while the other families politely applauded. The next day, the Western Union man became a familiar figure at our house, delivering dozens of telegrams from local politicians, beauty parlors, the church rector, even Chris Crump, whom I had beaten with the whiffle bat years ago. The note from one family friend summed up the prevailing sentiment: "As far as your parents and grandparents are concerned, you are already Miss Teenage America, as you are such a sweet, thoughtful all-American girl. If you stay this way, and I'm sure you will, you can never really become a loser!"

My prizes were a Sears wardrobe and a year's supply of Dr Pepper, which was stacked on our porch almost to the top of the pale green riveted plastic roof. But I also got to represent Memphis in the Miss Teenage America pageant, where the stakes were considerably higher: $10,000 in scholarships, a stock portfolio, and a car. All of the "young ladies" were to be accompanied to the contest in Dallas by their mothers. On one side of us was Miss Indianapolis, on the other Miss Spokane. Every time we left the hotel we were chauffeured in a cavalcade of turquoise blue Comets, escorted by cadets from Texas A&M to entertainments such as a Turtle Derby. (Each contestant got to keep her turtle and a supply of Gourmet Turtle Food.) My scrapbook from that week includes a recipe card for avocado dip and a coupon for dinner, noting in my scratchy penmanship: *Had to have meal ticket or couldn't eat*—always an important concern to me. The judges were introduced peremptorily at a cocktail party that featured a tomato aspic in the shape of an armadillo. I was thrilled to meet Dick Clark, but on a more practical level I was interested in the director of the American Airlines Stewardess College, something I'd always considered a viable career option, a last resort to get out of Memphis.

When the finalists were announced, I was not one of them. Instead I was named Miss Congeniality, one of the honorary but dubious consolation prizes that included Miss Personality and Miss Sportsmanship. Lying to a reporter from the *Memphis Press-Scimitar* who called for an interview, I gushed, "This is the greatest thing that ever happened to me. All the contestants are best friends already. Last night we had a slumber party, and tonight we're dancing at a go-go place, but no boys are allowed. It's a good thing the frug came along since the girls have to dance by themselves." Failing to make the cut as a finalist was devastating, reinforcing my lifelong anxiety about falling short of perfection. Sad and miserable, I had to swallow my disappointment and participate in the remaining festivities, rehearsing a group song about the spectrum of national contestants ("They're beautifying Baltimore and out in Santa Rosa, in Louisville and Buffalo and on the Ponderosa"). The winner was an "at-large" candidate from Milpitas, California, whose talent was an "authentic" hula dance performed to a Don Ho record.

Even though I returned to Memphis in defeat, something was changed and would never again be the same: I was famous, publicly acknowledged as beautiful and rewarded for it, different and set apart. I'd imagine a friend's voice getting a little crispy and impatient, disallowing me any complaint about fatigue or boredom or a bad hair day. The president of the pageant did offer me a summer job at the shows he produced for Six Flags over Texas—my first professional offer—but my parents wouldn't let me live away from home by myself. I was still somewhat useful to pageant officials, who asked me to appear at a party for the next year's Miss Teenage hopefuls. "Actually," said the letter from the director of public relations, "all we want you to do is smile prettily when you are introduced and mingle with the girls, convincing them to enter the contest." Smiling prettily seemed to be my talent.

---

*E*VERY CHILD OF MEMPHIS GREW UP UNDERstanding that it was the cotton capital of the world, that the crop had dominated the economy, even the society of the city since before the Civil War, when a major slave market provided the necessary labor of industry, and cotton brokers dotted the waterfront, transacting business at a cotton exchange that rivaled Wall Street. King Cotton still occasioned the biggest social event of the year, the Cotton Carnival. From the time I was a little girl, I stood with the crowd awaiting the Carnival king and queen, who were chosen from the wealthiest and most prominent families in town. They arrived on a flower-bedecked barge, blindingly lit and dressed in shiny rhinestoned costumes, at the historic downtown steamboat landing, lined with cobblestones that were said to have been brought to North America as ballast on Spanish galleons and towed upriver by mules. The local country clubs named royal princesses to the king and queen's court, and Chickasaw's board of directors appointed me their representative in 1968, a commission that could not be refused, whatever my disdain for pageantry. I had to make an appointment with the "modiste" who was making the princess costumes, after receiving a mimeographed sheet of instructions: "You are to bring sixteen (16) button white fabric gloves for evening and 'shortie' white gloves for day costume. You are to bring small button pearl earrings (no loops or 'dangles' please). . . . A rhinestone tiara is to be worn with your nighttime costume. A deposit of $5 will be required. . . . You will be responsible for furnishing two pairs of shoes—plain, closed heel (opera), closed toe pumps. NO FLATS OR BALLETS, PLEASE. Hose for your daytime costume will be furnished. . . . MOST IMPORTANT: Wear the foundation garment you plan to wear with your costumes when taking your measurements and for fittings."

There were no blacks represented in the Carnival—they had their own separate Cotton Makers Jubilee—and the only black people I knew were domestics or warehouse workers at Shobe, Inc. Memphis was still cleft along rigid color lines, with segregated barbershops and libraries, and there were COLORED ONLY signs with figurative hands painted in dark colors pointing to different drinking fountains and rest rooms. The local movie house had a colored box office and seating up in the nosebleed section of the balcony, a brutal sauna on humid summer nights. In 1965, when a maverick theater operator at the Poplar Plaza Shopping Center screened *A Patch of Blue* and Sidney Poitier actually kissed a white woman, the audience reacted with an audible "Whoooa." Blacks were admitted on a different day at the Mid-South Fairgrounds every fall and attended the Negro school a mile away from my own. There is still, in a public park across from the University of Tennessee Medical School, a statue of Nathan Bedford

Forrest, the first grand wizard of the Ku Klux Klan, founded in rural Tennessee. Despite an ongoing controversy, it's allowed to stand because he was a famous Civil War general. Once, when I was very young, my grandfather and I saw the hurried scattering of spectral white gowns and pointed hoods, illuminated by the glow from a burning cross, as we drove through the "other" part of town. The sight of the Klan in full regalia strikes fear in the heart of even a little white girl and an old white man.

"Da-Dee, who are the ghosts?" I asked.

"Don't bother your pretty head," he answered, but he put his foot to the gas pedal.

Like most of the people in that time and place, my family had a tacit code of "benevolent" racism: my grandparents treated their black housekeepers with familial fondness and support, dispensing hand-me-down clothes and leftover food with the fraudulent magnanimity of the times. Waiters and bellhops were addressed by their first names, whatever their age, and I shelled peas on the back porch of the lake house with a kind and dignified elderly lady named Annie who had to call me Miss Cybill. It would have been unthinkable for me to challenge the views and vernacular of the older generations. Even though I was enlightened by the climate of civil rights activity, I did nothing. There were black kids in my high school class, unknown to me and my circle of friends. Our connection to black culture was through the music of the times. Jr. Walker and the All-Stars spoke to us in a different way from how our parents had related to the Ink Spots or the Mills Brothers, although I hardly examined the societal ramifications of the soulful sounds.

In the spring of 1968, Martin Luther King Jr. brought his Poor People's Campaign to Memphis in support of the mostly black striking sanitation workers. Hundreds of men who hauled garbage and dug sewers gathered at a rally to hear him say "It is a crime for people to live in this rich nation and receive starvation wages," and strikers wearing sandwich boards that read I AM A MAN were maced and tear-gassed on Main Street. Local news reports portrayed King as an irresponsible agitator who had goaded the rabble to violence. Shops were vandalized, and we heard that the train from Chicago to New Orleans passed through Memphis without stopping. The National Guard was called out in armored tanks that moved through the streets on rubber tracks—my friend Jane and I went driving around to see them rerouting traffic, sending people home. Some of the locals acted as if the turmoil was a huge personal inconvenience, but others treated the presence of armed guards in our midst with a comically misplaced sense of southern hospitality, pressing sandwiches and doughnuts on them. Rubbish in sacks and cartons was piled everywhere, and delicate ladies swooned at the mention of rats. The Mississippi River and the network of open drainage ditches in the city combined to host a sizable rodent population—it was said that a rat could traverse the city more quickly by ditch than a person could by car. And they were big enough to mount and ride. I once went to a "Sunset Symphony" picnic near the river and remarked on a cute little cat wandering near the water. "Not a cat," I was told.

I was standing with friends on the colonnaded veranda of my high school in the late afternoon of April 4, just weeks before our graduation, when we heard that Dr. King had been shot, and within a few hours, the world way beyond Memphis knew that he was dead. The Lorraine Motel was a few miles away, too far to hear the firecracker blast of the assassin's bullet or to see Dr. King's friends trying to scrape his blood from the balcony, but too close for comfort to my family and a large part of the city's white population. My father made sure his luger was loaded, and Moma called to say that Da-Dee had moved a shotgun down to the front hall.

There was a pall over the city for weeks, a sense of fear and chaos, with stringent early curfews and the intensified presence of militia. High school proms were canceled by municipal decree, as was Cotton Carnival, and I was not displeased to be a princess in absentia. When I passed a black person on the street, I averted my eyes with a searing flash of shame. I felt absolutely responsible for the murder. I knew the expression "If you're not part of the solution, you're part of the problem," although I was not to assuage my guilt with action for another twenty years. But after the initial shock, nobody in my little microcosm talked about the shooting. It became unmentionable. Palm Sunday fell three days after Dr. King died, and there were green fronds decorating the white pillars of our church but no sermon from the pastor about healing the wounds of race relations in our community. Commencement exercises proceeded on schedule but I recall no mention of the assassination.

As a graduation present, my grandparents gave me a trip to Europe: the beginner's three-week tour with a group of students from the local high schools, through

London, Geneva, Madrid, Lisbon. We had to skip Paris because of the student riots against U.S. involvement in Vietnam, but that meant extra time in Italy and my first exposure to its masterly painting, sculpture, and architecture. I had inexhaustible energy for museums and basilicas, panoramas and piazzas, never-drying underwear hung on Juliet balconies and dark-haired boys who flirted in charmingly accented English limited to "Hello, beautiful." And the trip occasioned an epiphany. Looking up into the vaulted ceiling of the Sistine Chapel, I was overwhelmed by the power of those frescoes—the creation of Adam with God's outstretched hand and the last judgment of Christ—but my eyes drifted to the image of a half-clothed female.

"Excuse me," I asked the guide, "who's that big ol' muscular woman reading a scroll?"

"That is the Delphic Sibyl," he answered. *My* name, a name I'd hated and heard mispronounced all my life, was known to Michelangelo (albeit with the spelling tweaked). And why was a pagan symbol on the ceiling of a Christian chapel? Because it was a Sibyl who prophesied the coming of Christ. And there were lots of us. In Roman mythology, the guide informed me, Cybele was a supreme being called the Great Mother of the Gods, and a temple in her honor was erected on the site now occupied by the Vatican. The high priestesses known as Sibyls were named for her, and their oracles were so respected that they guided imperial policy for Roman emperors.

I know how pretentious and melodramatic this sounds, but something in me clicked at that moment in that place of such beauty and grandeur. I'd never been exposed to fine art—hell, the closest I'd gotten to classical music was 101 Strings of Mantovani. It was as if the world had been in black and white, and suddenly there was a new palette. There seemed to be a personal message in the chapel for me: the existence of a female deity before the time of Christ symbolized the limitless power and potential achievement of women. If God is a man, then woman is not created in his image, limited by a celestial glass ceiling. But if the holiest of holies is female, then women can do anything. I have a droll friend who says she doesn't believe in God, only in signs from God. I believe in both, and the Sibyls were a little calling card from the divine. The visual stimulus of great art was sensuous and powerful, and it made me long to do something creative. Modeling was not what I had in mind.

$\mathcal{M}$ODELING GOES BACK A LONG WAY IN OUR family: when my grandfather was a toddler, he wore a wide-brimmed hat and pulled a red toy wagon in a turn-of-the-century advertisement for Shapleigh's Hardware. My first paying job, in my junior year of high school, was for Coppertone, made by the Memphis-based Plough Corporation. (A dump truck backed up to a photography studio fitted with fake palm trees and poured in a load of white sand.) It must have been a slow news day when Ken Ross, a staff photographer for the local paper, asked me to pose, without pay, for a few seasonal photos in which I scared some Halloween goblins. He was a scout for the Model of the Year pageant, the brainstorm of a man named Stewart Cowley who owned a modeling agency in New York City, and Ken put my name on a list of suggested entries. When Stewart called, my parents thought I was too young to consider leaving home but decided it was only polite to meet Cowley at the Peabody Hotel when he came to look over the local pulchritude. Our appointment coincided with the ritual marching of the ducks through the Peabody lobby: In the 1930s the hotel manager returned from a weekend hunting trip having partaken of a little too much Tennessee sippin' whiskey and thought it would be fun to put some of his live duck decoys in the lobby's ornate marble fountain. The enthusiastic response from guests begat a tradition: every morning at eleven, under the care of an exalted bellboy called the duckmaster, a gaggle of English call ducks descend in the elevator from their home on the roof to spend the day splashing in the fountain, and every evening at five they return. It's one of Memphis's prime photo ops.

Stewart Cowley had been a theatrical agent before World War II and had a certain flamboyant flair—there were framed photos of two large standard poodles in his suite. I didn't know that his contest idea was contemptuously referred to as Stewart's Folly by his New York competitors—my parents simply told him, "Maybe next year." The first Model of the Year contest drew a huge audience when it was telecast on CBS—so much for Stewart's Folly, although another man claimed Cowley had stolen the idea, and he spent so much time in litigation that he was known as Suin' Stew. When he returned to Memphis the following year, I was planning to study art history at Louisiana State and was still disdainful of anything that smacked of a beauty pageant. My mother insisted that I show him the courtesy of turning him down in person, and I went to the hotel in defiant disregard for my appearance, wearing cutoff jeans, with skin tanned mahogany and unwashed hair too blond from the sun. We sipped sweet iced tea, a southern tradition with its overkill of sugar, while Cowley chatted about the rewards awaiting the contest winner: a contract with his agency and $25,000 guaranteed in modeling fees the first year.

I'd rehearsed a smug little speech about having a higher calling to study Italian art. "I'm really not interested in being a model," I said.

"I'm sorry to hear that," Cowley replied. "You have a good chance of winning here in Memphis and going on to New York." There was a twinkle in his eye as he dealt his trump card. "And you're a helluva lot closer to Italy in New York than in Baton Rouge, Louisiana."

My father was cutting the grass and my mother was sitting on the front porch in a wrought-iron chair when I returned from the local Model of the Year pageant. There was a huge pile of yellow roses poking out the window on the passenger side of the 1960 Ford Fairlane I'd inherited from my great-grandmother, which required putting your foot flat to the floor every time you accelerated.

"What in the world is all that yellow?" Mother called as I pulled in the driveway.

"I won," I said.

Stewart Cowley tempered my victory with a dose of reality. "You'll have to lose at least thirty pounds," he announced and handed me a mimeographed copy of the grapefruit diet. I consumed two strips of bacon a day, plus meager portions of canned tuna and cucumbers, washed down with black coffee and Tab, each meal followed religiously by half a grapefruit (occasionally, for a bit of exotica, broiled). Perversely, during this starvation routine, I lay around the house reading cookbooks and a twenty-five-cent booklet called "Count Your Calories" that detailed the difference between boiled pigs feet (185 calories) and pickled pigs feet (the way I liked them, at 230 calories). All I thought about was food. Once I sneaked into the kitchen at 3 A.M. to polish off some leftover lamb chops that hadn't been ravaged to my mother's satisfaction.

I lost twelve pounds but claimed twenty-eight on the Model of the Year application, and that September, instead of registering for Art History 101 at Louisiana State University, I went to New York for the finals. I was familiar with the skyline from the movie *King Kong*, one of my childhood favorites, but nothing could have prepared me for my first view of the city as the plane circled La Guardia Airport: Manhattan on a platter, rising from its slim, precarious perch between two rivers, with the crush of people and their island mentality, all wanting access and egress at exactly the same time. The other contestants were registering at the Waldorf-Astoria with their mothers, despite the fact that they all seemed stunningly grownup. I called home in a panic, and my mother was on the next flight. As she walked through the hotel lobby, she passed one willowy Miss Somewhere after another. "I swear," she declared when she called my father to report her safe arrival, "I don't know what Cybill is doing up here with all these beautiful women."

The walls of the Stewart Modeling Agency were

covered with intimidating pictures of Twiggy, Jean Shrimpton, Cheryl Tiegs, and Marisa Berenson, behind the "bookers" with telephones attached to their shoulders and big volumes of rate cards for all the girls, who were never called anything but girls. (The stars didn't have a rate. Their fees were unquestionable and unmentionable.) My outlook improved when I went to the CBS studio and started trying on various outfits. Looking in the mirror at my gold sequined bikini and long hot-pink cape with a hood trimmed in matching sequins by Oleg Cassini, I thought: *Maybe I have a chance.* I also thought: *Losing is really a drag—let's try winning for a change.*

I watched a tape of the pageant recently, and it feels like going on an archaeological dig, pulling up unfathomable shards of the past. The broadcast, which preempted *Mannix*, opened with a song: "Who's that walking along the street, so cool, keeping a groovy beat. . . . She doesn't mind you will have to stare, great in everything she wears." A silver pleated curtain rose to reveal a group of go-go dancers writhing in front of the contestants, who stood, frozen, on a stepped platform. The helmet-haired hostess, Arlene Dahl, sat at a table behind a pitiful arrangement of carnations that seemed to be strategically placed to conceal her bosom. The dimpled and equally helmet-haired cohost, John Davidson, commented, "This is a girl watcher's dream come true."

There was some speculation about the career ambitions of the contestants. "Do you think these girls always wanted to be models?" Davidson asked with some gravity.

"Not necessarily, John," answered Dahl. "Some

wanted to be nurses, airline hostesses, and more often than not, movie stars."

The emcee, Jack Linkletter, summoned each girl to center stage for an interview, each of us having been instructed to do a little pirouette as we reached him.

"Do you want to have a large family?" he asked one.

"No," she said without a touch of irony. "I think maybe six or seven."

He asked a girl from Iowa to make the noise of an egg-laying chicken and commented about another, "This is a very ambitious girl in the sense that she has a lot of ambitions."

Everyone was wearing so much eyeliner and shadow, such heavy false lashes, that we looked like sleepwalkers. Davidson and Dahl did the fashion commentary.

"The accent this year is on chains," said Dahl, "to circle the waist or wrist or just to call attention to a pretty face."

"Or maybe to keep a girl at home with the chains," chimed in Davidson.

When my turn came, I approached Linkletter, wearing a crushed red velvet coat with black gloves and boots and a cossack hat—actually a rather elegant look, considering the possibilities, which ran to tartan tam-o'-shanters and orange leather boots. I was terrified, exhausted, overwhelmed, and no doubt starving, and I looked it.

"In last year's Miss Teenage contest," Linkletter said to me, "you were Miss Congeniality. And you got to travel to Europe."

"Oh, yes," I gushed, "it was wonderful."

"Which do you like better: European men or American men?"

"Oh, I like them booooooth," I said in a breathy drawl.

"Are they different?"

"Oh, there's all different varieties, American men and European men."

"See how congenial she is?" said Linkletter.

Instructions were to walk as if I were floating, like a geisha, my heels never touching the ground, when I paraded down the runway in the "Fun" segment of the program. Other contestants were consigned to pseudo cowboy chaps and space suits. The girl who followed me was wearing a hat so hideous, all she needed was a dangling price tag to look like Minnie Pearl. I had practiced flinging open my sequined cape in front of every available shiny surface until I had the move nailed, and I sold that bikini. I thrust my hips into the turn at the end of the runway, exposing a slice of midriff that hadn't been so flat since I was ten and never would be again. Winning was nothing short of a calculated decision, but it was emotional beyond my initial contemptuous expectations. All that sentiment had been held in check until the moment of triumph while I smiled and made the right turns. There's something devastating about winning, almost like walking across the bodies of the others, feeling the responsibility of the torchbearer for the beauty olympics. It's almost too much to bear. When you see a pageant winner crying, those are not crocodile tears. You don't cry that way when you lose.

It was the lore about a young Grace Kelly, safely ensconced in the Barbizon Hotel upon her arrival in New York, that pacified my parents when Stewart Cowley suggested it as a place for me to stay. Perhaps

Grace liked pink. My room looked like the inside of a Pepto-Bismol bottle, with a narrow single bed and a gigantic bathtub down the hall. The decision was made in haste: I won the contest on a Saturday night, and that Tuesday morning I was shooting on the sand dunes at Jones Beach for Ship 'n' Shore blouses. My starting rate was $20 an hour, and during my first month of work I made $6,000, but I spent a small personal fortune on the arsenal of beauty props I was expected to carry: self-adhesive nails, hot rollers, braids, falls, ponytails, hair spray, a ratting comb, and enough makeup to spackle a driveway. To haul it around, I bought a khaki fishing bag at Abercrombie & Fitch — a store on Fifty-seventh Street that celebrated patrician leisure activities — and took out the plastic lining meant for the fish. One of the women at the model agency informed me that I needed fur to look glamorous in New York and set up an appointment at Mr. Fred's Fur and Sport, where I bought three, count 'em, three coats: rabbit, possum, and curly white lamb. My shopping expedition was given six column inches in my hometown newspaper, but the midi length of the possum I'd chosen was deemed "overpowering for her delicate blond beauty." (I wore it to wave from a float in a Thanksgiving Day parade in Charlottesville, North Carolina, much to the consternation of the officials, who were upset about not being able to see tits and ass. They gestured frantically for me to remove the coat and reveal the skimpy gown underneath, but this particular set of tits and ass was freezing.)

I quickly learned the art of the go-see: I was told to buy a little notebook for my appointments, and every day I'd call the agency for a list of perhaps a dozen magazine editors and account executives who wanted to look me over. Getting the lay of the land required reciting a mantra: the Hudson River is to the west, Greenwich Village is to the south, Fifth Avenue's in the middle. . . . Often I'd realize that I was on West Fifty-fourth Street when I was supposed to be meeting a client on East Fifty-fourth Street. I felt a discomfort akin to the theme of my childhood, when I knew that physical attributes were all that counted, but my early foray into modeling was a wonderful opportunity to become accustomed to rejection. Sometimes I knew the reason, sometimes not. I never got the Dentyne chewing gum commercial that I went up for three different times. The ad agency executives ordered "Smile harder," then "Wider," then "Less." Apparently I chew funny.

One day I was summoned to the office of Diana Vreeland, the flamboyant editor of *Vogue*. She handed me a bikini that looked like three slices of bread strung together and told me to change in a closet. My ass hung out the back, which did not go unobserved—rather rude, I thought, since she had such an odd-looking body herself: all limbs with no waist and a face that seemed to have been ironed.

What many people don't know about modeling is that the editorial shots in fashion magazines are the worst-paying jobs. Catalogs are the bread and butter of the industry, photographed in formulaic ways that were thought to show the cheap clothes at their best advantage. Usually we worked in a studio against a huge roll of paper called no-seam hung from the ceiling. If I tried to make an impulsive, spontaneous gesture, the clothes tended to wrinkle, and the photographer would bring me back to the standard pose— "One hand on your hip, please, one hand on your throat."

Location shoots were more interesting, although there was seldom time to explore and enjoy the locations. I was required to make a personal appearance as Model of the Year in Caracas. (I mostly remember the sweet, thick coffee, which jolted me out of jet lag.) I made an Ultra Brite toothpaste commercial in Los Angeles, staying at the Continental Hyatt on Sunset Boulevard, which got a reputation as the Riot House after it was trashed by rock groups in residence. (I mostly remember worrying about my eyes, puffy from crying out of sheer loneliness, plus I had a zit on my face that looked like a third eye.) I made a Cover Girl commercial in Bavaria, where the big brewing companies made extra-strength beer for Oktoberfest and waitresses carried three steins on each arm as people danced on tables in steamy beer halls. (I mostly remember wrapping myself in a feather bed in my freezing room at the inn.)

I didn't make many friends while I was modeling. Competition turned the other girls into enemies—even on a location shoot where we were all working, there was a sense of rivalry about who'd end up with more pictures in the magazine. On-camera "talent" must be protected, which made people suck up, but only until they'd gotten what they wanted. I didn't trust the editors and account executives, who acted as if I was going to be their best friend for life while we were working together, and then vaporized when the day ended. In the beginning I was afraid to look at the camera for fear that the photographer would think I was looking at him and giving him sexual license. It took me a while to acknowledge that photographers didn't *necessarily* want to sleep with me. I felt utterly intimidated about talking to northerners; many people took my thick Memphis accent as evidence of mild retardation.

One who didn't make those assumptions was a young executive at CBS named James Cass Rogers, newly graduated from Yale Drama School and assigned to the Model of the Year telecast. During a rehearsal break one day, I was sitting in a corner with my nose in a book when he approached. "You don't look like the sort of girl who'd be reading *The Confessions of Nat Turner*," he said.

"Oh, really," I said, "what does that sort of girl look like?" Our friendship is now in its third decade. Jim always gave me loving criticism—there's probably nothing more valuable. And he understood that I felt diminished by modeling. It made me financially independent and was occasionally creative, but most of the time I was treated like a prize steer being groomed and readied for a county fair (except I wasn't supposed to bulk up). He encouraged me to find out what delighted and excited me by taking some college courses, a proposal that was greeted with derision by everyone at my agency. "Models always say they want to go back to school," said the same person who told me to buy fur, "but they never do. Modeling money is too good, and the life's too cushy." Removed enough from childhood tutelage about being a good girl, my new reaction to the words "You can't . . ." became "Watch me."

Stewart Models demanded three days of work a week to fulfill my contract, so Jim suggested that I start with a single English literature course at Hunter College night school. Books had been my best friends in a chaotic household where people said they were happy but didn't act like it. Books never talked down to me, didn't care what color my hair was and, to this day, are my most treasured possessions. College was an opportunity to devour the classics, to live inside them: in Oscar Wilde's *The Picture of Dorian Gray*, I learned the tragic bargains people make for eternal youth and beauty.

In *Heart of Darkness*, Joseph Conrad exposed the sinister unexplored and unowned areas of my psyche. In *What Maisie Knew*, Henry James let me into the turbulent world of a girl whose parents, just divorced, compete for her affection and approval, a parallel universe to my own. In *The House of Mirth*, Edith Wharton seemed to speak directly to me about a beautiful outsider trying to fit into fashionable New York, recognizing "a new vista of peril." (One book I couldn't relate to was *Beowulf*, written in Old English, which might as well be Old Swahili.)

The next semester I enrolled in the College of New Rochelle, a small progressive Catholic school for women in Westchester County, an hour north of Manhattan, which was more willing to accommodate my full-time work schedule. I spent only one night in the dorm, which seemed to vibrate with stereophonic noise. I tried blasting the opera *Carmen* to counteract Grace Slick down the hall and experimented with waxy earplugs that got stuck in my hair, but I had been out in the world too long to put up with the indignities of shared showers and toilets. I had moved out of the Barbizon (I wouldn't last long anywhere that men weren't allowed) to share an apartment with other models, so I made a reverse commute for my classes, taking the train up from Grand Central Station. Blessedly, I was excused from taking statistics and was allowed to bypass the generalized Introduction to Art, proceeding right to History of the Italian Renaissance. It was a highly charged time on campuses across the country, and I voted along with my classmates for a student strike against the Vietnam War—my first political protest. I was an anomaly: a passionate student who didn't care about grades or earning a degree, and I wanted to learn. I was required to think, and it was one of the happiest times in my life.

Feeling like a frog that needed a bigger pond, I enrolled at Washington Square College of New York University and switched my major to English literature. Studying art history means reading art criticism, much of which is dry as a bone. At least literary criticism uses the same medium it is commenting on. I wouldn't be studying what other people said about the creative people, but the words of the creative people themselves. Sitting through a Shakespearean play had never been my favorite pastime, but my class on his works was a chance to read and discuss the universal Sturm und Drang still pertinent today—hardly a week goes by that I don't refer to the lies and betrayal in the unholy trinity of Othello, Desdemona, and Iago.

An anthropology course imparted a daring bit of knowledge: somewhere in the world there were women uncovering their breasts with impunity and covering up their ankles. I knew the stereotype that you could identify a woman's nationality by noticing which part of her body she tried to hide if naked: an American would cover her breasts, a European would cover her genitals, an Arab would cover her face. Whatever part a woman believed she'd be struck down dead for exposing depended on country, culture, god, or tribe. The idea that there was nothing inherently right or wrong about nudity would justify one of the most important decisions in my future.

Stewart Cowley's attorney's best friend had a best friend whose best friend was John Bruno, a wealthy restaurateur who raced Ferraris and ran a family-owned steakhouse called the Pen and Pencil. He seemed both suave and down-to-earth to me: ten years older, Italian, born and raised in Manhattan. On one of our first dates he put on a white lab coat and took me into his meat locker, showing how he had inspected the beef himself, stamping it in purple ink with the restaurant's insignia. One night we parked half a block from the restaurant after it closed to spy on employees who were stealing meat. (John said that all employees steal, that part of running the business was figuring out how much he could afford to have stolen and still make a profit.) He loved New York, and I got my feet permanently planted in the granite, in the subway and the theater, in Central Park and in the fountain on the plaza of the Seagram Building, where we went wading on a deserted Fourth of July when it felt like we had the city to ourselves.

I was sharing an apartment on Sutton Place with three other models (two bedrooms, two bathrooms, two locks on the door). When I got a bad strep throat, John brought me an Italian chicken soup called *stracciatella* and held me until I fell asleep. I've always felt that foreplay should be like a good meal, going from soup to . . . nuts, and we consummated the relationship when I recovered. Leaving the apartment, a chorus of "You Make Me Feel Like a Natural Woman" ringing in our ears, we danced our way toward the East River, not caring that the sky was gloomy and certainly not noticing the piles of steaming dog shit before we stepped in it. (Pooper-scooper laws were not yet in effect, but I later learned the traditional theatrical superstition that stepping in dog doo on the way to a performance will bring luck.) Eventually I asked John to help me find a small apartment of my own and moved into a studio in the East Sixties, with a sleeping loft and a pullman kitchen that cost $500 a month (my day rate was up to $60). I indulged my innate disordered slobbiness, with nothing in the refrigerator but unrecognizable leftovers. (Could it be that the green fuzz ball was once a piece of cheese?)

I'd never even heard of brownstones, the nineteenth-century town houses built from the stones of river quarries up the Hudson, until I saw where John lived on the Upper East Side. When he led me up the spiral staircase for the grand tour, I gasped at a room with grand gilded mirrors, plush curved couches, and Victorian bibelots. "That's where my mother lives," he explained. "I'm upstairs."

He lives with his mother . . . ? I was reassured when I saw his own bachelor quarters, complete with bearskin rugs and leopard upholstery, even as a cover for the bathtub. And John's mother turned out to be one of his best assets. Frances Bruno was a good head shorter than I and shaped like a Sumo wrestler—she looked as if she could roll right over anyone who got in her way. She had a big nose, short brown hair, and the gravelly voice of an ex-smoker, with an earthy, unedited laugh. She was involved in almost every aspect of the restaurant business, and no task was too insignificant: she had even reupholstered the chairs in the powder room herself. She suffered from bad arthritis and sometimes joined me in the basement swimming pool at the Barbizon, even after I was no longer living there, wearing a thick white rubber cap (although she didn't put her face in the water) and a bathing suit with a "modesty panel." Her street wear was more fashionable. Years before, she'd been the head fitter at Saks Fifth Avenue and took me to see how, in the days before computerized everything, the salespeople would send a customer's money up to the cashier through a system of polished brash pneumatic tubes. She loved to shop, sometimes handing me a suede jacket or a pearl necklace with an apology: "Forgive me, I just had to buy this for you."

Everything Frances did seemed sophisticated too, not just going to the Metropolitan Opera House at Lincoln Center but eating *afterward*. (Dinner was at six o'clock when I was growing up.) She ordered steak tartare and so did I. I didn't know from tartare; I figured it was steak, and how wrong could you go? When the plate of ground raw meat arrived at the table, I didn't want to admit that I had no idea what I'd ordered. I took a bite, managed to swallow, and asked, "Isn't this too rare for you?" Frances always poured water into her wine, saying, ". . . or else I'll be tipsy." And she was so easily, physically demonstrative. I felt that her hugs were untainted by any envy or reservation. That time had passed with my own parents, who conveyed a subtle discomfort about physical affection. Puberty and lies had distanced us.

Christmas 1968 should have been a triumphant homecoming for me. When the *Commercial Appeal* was delivered to our house, I was on the cover of the magazine supplement. After dinner, my father and I took one of our traditional walks around the neighborhood, where a suburban building boom had created lots of new construction. We hadn't gotten out of our yard before he said, "Your mother doesn't turn me on anymore."

Long pause. My first thought was: *I don't want to hear this.* I felt as if I was outside the scene, which looked small and distant, as if viewed through the wrong end of a telescope. But I said, "So who does?"

And he answered. "Her name is Ellen. She's my secretary. She's quite a bit younger than I am."

My father was never supposed to leave, no matter what his behavior to my mother, no matter how she might have failed him. They were, after all, the best jitterbuggers in Memphis. For years I asked my mother, "Why did you and Dad stay together if you were incompatible?" and she always answered, "It was a perfect relationship. We were so in love." I remember reading somewhere that the urge to defend your failures can be so strong that you invent another world to inhabit, a cocoon of denial in your own head and in the public eye. My mother had invested in a kind of fantasy goodness about my father, and it wasn't until years later, when I'd confided the worst heartache of my life, that she acknowledged her futile convictions about her husband and the societal pressure to stay married. You get to know the bad mask of a person, she would say, and you stay, hoping there is a good person underneath who really loves you and will never leave.

My father always said he left Memphis with nothing but the shirt on his back. In truth, he drove away in a white Ford LTD, with a nice severance package, having failed to usurp control of Shobe, Inc., from Da-Dee. He married Ellen, then divorced her, then remarried her, and along the way they had a daughter, Mary Catherine. They were living in St. Louis and he had stopped paying my mother alimony. I begged her not to have his wages garnisheed, which got him fired because of the corporate policy at the company where he worked. A lifetime of heavy drinking caught up with his liver, and the doctor said he'd be dead within the year, a censure that seemed to impress him. He stopped drinking, and when he rented a vacation cabin in Ponca, Arkansas, deep in the Ozarks, I went to see him. The opposite of *in vino veritas* is that liquor can camouflage the true person, and in sobriety my father turned out to be lively, kind, intelligent, unpretentious, fun. But mostly he was alive.

JOHN BRUNO LIKED SKINNY MODELS, BUT HE fed me a little too well. He belonged to the oldest gourmet society in the world, called La Chaine de Rotisseurs, and wanted to eat in a different restaurant every night. The meals were glorious—silken smoked salmon with fat capers at The Colony, foie gras and duck à l'orange at Quo Vadis—but disastrous for my figure. The paradox of modeling was that I represented the cynosure of female beauty, selling an illusion of perfection, and the tacit promise of an ad or commercial with my likeness was that those products and services would make other women look like me, but in my private life, even *I* couldn't look like that me. The moment the Model of the Year contest was over, I started gaining weight, back up to my prestarvation pounds. On weekends I went running around the Central Park reservoir with John, but he couldn't join me on the days he worked, and I felt unsafe going alone.

Every week I'd pass thinner, younger, prettier girls on go-sees, and John made disparaging comments about my ample hips and thighs, even as he was ordering a Grand Marnier soufflé from one of his gourmand buddies. Twice I stuck my finger down my throat after a meal but fortunately found the experience too repulsive to make it a habit. The average model of my height weighed no more than 108 pounds (110 was considered fat), and I weighed 150. Nothing ever fit. *I* didn't fit. On a photo shoot for *Vogue*, the editor had to cut the dresses up the back and affix the butterflied pieces to my skin with Scotch tape.

Sometimes when we were shooting on the streets of New York, the magazine would rent a big black limousine, the driver would look the other way, and that would be the changing room. I'd jump out, do the picture, and jump back in again. Once when I was doing a *Glamour* shoot, the editor handed me a long-sleeved shirt that would not go past my elbows and pants that would not go past my knees.

"What size are these?" I asked, poking around for a label.

"These clothes are French," she said with a sniff.

"Well, these are not French shoulders," I said. "My elbow must be the size of a French woman's thigh."

"You can go home," said the editor with a sigh. Getting paid to go home was one of my favorite days of modeling.

On a shoot in Saint Martin, the other model had spent much of the past year in Mexico, obviously sitting in the sun with iodine and baby oil, and it was the middle of winter in New York. When we lay on the beach together, we looked like the black and white keys on a piano, and I was told to stay out in the sun so we would "match." I had baked myself for years, but this time I had an allergic reaction, and the next morning, my eyes were swollen shut. I stayed indoors for twenty-four hours with compresses of wet tea bags, but it didn't do any good. I got paid for not working that time too.

Most models casually took appetite suppressants that were pure speed, professing satiety after nibbling what I considered hamster food. Practically everyone smoked, a habit I'd avoided because of childhood pneumonia, with the added incentive of my mother's hacking cough as morning reveille and evening taps from her three packs a day. On location for *Glamour* in Key West, my roommate was a former Miss Universe who convinced me to try her doctor-prescribed amphetamines.

"Are you sure they won't make me feel weird?" I asked. "And aren't they addictive?"

"Not at all," she answered. "I take them every day."

She assured me there'd be no unpleasant side effects, and I'd watched her sleep sound as a baby, so I swallowed a few pills. I lay awake all night, sweating and staring at the ceiling, my heart pounding as if it was going to pop out of my chest and my teeth gnashing like a hungry beaver. When she woke up and asked, "Would you like—" I quickly said, "No, thanks."

The photographer on that shoot was a man named Frank Horvath—scruffy and obese, partly shaven before it was chic, wearing supersize dark army fatigues, utterly unappealing and initially uninterested in me. At our first meeting at the magazine offices, he'd looked me up and down for about two seconds, shrugged, and muttered, "Okay, she'll do," and left the room. We were working at Hemingway's house in Key West, with a resident collection of six-toed cats living in the garden, and Horvath didn't bother to knock when he came into the room where I was being dressed by the editors, demanding of no one in particular, "Is she ready yet?" We were working on a second-story veranda, and he hadn't even shot a whole roll of film before he said, "You're not very good at this." I stared at him, struck dumb by his blunt candor. "Stop posing," he said. "You're trying too hard, and you've developed some bad habits. Just think, be in the moment, actually see what you're looking at." I didn't know it at the time, but he was giving me my first acting lesson. The camera captures what you're thinking, so it had better be something besides: *if I hold my hands like this, I'll look thinner*. Jimmy Cagney said that acting was easy: stand up tall, look the other guy in the eye, and tell the truth. What Frank Horvath led me to that day was a kind of *photographie vérité*.

Glamour put me on the cover and used 101 photographs of me inside that issue (my grandmother counted) followed by seven more *Glamour* covers that year. The era of Twiggy and Jean ("the Shrimp") Shrimpton was over, and there seemed to be a little window of opportunity for a healthier look, personified by Cheryl Tiegs and me. Everybody is supposed to have a better side, and I was always photographed from the left for covers, but Richard Avedon took this as a challenge. "Let's try the right side," he'd say each of the half dozen times we worked together, but his "cover tries" were never used because editors were unaccustomed to seeing me that way.

Sometimes the photographs looked like another person altogether. By the time they'd been retouched, there were no flaws, no asymmetry of any kind. Things you didn't know you had were eliminated from your face. I'm still shocked at what Kodak did on the full-length cutout of me that stood in drugstores to introduce the first Instamatic camera—there wasn't a dimple or ripple of flesh. The countertop version had a mechanical arm that swung the camera up and down, rubbing an unfortunate line across my face. I inherited the cutout that my grandmother kept in her garage (she said "Hi" to it every time she pulled in), and one year my caretaker stuck a Santa hat on its head and a sign that said MERRY CHRISTMAS TO ALL. I still have my original "Breck girl" portrait too, an idealized vision of a woman, all misty and dew-eyed like a Stepford wife. These relics seem to migrate to my home in Memphis. Maybe they talk to one another when I'm not around, like the toys in Santa's workshop that come alive at night.

I was clueless about the future beyond modeling, but not out of contentment with the status quo—I was frantically trying to figure out what was my Job in the universe. Stewart Cowley was opening a talent division to maneuver models into lucrative television and film work. He suggested that I meet a man who'd made a violent, low-budget, successful movie and was preparing to direct the sequel. The gold-leafed hotel suite was far more sumptuous than I expected for a B-list mogul. Stewart brought me upstairs but left quite abruptly, whispering "I'll be right back" while I arranged myself on the sofa. As we were talking, Mr. B-list took my elbow and steered me to one of the tall windows overlooking Central Park. Then his hand moved from my elbow to my shoulder, he leaned in close and thrust his tongue down my throat. Naively, I asked what was going on.

"This is a scene in the new film," he said. "I thought we'd rehearse."

I pushed him away, saying, "I don't think this is working for me," just as I heard a knock at the door signaling Stewart's return. I made an excuse about needing to be somewhere else, and the moment we were in the hallway, I hissed, "Don't ever leave me alone with one of those creeps again!" I never knew whether his sudden departure was prearranged or an innocent mistake.

With the memory of that lechery still fresh, I learned with some trepidation that Roger Vadim had offered me a screen test for a film called *Peryl*, and I insisted that a chaperone accompany me to Los Angeles: my booker at the agency, Donna DeCita, whose sister is Bernadette Peters. We stayed in the grizzled old Chateau Marmont on Sunset Boulevard, where some of the regulars were wandering around the lobby in their bathrobes. Because there was no script yet, I was instructed to rehearse a scene from *Cat on a Hot Tin Roof*. I sat on the lawn reading lines with Vadim's assistant, who then drove me to Malibu for the screen test. Vadim was tall and slender with thinning hair, wearing a creamy shirt that he said was made of Egyptian cotton. Three years of Memphis high school French didn't help me understand a word as he conversed with a French actor named Christian Marquand (also tall and slender with thinning hair), whose home we were using for the audition. I definitely knew what the term *ménage à trois* meant and was glad for the chaperone.

Most of the test consisted of filming me, with no sound, dancing to the Rolling Stones singing "(I Can't Get No) Satisfaction." (The old-time Hollywood producers, many of them German, would refer to this as "M.O.S."—*mit* out sound.) The film never got produced; I was told that the financing fell through. But I had started something interesting with the assistant (younger, hairier, and shorter than either of the Frenchmen), and as my friend Wanda used to say, "How do you know if a shoe fits unless you try it on?" A few weeks later, I lied to John Bruno and flew to San Francisco for the weekend. The assistant picked me up on a motorcycle and strapped my suitcase to the back. I kept looking over my shoulder as we rode, expecting to see the highway littered with my bras and underpants. Vadim later offered me a role in *Pretty Maids All in a Row*, but the character was set to die, early and gruesomely, in the girls' rest room of a high school. I declined, thinking surely I could do better than death on a toilet seat, and my acting career was stalled at the gate.

CHAPTER FIVE

"Make Sure There's a Lot of Nudity"

IT'S A NOD TO THE HYPERREALITY OF THE FILM business that everybody in Hollywood knows the maxim: no names on location. Cast and crew conspire in an implicit acceptance and discretion about the phenomenon of musical beds, about who is seen emerging from which star's trailer or which grip's room at the Motel 6. The set is like an office Christmas party, where indiscretions are absolved when the party's over, or like the miniature village around the model trains that I coveted as a child, a bantam community assembled for fun. Everyone has a common purpose, everyone is paid to be creative, and everyone can pretend to be someone else. It's a dreamscape of sorts, basically free of familial and adult responsibilities. I was twenty years old when I entered that world, mischievous and recklessly self-absorbed.

In the spring of 1970, there was a mounting pile of scripts in one corner of my apartment, so daunting that I virtually ignored them. I was content to give the movie business a wide berth anyway. The Hollywood people I'd met so far were creeps, and every model I knew was taking acting lessons. I was determined to be different. My friend Jim Rogers offered to help sift through the scripts and found one he thought I should consider. It was called *The Last Picture Show*, from a coming-of-age novel by Larry McMurtry about the lives of small-town Texas teenagers in 1951. I would be considered for the part of Jacy Farrow, the character whose imprudent promiscuity wreaks havoc with her friends and neighbors.

I went to meet the director, Peter Bogdanovich, in his suite at the Essex House facing Central Park, and my deportment conveyed an intentional lack of interest: jeans and denim jacket streaked and softened in the washing machine with rocks and bleach, Dr. Scholl's wooden sandals, and a paperback book. Zen philosophers talk about hitting the target without aiming at it, which is surely what I did. I hated the idea of playing Jacy, a self-absorbed ice princess whose persona had often been assigned (erroneously, I thought) to me. She stings men and moves on, making them sexual objects as men traditionally do to women, but she never finds anything satisfying. Plus the script called for two nude scenes, which seemed anathema. Nudity as an inherently moral concept is one thing; actually dropping my skivvies was another.

Peter opened the door to his suite. He looked to be thirtyish, six feet tall with a high forehead, dark eyes, a shock of thick near-black hair, and a goofy smile. The immediate attraction was so strong, I was flummoxed.

"What are you reading?" he asked.

"Dostoyevsky," I said.

"Which one?" he asked.

"*War and Peace*." I was so unnerved, I might have fumbled my own name, let alone Tolstoy's. But we both laughed out loud, and he invited me to sit down. As he headed for the couch, I curled up on the floor next to a coffee table with a tray that held the remains of a room-service breakfast and a small crystal vase with a single red rose. During the course of our conversation about the film, I picked up the flower and slowly plucked the petals off one by one, making a little pile of vanquished foliage. Peter later told me that he imagined Jacy could do to any man what I had done to that rose.

Pages of a new script shuttled between Peter in California and Larry McMurtry in Texas, a virgin screenwriter who typed scenes on cheap yellow paper. They established a basic construction for the story that was not in the book (a year that spanned from one football season to the next), added some important material (like a graduation scene), and began casting pivotal roles. Cloris Leachman and Ellen Burstyn were to play two middle-aged women assuaging loveless marriages with infidelity. Ben Johnson, who'd played opposite John Wayne in several of John Ford's seminal westerns, turned down the part of Sam the Lion, the ethical heart of Anarene, Texas. He didn't like the four-letter words in the script, said he didn't talk that way in front of women and children. So Peter had Ford call him.

"Are you gonna be the Duke's sidekick for the rest of your life?" Ford demanded.

"Well, they've got to rewrite the dialogue," said Johnson.

Peter complied and called to tell Johnson that some of the objectionable language had been removed. "I hope you understand," Peter said assuredly, "you're going to get an Academy Award for this picture."

"Goddammit," Johnson said, "I'll do the goddamned thing."

Peter chewed on toothpicks in those days, part of his program to quit smoking, and had stopped to pick some up at a Food Giant in the San Fernando Valley. While standing in the checkout line, he saw my face on the cover of *Glamour*, my hair in tendrils over the collar of a pink and white shirt imprinted with the words "I love you" over and over. There was a fresh sexual threat in the photograph that made him think of Jacy Farrow. He'd considered two Texas girls for the part: one was Sissy Spacek, and the other was named Patsy McClenny until she started working in soap operas and reinvented herself as Morgan Fairchild. But I learned much later that his immediate reaction to that magazine cover was the kind of disorientation that Jacy engendered in men. If anybody ever projected an image of completeness when at the core was emptiness, it was Jacy Farrow. Peter couldn't know it was also me.

He was convinced that not only would my lack of acting experience not prevent me from playing the role successfully, it might even enhance my work because I wasn't coming into the process with preconceived notions about the character. I was a blank slate, fresh clay. He didn't want me to do a screen test, but the producer, Bert Schneider, was less assured. He even dug up the test I'd made for Roger Vadim in an effort to convince Peter that I didn't have enough innate talent to compensate for my amateur status. It was the only time Peter would ever doubt me. I was asked to do a reading in California with Jeff Bridges, who'd already been cast as Duane Jackson, the callous boy on his way to war, and two young actors who were up for the part of the more sensitive and vulnerable Sonny Crawford: John Ritter, son of the country music star Tex Ritter, and Chris Mitchum, son of Robert Mitchum. Eventually the part went to Timothy Bottoms, who had just played the lead as a quadruple amputee in Dalton Trumbo's World War I film *Johnny Got His Gun*.

My modeling agent Stewart Cowley arranged for his Los Angeles representative to pick me up at the airport, where he announced, "For your first lunch in town, I'm taking you to Pinks," a local landmark for chili dogs. I'd been to L.A. before on modeling assignments, but this was *Hollywood*. Tinseltown. Take the sunshine, mix in a little smog, and the city actually looks tan. I was anxious, excited, and hungry, wolfing down several chili cheese dogs with sauerkraut and mustard. I was fumbling in my purse for breath mints when we got to the BBS office. A young man with a lean face, receding hairline, and dazzling smile was reclining in a swivel chair with his feet on the desk, smoking a joint. I'd seen *Easy Rider* and *Five Easy Pieces* so I recognized Jack Nicholson, who lurched to his feet and made an elaborate attempt to bow in greeting, making jokes I didn't get but laughed at anyway.

I got the job but not without Schneider's growling

insistence to Peter, "Make sure there's a lot of nudity." My entire salary was $5,000 for twelve weeks of work, an amount I could have earned in a week of modeling, but by this time I began to believe that the compelling story of these teenagers whose options seem so limited by their dusty small town would be painful but important to tell. By thinking back to the paintings of the bare-breasted women I'd seen in the great museums of Europe, I'd determined that the nude scenes had nothing to do with morality. But my boyfriend, John Bruno, had other ideas. "You do a nude scene and I will never marry you," he declared. "If everybody in the world sees my future wife naked, you won't turn me on anymore." This from a man supposed to be *so* sophisticated? I was never really interested in marriage to John or anybody else: it represented a kind of indentured servitude, and I was hardly alone in rethinking the institution. The atmosphere of the late 1960s was one of sexual libertinism, from the bumper stickers that said MAKE LOVE NOT WAR to the newly endorsed forms of socializing (mate swapping, orgies, and "key parties"—couples played grab bag with their car keys, throwing them in a bowl from which the wives fished out a set and went home with the owner).

I don't need to hear Billie Holiday's "God bless the child who's got his own" to know that I had to make sure I could take care of myself in the world so I wouldn't be beholden to men. I was disturbed by John's possessiveness and his insistence, from the beginning of our affair, that if either one of us was in the mood for sex, the other had to comply—not a great basis for passionate lovemaking. But it was Frances

Bruno who provided the final impetus for me to leave. "If you wanna do this movie, you gotta do this movie," she said. "You know I love ya, but don't let Johnnie hold you back." I knew enough not to do *Pretty Maids All in a Row* and enough to do *The Last Picture Show*.

Production began that October in north central Texas, a time of golden Indian summer sunlight combined with fierce freezing winds. To a large extent, we were persona non grata in the community. The locals resented Larry McMurtry's portrayal of their foibles—when Peter met Larry's father, the elder McMurtry said, "If you'll pour kerosene on him, I'll light the match"—and the real town, called Archer City, was given the pseudonym of "Anarene" for the film. Our provisional home was the Ramada Inn in Wichita Falls, a two-story construction of red brick built around an unheated pool. Every day for two weeks I worked with an accent coach in my cheerless room right next to the soft-drink machine and rehearsed in the optimistically named Presidential Suite, an orange nightmare that Peter shared with his wife, Polly, the film's production designer. Peter was twenty-three when they married, and just three weeks before filming began, she had given birth to a second daughter, Alexandra, who was left in the care of Peter's parents in Arizona along with three-year-old Antonia.

I sometimes ask guests in my home to take their clean hands and touch the patina on my treasured canvases from Borislav Bogdanovich, Peter's talented and eccentric Serbian father, a painter who worked in his pajamas and allowed no one to touch his hair. His wife came from a prosperous Jewish family in Vienna, and though many of her relatives perished in the Holocaust, she managed to escape to America in 1939, already pregnant with Peter. Her first child had died after a horrifying accident, scalded by the hot soup she was making and succumbing to anaphylactic shock. Peter knew that an elder brother had died, but Herma Bogdanovich mentioned it to him only once toward the end of her life, barely able to get the words out, and I can't help but think that Peter suffers from survivor's guilt.

Peter once had a perforated ulcer and has had to be very careful about what he eats ever since, so he didn't accompany the cast and crew each morning as we ate eggs and grits at the motel diner, opened especially early for us. We rode to Archer City in a circa-1950 bus—the chug of its diesel engine in the predawn stillness was my wake-up call. I spent twenty-five dollars on a used bicycle with fat tires and no gears so I could explore the area, but there wasn't much to see except trailer parks and junkyards. We had so much time on our hands that I read voraciously Kate Millett's *Sexual Politics*, Germaine Greer's *The Female Eunuch*, and Betty Friedan's *The Feminine Mystique*. These three feminist books revolutionized my thinking and put his-story into perspective. I was born again as a radical feminist, and began a search for her-story.

My dressing room was on the second floor of a seedy old hotel whose street-level space was a hamburger joint—the burgers were put in paper bags that would be dripping with grease within moments. My wardrobe consisted of thin cotton dresses from a vintage clothing store and a pair of jeans from the Columbia wardrobe graveyard erroneously labeled "Debbie Reynolds"—many inches shorter and pounds lighter than I.

For my first scene as an actress, I was in a convertible parked in an open field, making out with Timothy Bottoms, who was to reach under my halter top and grab a handful of breast. There was a rumor that Tim refused to bathe in protest before his love scenes with Cloris Leachman, but he smelled fine to me and seemed almost as nervous as I was, furiously chewing gum all during rehearsal. The mid-autumn sun of the Texas plains was so blinding that I couldn't keep my eyes open, and it seemed like half the town was recruited to hold blackout flags made of a heavy opaque material called dubatine to block the glare. Right before he said "Action" Peter leaned in close to me and instructed, "No tongue." I disobeyed.

But for the most part I listened attentively to everything Peter said: how to do a double take or overlap dialogue with another actor, how to brush my hair lightly between takes so it would match in the next scene, how a task (called a piece of business) or an article of clothing or the town itself could help to capture and reflect the character. Casually taking Sonny's milkshake away from him, loudly slurping the last drops out of his cup, all the while professing my devotion, showed in a humorous way that Jacy always gets what she wants — like a spider sucking the innards out of her victims. Peter often repeated Orson Welles's dictum that a good director presides over accidents. During the scene with Sonny and Sam the Lion at the water tank, the sun was doing gymnastics, in and out of the clouds. Instead of saying "Cut!" Peter motioned for everyone to keep going. He loved the moody chiaroscuro created by the contrasting light. It became his homage to the great American director John

Ford. More than twenty years earlier, when Ford was filming *She Wore a Yellow Ribbon* (with a much younger Ben Johnson), a terrible rainstorm approached. Ford liked the threatening look of the dark sky and decided to shoot anyway. Fearing for his reputation the director of photography wrote directly on the celluloid, "Shot under protest." He won the Academy Award.

I witnessed the quintessential oblivious wielding of power of a passionate director: in one outdoor scene, two children were playing behind a house that was in the camera's frame, and Peter called to them, "Hey, you kids, get out of your yard." With each passing day I began to feel more and more invested in every scene, worrying: *Oh, God, is he going to get this take?* or *Has it stopped raining so we can finish this scene?* Every chance I got I stayed up all night to watch the shooting, drinking Dixie cups of coffee and brandy to stay awake. I loved to see the cables snaking across the wet streets (always hosed down for night filming because the reflection makes them more visually exciting), the huge wind machines that had to be moved by three brawny grips, the smoke wafting out of chimneys above the bulbs of the arc lights in the cold night air. Peter had decided to shoot the film in black and white because it would portray the 1950s more convincingly and because color can distract the audience. Gradations of gray allow people to concentrate on dramatic content and performance, rather than the tone of red in an actress's lipstick or dress. The sharpness and depth of field in black and white have never been surpassed in color photography.

Several weeks into the shooting, Peter got a request

from Bert Schneider: Could Stephen Friedman visit the set? He was a producer only because he owned the movie rights to the book and Peter reluctantly agreed to let him observe for a few days. Friedman asked me to take a walk with him one afternoon and gave me notes on my performance. Returning to the hotel, I saw Peter.

"Do you think my acting is enthusiastic enough?" I asked.

"Who's been talking to you?" said Peter. When he learned that it was Friedman, I thought smoke would come out of his nostrils. Then, crossing the lobby, he ran into Ellen Burstyn.

"Who's this Friedman character?" she asked. "Is he a producer or what?"

"Well, he's a nominal producer," Peter said.

"He's giving me line readings," said Ellen. "He told me about one of his favorite lines in the book, how he always imagined it being said like—"

Peter exploded and ran for a phone to call Bert Schneider. "If that cocksucker isn't out of Texas by tonight," he screamed, "I'm going to borrow a hunting knife from one of these good ol' boys and kill him."

Friedman was gone the next morning, and we didn't see him again until the Academy Awards, where he was dressed in a green tuxedo. When a still photographer on the set talked to me about my scenes, Peter sent him packing too. The joke was: if you want to get fired from this picture, talk to Cybill Shepherd.

Jacy makes her initial appearance in the movie theater where *Father of the Bride* is playing. Sonny is necking with his girlfriend in the back row, keeping one eye on Elizabeth Taylor, whom he really wants to be kissing, and Jacy walks up the aisle with Duane to ask teasingly, "Whatcha'all doin' back here in the dark?" I was sitting in a row just ahead of Peter as we waited until the shot was lit to the satisfaction of the Oscar-winning director of photography Robert Surtees. Peter leaned over the worn velvet seat and spoke in a low voice right next to my ear.

"How are you doing?" he said.

"I'm a little nervous, but I'm okay," I answered. "How are you?"

He bent an elbow on the seat and rested one cheek in his hand. "I don't know who I'd rather sleep with," he said, "you or the character you're playing."

The moment was so intense that I covered my face with my hands to hide the rising color. Just then I heard from the back of the theater, "We're ready for you, Cybill."

Even if he hadn't meant it, Peter's words would have been terrific motivation for the scene. I felt sexy, playful, inspired. And I couldn't stop thinking about him, about the corners of his mouth as he spoke before I covered my eyes.

Not long after, Polly was away scouting locations, and Jeff Bridges had left for a week of army reserve duty. As we wrapped for the day, Peter said, "I guess you're going to be alone tonight." It was his first reference to the open secret that Jeff and I had been keeping company after hours.

Jeff was adorable, but nobody could compare to Peter. What he had to offer was authority, maturity, guidance, and a palpable attraction. The force field that had started in the Essex House, when I didn't know what book I was reading, would grow to the point that even Polly remarked on it—she said facetiously that Peter was always drawn to women with big breasts and small feet (neither of which she had).

There was a moment of silence and expectation before I responded to Peter's comment.

"I'm alone every night," I said. It was as if the lighting in the room changed, everything fading to black until there was just one spotlight on the couple.

We made plans for dinner that night at a cowboy steakhouse outside of town that we hoped would not be frequented by any of the cast or crew. I nervously tried on every outfit in my suitcase, finally settling on blue jeans. It was the time of night when the ambient temperature in Texas seemed to drop like a stone, but the shiver I felt down the back of my neck as I saw Peter at his car wasn't meteorological. In that flat country, the sky gets bigger and the sunset surrounds you like a dome. We stopped and stood by the bridge that crosses the Red River, watching the ball of fire drop behind the horizon. He sang a cappella to me in the car on the way home—"I'm a Fool to Love You" and "Glad to Be Unhappy." No suitor had ever serenaded me like that, and it felt like the most romantic kind of wooing. When we got back to the motel, we both went to my room.

An emotional archaeologist might speculate about how much I bought into the mythology of *The Last Picture Show* and a character who represents the height of narcissism: damaging other people but focusing on how bad it makes her feel. Jacy was doing that in the film, and I was doing it in real life, aware of the pain we would cause but unable to resist causing it. The inability to tolerate the truths about oneself is an essential element of narcissism, and I had a blithely unexamined life. The participants in a love triangle are often neatly categorized as innocent victim, faithless destroyer, and erotic enabler. But the roles are mutable, and I don't think you can play one without ending up playing them all.

When Polly returned from her scouting expedition the truth became impossible for her to ignore. We weren't doing anything obvious—on the contrary, we were even more guarded, trying to stay away from each other—but the energy changes when an illicit affair is consummated. Polly would later tell Peter that she knew for sure when she saw a box of pralines in their room that were not meant for her, even though they were her favorites. One night she was eating dinner in the restaurant at the Tradewinds Motel when she saw us come in. Knowing it was best not to have a confrontation until the work was done, she crawled out of the restaurant on her knees. She moved to another room at the Ramada Inn, hoping that she could resurrect her marriage after a location affair had lost its heat.

On those charts that measure stress in life, where the death of a spouse rates 100 and a bad haircut is a 3, Peter was hovering near the top, and he went off the chart entirely when he got the news that his father lay in a coma after a catastrophic stroke. He went to Arizona for the weekend, but three days after he returned to work, Borislav Bogdanovich died.

Peter's father's death drew us closer together as I made myself available to hold and comfort him. But it would have been completely inappropriate for me to accompany him to the funeral—I was the chippie who had broken up his marriage—and Polly declined to go, so he had no support for the trip. When he returned, he had to shoot the funeral scene for Sam the Lion, a brutal piece of bad timing. It would become one of the most powerful sequences of the film, informed by Feter's personal loss and infused with an extra dimension of raw emotion that affected all of us.

My whole life I'd been told I could use my beauty, but it had been slippery footing: I was never thin enough, my breasts were not the right shape, and the area under my eyes was too puffy. But in 1970 I had the right look for the right time—a genetic roll of the dice in my favor. If I had resembled one of Modigliani's fragile waifs rather than Botticelli's ample voluptuaries, maybe nobody would know who I am today. Peter told me, "Don't you dare lose weight," and for the first time in my life, I felt confident about my looks. But I was still petrified by the thought of the striptease on a diving board at a midnight pool party and the deflowering at the Cactus Motel that has all the romance of root canal.

An assistant director was given what he considered the plum assignment of going to talent agencies in Dallas and finding a body double for me, in case I refused to do the nude scene. But I wouldn't let him see me naked or pose for photographs, so I was put in the bizarre position of describing my breasts to him. (Wildly embarrassed, I said "eggs over easy.") Peter kept reassuring me that there would be only a skeletal crew, that none of the other actors would be present when we filmed, and that it wouldn't mean the end of my career before it even started. A friend had pointed out to me that once an actress appears nude on film, the stills often fall into the wrong hands, and I wanted a signed affidavit from Peter and the producer Bert Schneider that no still photographs would be printed. I continued to nag Peter about this until one day he snapped, "If you ever mention this again, I will never give you another piece of direction." I never did speak of it again. The day we shot the diving board scene, I wore two pairs of underpants so I could remove one and still be covered. My anxiety was impeccable motivation, since Jacy's bravado covers up sheer terror.

I had another naked moment of truth in the scene at the motel. As an impotent Duane keeps mumbling, "I dunno what happened," Jacy finally explodes, "Oh, if you say that one more time, I'll bite you," throwing her panties at his head. Since Peter was framing the shot for a close-up, I was thrilled to get to put my bra back on. There's a comic juxtaposition of music and action in the scene, a florid arrangement of "Wish You Were Here" mocking Duane's inability to get it up. Nudity and comedy in the same scene is a rare combination in film.

(Years later, when Peter reedited the movie for a new release, he reinstated a scene where Jacy has sex on a pool table with "Abilene," a callous older man who works for her father and has an affair with her mother. The sex is not violent or coerced but so cold and bloodless that it seems tantamount to an act of aggression against Jacy, stopping just short of rape. Including this scene makes my character more sympathetic, gives her more dimension. The original sound had been lost, so I had to go into a studio and rerecord the audible implications of lovemaking, looking at footage of myself from twenty-five years earlier while Peter stood next to me giggling.)

At the time I thought that God was going to strike me dead for appearing nude in a movie. But the morning after, I got up and ate oatmeal and realized that I was going to live. I thought surely I'd be struck down after I had sex with a married man. But the morning after, I woke up quite healthy. I knew the affair was wrong, but I rationalized it by thinking that I hadn't exchanged any vows with Polly, and that I was only doing what men have been doing for eons, taking their pleasure wherever they find it. John Bruno, who had come for one visit, sent me a pithy present: a shiny steel heart-shaped dog tag on a chain that said: MY NAME IS CYBILL. I BELONG TO NO ONE. Now it seems like an estimable motto, but at the time it saddened me.

When a film wraps, the actors often like to keep some of their props or wardrobe as mementos. I wanted the heart-shaped locket and the brown and white saddle shoes that Jacy wore, but Polly was in charge of costumes and wouldn't give them to me. I guess she figured I had enough of a souvenir: her husband.

Peter and I had made no promises to one another beyond the boundaries of Texas. I'd never experienced anything so powerful before and didn't know where it would lead. I still thought of marriage as an outdated institution left over from the era of chastity belts, but Peter said he had to give his own marriage a chance. I went back to Memphis before returning to New York City, and Peter and Polly returned to their home in Los Angeles. Right away he began sneaking out to phone me, and Polly finally said, "If you can't stay away from her, why don't you just go with her?" He called me from his room at the Hollywood Roosevelt Hotel.

"Do you want to come out here and live with me?" he asked wearily.

"Okay," I said, the calmness of my voice belying the joy and trepidation in my heart. "When do you want me to come?"

"On the next plane," he said.

We rented a furnished apartment on the seventh floor of a landmark Art Deco building on the Sunset Strip. But many nights I camped out on the couch at the production company, living on those chili dogs from Pinks and watching Peter edit *The Last Picture Show* on an old Moviola. Since he had no assistant, he assembled the raw footage himself—twenty-four frames per second, like twenty-four still photographs. He marked with a white wax pencil between the frames where he wanted to cut. Then he rolled his chair over to a splicer table, reassembling the film with a special Scotch tape that had sprocket perforations. He would then run the scene for me, demonstrating the powerful effect of adding or removing even a single frame to the "head" or the "tail" of the shot. Watching Peter work was an education in film, and it served me well when I got involved in the editing of the *Cybill* show. I like it when I hear this process called "montage." It seems to convey the hope that the whole will add up to even more than the sum of its parts. Film is visual music. It's put together with more than logic and announces when it's right. Many a performance can be made or destroyed by what is left in or cut out.

Columbia fought hard to rename *The Last Picture Show*, afraid it would be confused with *The Last Movie*, Dennis Hopper's follow-up to *Easy Rider* that was to be released just a few weeks earlier. Studio executives submitted about five hundred alternative titles, all of which were resoundingly rejected—it was, after all, the title that had originally attracted Peter to the project. Bert Schneider called with the disheartening news that the picture had been given an X rating because of the nudity, but Peter said, "I don't see how we can cut any of it. Tell them to look at it again." Bert appealed to his brother, Columbia's head of production, who had been an earlier advocate, arguing against the corporate executives who questioned why anybody would want to see a black and white film, much less make one. The rating was changed to R. We never knew why this happened.

My mother's response to the news about Peter and me was "If you're going to be with a married man, you might as well be a whore." But her moral stance didn't prevent her from accepting my invitation to the premiere at the New York Film Festival or from sharing the suite reserved for Peter and me at the Essex House. (In a romantic gesture, he had tried but failed to get the same suite where we first met.) There was only time for brief introductions because we had to leave early for the requisite media interviews, and Mother was not happy that she didn't get to ride to Lincoln Center in the same limousine with us and share the glory. I was ambivalent about her presence: I wanted her to participate, but she'd already declared me a harlot, and I knew she'd have a hard time watching a movie featuring my bare breasts.

The Last Picture Show starts in silence that continues for a long time—no music, stark black lettering for the credits, and a slow pan during which the only sound is a blowing wind. The first voice you hear is Peter's, as an off-camera disc jockey with a thick Texas drawl introducing Hank Williams's recording of "Cold Cold Heart." Peter and I held hands as the lights dimmed. I didn't relax until Jacy's first line—"Whatcha'all doin' back here in the dark?"—and for the first time, I felt the magic of an audience laughing at something I said.

There was a postpremiere party at Elaine's, a popular place with the New York media crowd. When I walked into the room on Peter's arm, people stopped talking and snapped to attention. But I was also aware that they weren't much interested in what I had to say. I felt like a paper doll: I looked good on a flat surface, but if I turned to the side, I wasn't there, like the cardboard cutout of me used to sell Instamatic cameras. I listened rather than talked for most of the evening, burying myself in my lamb chops.

When we got back to the hotel, my mother was standing slightly out of the doorway to her darkened room, wearing a bright floral robe.

"What did you think?" Peter asked.

She directed her answer to me, as if I had asked the question. "Maybe you'll do better next time," she said, then turned her back and shut the door. I giggled a little uncomfortably (after all, we'd gotten a standing ovation), but Peter winced, as if he'd been slapped in the face and muttered "shit" under his breath. They never spoke again.

Newsweek called *The Last Picture Show* "a masterpiece . . . the most impressive work by a young American director since *Citizen Kane.*" It was nominated for eight Academy Awards and won two, for Best Supporting Actress and Actor (Cloris Leachman and Ben Johnson). It won seven New York Film Critics awards, three British Academy awards, one Golden Globe, one National Society of Film Critics award, and was selected by the Library of Congress for the National Film Registry. Although the Oscars for Best Director and Best Picture went to William Friedkin and *The French Connection*, I had become an actress under the tutelage of a great teacher. Like the song about dancing with the man who danced with the woman who danced with the Prince of Wales, I was taught by the man who was taught by Stella Adler who was taught by Stanislavsky. He surrounded me with people who were the best in the business, helping me avert the kind of early career embarrassment that comes back and bites you in the ass. My ass didn't show teeth marks until later. As Orson Welles said about his career, I started at the top and worked my way down.

CHAPTER SIX

"White Boys Don't Eat . . ."

MUTUALLY AND ENTHUSIASTICALLY, PETER and I rejected marriage vows—but both of us will always regret not having had a child together. When we moved into Sunset Towers, there was a period of time when he went "home" each night to put his two young daughters to bed. He usually returned beaten down by Polly's recriminations. Later his girls would visit us on weekends, and for the first twenty-four hours, I was the enemy, but I never tried to woo them or be their mother, just included them in games of Parcheesi and croquet and took them swimming. Eventually we would all relax—just in time for them to go back "home."

I had no more than the occasional bloodless telephone conversation with their mother. Polly was a great help to Peter in his work, but when the marriage was over, their behavior toward each other reinforced a sense of the singular creative hostility between them, still fresh in recent interviews. According to Polly, she not only discovered the novel of *The Last Picture Show* but also me. When Peter began work on *What's Up, Doc?*, a screwball comedy with Barbra Streisand and Ryan O'Neal intended as an homage to *Bringing Up Baby*, he decided to hire Polly, who accepted the job of set designer on the condition that I be banned from the set, bravely joking that she refused to be "Cybillized." I visited in San Francisco anyway but was relegated to swimming laps at the Nob Hill YWCA and hearing stories about la Streisand secondhand. (Peter asked her to cut her famously talonlike fingernails, but she would only comply on her right hand, so in most of the movie, she's holding a raincoat or some other prop in the left.) The closest I got to the set was watching the "gag reel," with Peter playing Barbra's part to show her what to do in the scene where she sings "As Time Goes By." He hides under a drop cloth and slithers off the piano, stopping just short of kissing Ryan on the mouth.

My relationship with Peter felt as if it was built on shifting tectonic plates. Our only rule was "Don't ask me what you don't want to know," and the corollary was "Never cheat on me in the same city." I'm sure part of my appeal for Peter was that I was attractive to other men. He'd watch from down a drugstore aisle or across a theater lobby as some guy would circle in pre-flirting formation, then he'd appear beside me with a smug kiss or gesture of intimacy that announced squatter's rights. I wonder now if he didn't unconsciously condone me having relationships with other men.

The summer of 1972, while back in Memphis, I got

a call from George Klein, the local television host who'd emceed the Miss Teenage Memphis pageant. A friend of his had admired me in *The Last Picture Show*. He was an actor too. And he lived at Graceland.

I'd been crazy jealous when my sister got a record player and a small collection of Elvis Presley 45s back in the mid-1950s, playing "Hound Dog" and "Don't Be Cruel" nonstop and singing along in a tinny voice that I tried to overshout. Everybody in Memphis felt jingoistic pride in the native son who hung out with the black musicians like Big Joe Turner and Ivory Joe Hunter in the juke joints of Beale Street, adapting their moves and their music. (It was Willie Mae "Big Mama" Thornton who recorded "Hound Dog" first, and she was talking about *men*—"You ain't lookin' for a woman, all you lookin' for is a home.") Sam Phillips, who engineered the radio broadcasts on the Peabody roof, had started Sun Records, signing up Jr. Walker and Little Milton and B. B. King, and he was looking for a white boy who could sing like a black one. A local disc jockey at WHBQ named Dewey Phillips was playing black and white artists on the same station for the first time. He'd spin anything from Hank Williams to Sister Rosetta Tharpe, and he put Elvis on the map. But when Elvis went from radio to television and live performances, his music wasn't considered polite (you never saw Sinatra bump and grind like a stripper), and I could recall with clarity the furor when Ed Sullivan consented to show him only from the waist up, fearful for the overwrought libidos of the nation's youth. In 1972 I was not too interested in Elvis Presley or his moves. He'd become a little passé, supplanted by Motown and the British invasion of the Beatles and the

Rolling Stones. But he was, after all, the King.

"He's got to call me," I told Klein, "and he's got to pick me up himself."

"Fair enough," he said.

One of his people tracked me down at Jane's house. "It's for you," she said, handing me the receiver with demonstrative boredom. "Some weirdo pretending to be Elvis Presley." When she grasped from my stunned mien that this was no impersonator, she pressed her own ear to the receiver next to mine, the two of us listening to a voice that sounded like melted Kraft caramels.

"I've wanted to meet you for a long time," he said, "ever since I saw you in that movie."

"That was two years ago," I said. "What took you so long?"

He gave an appreciative little laugh. "I'd like to see you sometime," he said.

"Are you sure you're not still married?" I asked. Like the rest of the world, I knew about Priscilla and their daughter, Lisa Marie, and I'd already taken hits for breaking up one marriage, but he assured me he was separated and in the throes of a divorce. He asked me to join him for a movie that evening—Elvis regularly rented local theaters at midnight for his entourage, unflatteringly known as the Memphis Mafia. Jane was flailing her arms in a silent entreaty, "Take me! Take me!" I asked if I could bring my best girlfriend. Sure, he said. Elvis never did have a problem with two girls.

I dropped my demand about being picked up, since Jane and I were driving together. When we entered the Crosstown Theater, the phalanx of good ol' boys wouldn't let us past the lobby. So Jane and I started tangoing together in front of the popcorn machine, ignoring the people who were trying desperately to ignore us. Word that Elvis had entered the building through a side door filtered into the lobby like a game of whispering down the lane, and we were granted admission, sitting in a row with the bubbas. As if on cue, everybody in the row to my right got up and moved one seat over.

I smelled him before I saw him, but I couldn't for the life of me identify his cologne. Let's just call it Eau de Elvis. His luminous olive skin glowed with what I later learned was bronzing makeup. He was chewing Fruit Stripe gum and offered me a piece, graciously sending another down the row to Jane. As others arrived for the screening, he pointed out a distinguished-looking man. "That's an eye surgeon," he said. "He treated me for an infection by driving a needle straight through my eyeball, and I was awake every minute." Then he opened his jacket and revealed a pearl-handled revolver stuck in his belt. "I carry this little girl everywhere I go," he said. When these preambles were over, we watched *Goodbye Columbus* in silence, while I tried to sneak peripheral glances at him in the dark. There was a second feature scheduled, but partway through *Sunday, Bloody Sunday*, there was a kiss between two men. Revolted members of the Mafia yelled, "That's gross, man," and Elvis ordered, "Stop the movie." And then he was gone, uttering a barely audible "See y'all later."

Jane and I had just reached the sidewalk in front of the theater when a white Lincoln made a U-turn and pulled up to the curb. Elvis strode toward us and asked, "Y'all want to come back to the house?" Jane and I exchanged glances, read each other's thoughts, and declined. With the barest trace of good night, Elvis pulled away and proceeded right through a stop sign, within spitting distance of a motorcycle cop. We watched as the officer signaled the car to pull over and Elvis flashed his Special Deputy badge from the Memphis Sheriff's Department. (Later I got a badge too. It lived in the bathroom drawer until somebody in the sheriff's office was indicted on sixty counts of fraud and bribery, and all special badges were revoked. Fortunately I tend to get in the kind of trouble that doesn't involve law enforcement.)

A few days later I was invited to Graceland for lunch. One of the bubbas rang the bell of my childhood home while Elvis waited out front. Mother was oblivious to my caller, and my brother was in his "Everything-in-my-life-is-terrible-because-you're-my-sister" stage. I'd been in swanky homes of famous people (in fact, I now lived in one with Peter), but Graceland had a special glow behind its wrought-iron gates, with a tree-lined driveway winding up to a portico fronted by tall white columns and two white stone lions as palace guards. There was a rather formal dining room, but we ate in the kitchen with Elvis's father, and with little conversation. (Southern folk are brought up not to talk with their mouths full.) The meal included the first three of the four southern food groups: salt, fat, sugar, and alcohol. Chicken-fried steak was cooked well done by a housekeeper who called me Missy and sent plates out to the bodyguards waiting by the cars. One of them drove me home shortly after dessert: slices of devil's food cake colored an unnatural red.

I was back for dinner the next day (deep-fried sandwiches made of peanut butter, bananas, and mayonnaise), and it was just the two of us. Elvis led me on a
tour ending in his bedroom, all red and black with a
fake leopard cover on a king-size bed, four TVs, and
smoky mirrors on the walls and ceilings. I had no
doubt about how the evening would end—there was
soft kissing on my neck and arms, pulling off layers of
clothing to reveal new naked places—while I kept
thinking: *Do I want to do this?* I'd been treated like a
hot piece of ass in New York, and I resisted the idea of
being a notch on the belt of a renowned lover boy. But
his kisses were so slow and deliberate, his skin so
smooth—a little soft around the middle but hard in
the right places. He nibbled down my body, virile and
playful, then stopped abruptly at my belly button.

"Is something wrong?" I asked.

"Uhh, well, you see, me and the guys talk, and,
well, white boys don't eat pussy," he said.

This was an interesting concept: that the frequency
and popularity of oral sex broke down along racial lines.

"You don't know what you're missing," I said playfully, emboldened by the prospect of shaming him
into action with my sheer disbelief. "I'm used to men
diving for it. Would you like me to show you how?"

He warmed to the subject, as did I. But I had the
feeling of being outside myself, watching. Sex with another man didn't feel like I was cuckolding Peter—I
figured I couldn't cheat on someone I didn't have, and
Peter wasn't mine in any real, permanent sense. I kept
earnest, copiously annotated diaries in those days,
written in code in case Peter happened upon them.
The musings of youthful, self-absorbed angst are fairly

insufferable to read now, but there's one passage that still resonates: "Elvis's stupidity is rejuvenating against Peter's superiority. I don't think Peter takes me seriously, but going with him has a lot of prestige."

I had fun in Elvis's bed, but I couldn't sleep in it. Shortly past midnight, he drove me home, my face rubbed raw from kissing.

Although I'd made TV appearances as Model of the Year, *The Last Picture Show* really inaugurated what becomes almost a tangential career for any actor: working the talk-show circuit. At first I was stiff, calcified, afraid to open my mouth. Then I became awkwardly flirtatious, trying to amuse, drinking too much coffee and talking too fast. *Then* I would adopt Peter's hauteur, minus his raconteur skills. One of my appearances almost derailed my career. In 1971 Neil Simon, the most popular American playwright of his time, had written his first screenplay called *The Heartbreak Kid*, from a short story by Bruce Jay Friedman. Charles Grodin was to play the nice Jewish guy who falls in love with the classic icy shiksa of his sexual fantasies on his Miami Beach honeymoon and ditches his bride, played by Jeannie Berlin. (Director Elaine May had cast her real-life daughter as the jilted bride, although nobody knew they were related until filming had begun.) The shiksa role went to the dark-haired girlfriend of Freddie Fields, a powerful Hollywood agent who looked like an early Austin Powers. ("Let me give you some information, kiddo," Fields once said to me, leaning uncomfortably close and breathing hot agency breath on me at a screening in his house. "It's not the directors or the producers who are the real powers in this business. It's the agents.") The brunette had to become a blonde, and rehearsals had already started when her stripped and bleached hair began falling out in clumps. I got a call: could I go for a reading tomorrow?

Although I didn't learn about it until later, Elaine May had seen me chattering mindlessly on Dick Cavett's show and decided I couldn't play this or any part. (In partial defense, Cavett had started the interview by saying, "I haven't seen your film, but it's supposed to be very good.") The reading for May and Simon took place in a small generic office building in New York. Most of the time when I enter a room for an audition, I know if I've got the job, and I didn't feel like I had this one. But I started to read, and they started to laugh. As we said good-bye, Simon clasped my hand in both of his and said, "I always knew you'd be perfect."

Simon had a contractual guarantee that the dialogue would be used exactly as he'd written it, and we knew that not a word could be altered. (There's nothing wrong with cleaving to good writing: Katharine Hepburn and Spencer Tracy always said they were "script technicians" hired to make the lines on the page work.) But May liked to use improvisation as an acting exercise during rehearsals, although she didn't call it that. She spoke about the exploration of subtext, the meaning beneath the lines. And she gave me a wonderful piece of advice that sounds dumb but works. "When you deliver a line," she said, "say it as if you expect the other character to be hearing you, getting it."

May seemed to think that Grodin was hysterically funny and laughed at everything he did. He had lost a lot of weight to do this role, so his skin was kind of hanging off his bones. In a scene where we were lying in bed together, the script called for me to play with his hair, but when I reached up to push a strand off his forehead, he blocked my hand and hissed, "Fake it. This is a rug."

"You're kidding," I said, assuming that he was making a joke to catch me off guard and provoke an interesting facial expression. (I'd never come within calling distance of a toupee before.)

"No, really," he said.

"You can't be serious," I persisted.

"I'm serious," he said. The exchange did not endear me to him, or him to me.

The Heartbreak Kid was a continuation of The Great Breast Hunt: I didn't want to do the nude scene clearly indicated in the script, but if I'd said so up front, I wouldn't have gotten the part. I still didn't quite trust that stills from *The Last Picture Show* wouldn't fall into the wrong hands and had no wish to enrich any celluloid archives that could haunt me in the future. I was bothered by the objectified use of naked women, an issue of power, not morality. If Harrison Ford had to expose his balls on-screen, I don't think he would make as much money. In the past, when nudity was verboten, directors had to be more clever. Alfred Hitchcock hired a double for Janet Leigh's shower scene in *Psycho*, then used seventy-two different shots in forty-two seconds without ever exposing an erogenous zone.

One of the producers of *The Heartbreak Kid* was Eric Preminger, the love child of the director Otto Preminger and the burlesque queen Gypsy Rose Lee, who said of her career, "I wasn't naked. I was covered with a blue spotlight." Perhaps Preminger was deemed to have a special affinity for female strippers because he was recruited to visit the Playboy mansion in Chicago to audition the bunnies, inspecting their breasts and selecting a body double for me. When he found the pair he'd dreamt of, he came to my dressing room with a contract and said, "Sign this right away."

I didn't know it at the time, but an actor has the right to give written approval of a body double, guaranteed by the Screen Actors Guild. I just knew not to sign anything without a lawyer looking at it (a precaution I have drummed into my children since they were old enough to hold a pen). When I finally saw the scene cut together, Grodin was shown looking at my chest, followed by a shot of the proxy's breasts (nice ones, by the way) without my head attached. I found the nudity disruptive, but there was a lot of pressure on me to approve the use of the body double, since Preminger had spent considerable production money on the Chicago trip and had paid the bunny. But I held my ground, and Elaine, the director, agreed with me.

Elaine May chewed No-Doz by the fistful to stay awake. Shooting in a frigid Minneapolis winter, her feet got frostbitten, and we got to keep warm inside, while her toes thawed out. The weather was more accommodating in Miami. I was staying with the rest of the cast at a low-rent Holiday Inn nowhere near the fancy beach hotels and got stuck in the decrepit elevator. I was more bored than scared—which is why, to this day, I never approach an elevator without thinking *I should have a book with me, just in case.* So it wasn't just languishing for Peter that made me anticipate his visit so eagerly: for a few days I would get to stay in the Fountainbleu. Big breakfast buffet. Big swimming pool. Big Atlantic Ocean. Peter was not one for slumming.

Larry McMurtry came to visit too. Peter had suggested that they collaborate on a new script, called at various times *West of the Brazos* (which is a river), then *Palo Duro* (which is a canyon), then *Streets of Laredo* (which, it turned out, had been the title of a mediocre movie starring William Holden and Glenn Ford). "What kind of western do you want to make?" Larry had asked Peter.

"Some kind of a trek," Peter said. "As long as it's not about cows because Howard Hawkes did the quintessential cattle drive in *Red River.*"

From the beginning, the film was conceived as a vehicle for Jimmy Stewart, Henry Fonda, and John Wayne. Peter acted out all the parts while he and Larry wrote the script, and nobody does a better Stewart, Fonda, or Wayne except Stewart, Fonda, and Wayne. But Wayne apparently asked John Ford's opinion, and although Ford had been instrumental in getting Ben Johnson to do *The Last Picture Show*, this time he told Wayne not to do the film, knowing full well that if he backed out, the others would follow. "The old man doesn't like it," Wayne said to Peter.

"That's not what he told me," Peter said, but for some reason he never confronted Ford. Maybe he didn't want to ask another favor. But Peter would often repeat what James Cagney said about Ford after the director had knowingly let him crash in the sidecar of a motorcycle driven by the character actor William Demarest, who had never been behind the wheel,

"There's one word to describe John Ford and the Irish: malice."

The ideas that germinated in the Fountainbleu were eventually reworked into Larry's Pulitzer-winning novel *Lonesome Dove*. Despite the warning that cows had been done, the book centered on the last daring cattle drive from Texas to Montana in the late nineteenth century. But Peter was never given credit for many of the ideas generated at the hotel, which saddened and angered him. "Larry used every part of the pig," he would say.

I hadn't heard from Elvis since Graceland. But when I was back in Los Angeles, he called, offering to send his plane for me for a weekend at the house he'd rented in Palm Springs. One of his henchmen picked me up at the airport, looked at my jeans and tie-dyed mirrored vest and said, "Next time we're in L.A. we're gonna arrange a shopping trip so you can get some nice new clothes because Elvis likes his ladies to look a certain way." *Only if I can help pick out his clothes*, I thought. The house was luxurious in a rental sort of way, sprawling and devoid of personal taste. Everything had a metallic glow. All the King's men were in residence, wearing pins that said TCB, code for Elvis's catch phrase "Taking Care of Business." They spent the afternoon competing to see who could make the biggest splash into a murky swimming pool. I really didn't want to go near that pool but couldn't resist one-upping the bubbas by doing a "can opener" leap I'd learned from the lifeguards at Chickasaw Country Club. The guys raced in dune buggies three or four abreast while shouting into walkie-talkies or sat around a long table with a thick top of beveled glass, eating their favorite deep-fried sandwiches. Elvis was the first person I ever saw drink bottled water, which he had imported from the Ozarks. "You drink enough of this," he said, "and it'll keep you regular."

I thought it was a little odd that he slept during the day, and I didn't learn until many years later that he was actually terrified of falling asleep in the dark. He had heavy drapes, blackout shades on the windows, even aluminum foil taped to the glass to block out every bit of daylight. The sweet charm that I had seen in Memphis seemed to be draining away, replaced by unfortunate frat boy humor. When I emerged from the bathroom before dinner, he said, "I never knew a girl to take so many baths," which caused great guffaws among the cronies, even though his own bathroom had a six-drawer black box of cosmetics — he wore more makeup than I did. We were hardly ever alone and didn't talk much when we were, not about his music or his marriage or his daughter or the lunacy of spending $40,000 to fly his entourage to Denver for a certain kind of sandwich (this, from a man whose father was once sentenced to three years in jail for forging a forty-dollar check). He didn't seem too interested in anything I said either, and he acted as if I was putting on airs if I mentioned the book I was reading. I was seeing the morbid cheese ball side of him, and it made me slightly nervous, as if I'd better not displease him or I could get myself in trouble. Fortunately, I was never asked to enact what I heard was one of Elvis's favorite erotic scenarios: putting on waist-high cotton panties, eating cookies and milk, and wrestling with another girl.

Toward the end of the summer, Elvis invited me to

see him perform at the Las Vegas Hilton. I told Peter that I was spending the weekend with a girlfriend in San Francisco. The spectacle began with the orchestra playing the tone poem "Thus Spake Zarathustra" by Richard Strauss, better known as the theme from *2001: A Space Odyssey*. If ever there was music announcing the arrival of a god, this was it. A noisy procession of motorcycles swept onto the stage before Elvis appeared in a jeweled cape and jumpsuit— splendiferous but a little chubby. I'd always admired his voice, but now I was moved in a way I had not expected, as if he were singing directly to me, and without thinking, I rose to my feet just like the rest of the audience. After the show, he sat at the piano in his suite and sang gospel songs with his background singers, wearing a custom-made blue velour lounging suit. Then he walked through curtained French doors into the bedroom and collapsed on an enormous fourposter bed.

I didn't know it, but what I was seeing was the fullthrottle effect of drugs. I had an adjoining bedroom, and I wasn't sure what I was supposed to do. Any possibility of nooky had evaporated—he seemed faraway and woozy, his eyes half closed, his speech slurred. Holding out a handful of pills, he said, "Here, take these."

I was confused. "Are you going to take some of them?" I asked.

"Oh, I already had mine," he said. "These are all for you."

I went to my room and flushed them down the toilet. As I got into bed, I noticed a small black velvet box on the nightstand. I opened it to find a diamond and emerald ring that looked like a glob of porcupine bristles—too large, too elaborate, too hideous even for Liberace. I went to the desk and wrote Elvis a note on Hilton letterhead, thanking him but declining his generous and extravagant gift. Then I called the airline to change my return reservation.

Earlier that day in Los Angeles, Peter was driving on Santa Monica Boulevard when he noticed a billboard announcing Elvis's Vegas engagement. He'd been hearing me say that I was fascinated with Elvis (Peter deemed him boring) and had a purely intuitive feeling that I was with him. He called the Hilton, asked for me, and when I answered, he screamed, "You're a goddamned liar!" Then he hung up. I called back to hear more of his invective. "You know what happens to liars?" he shouted. "They get their mouths washed out with soap. You get your ass back here, and I'm going to wash your mouth out with Ivory Soap."

I only heard that he wanted me back, that the damage wasn't irreparable. When I got home, he screamed and stomped so hard that the fake crystal chandeliers of the apartment shook, then issued a summary judgment: "That's what I get for being with an actress." Fortunately, he wasn't home a few days later when I got a call from one of the Memphis mob saying that Elvis needed to talk to me.

"I can't do that," I said.

"He's right around the corner," said the bubba. "Do me a favor, just talk to him because he's really upset."

When Elvis pulled into the oval driveway at Sunset Towers, he seemed sulky and remote—no kiss in greeting, no concern about my disappearance of a few nights before, just a statement of intention and an ultimatum.

"I really enjoy spending time with you, but you've got to get rid of this Dogbanovich guy," he said, mangling the name a little. "It's either him or me."

I was thinking: *What's he talking about?* Watching someone pass out cold when I was expecting a rollicking sexual romp was not my idea of fun. Perhaps it was a bit of posturing from a wounded ego, an attempt to regain control after my rejection of his ring and his drugs. Later I learned that I was a temporary filler for Linda Thompson, who was Miss Memphis State, Miss Liberty Bowl, and Miss Tennessee—a self-described virgin who quit college twelve credits short of her degree, gave up her acting ambitions, and let Elvis make all her decisions, even changing her sleeping habits to become what his buddies called a "lifer." Elvis was a goody I couldn't resist, but I had a life with Peter I wasn't about to give up. I wanted to make decisions, some of them foolish, on my own.

"Well, that's it for us," he said. Those were his last words to me. We circled the block in silence until we got back to Sunset Towers, and he paused at the curb barely long enough for me to exit under the yellow and white awning. I said "Good-bye," but he didn't answer. I never saw him again. Five years later he was dead. Peter, unrepentant about his opinion of Elvis, said it was the best career move he ever made.

WHEN PETER WAS ENVISIONING DIRECTING A McMurtry western, he wanted Polly Platt to do the set design, but only on the condition that she knew I would be in the movie, and in her face. The western never got made, and instead they began working on

Paper Moon, with Ryan O'Neal playing a Bible-selling con man and his daughter Tatum as the sharp-witted progeny he never knew about but unwittingly befriends. In the late fall of 1972, days before principal photography began in Hays, Kansas, Polly announced to Peter, "I can't handle Cybill coming to the set." It was the end of any pretense of civility between them, and their relationship never healed, although I schemed to defy her, wishing I could make her deal with my presence just once. Peter's whole life was his work, and I was excluded from it because he was working with his ex-wife again. She wasn't even his ex-wife yet. (Their divorce would not be final for three years.) I spent most of my time driving around the depressed prairie towns, photographing dilapidated buildings, railroad yards, and old men's faces, practicing my tap dancing on the linoleum flooring of our hotel room until the people below pounded on their ceiling with a broomstick. We were staying in the utilitarian Pony Express Motel in Elwood (still resting on its laurels of being the first Pony Express station in Kansas) because Polly and the crew were in the marginally better Ramada Inn. The tension must have gotten to Peter because the next to last day's worth of footage was shot with a hair stuck in the "gate" as the raw film passed through the camera. (That's why someone yells "Check the gate" after every take.) All these scenes appear slightly soft-focus in the movie, since Peter enlarged every frame just enough to eliminate the hair, but he refused to go back and reshoot, declaring, "It beats spending another day in that hellhole with Polly."

Peter met Marlene Dietrich on his way to Kansas—

the plane stopped first in Denver, where she was doing a one-woman show. He was not the sort of man who imagined that women were coming on to him when they weren't, and he knew she had something in mind even before he walked into his Kansas hotel room. The phone was ringing: Dietrich saying in a smoky voice, "I found you." When *Paper Moon* was completed, he invited her to its New York premiere, and she was not pleased when she saw me in the limousine, obviously anticipating a "date" with Peter. She sat between us, cooing into Peter's ear and digging her left elbow into my side. Marlene Dietrich was the closest thing I had to a role model—a working mother who created sexually powerful roles (she wore pants before Katharine Hepburn) and ended her career with a triumphant cabaret act. I was so excited to be in her presence that I was happily impaled.

The next day, a bellman knocked at our suite in the Waldorf Towers. "Flowers for Miss Shepherd," he said.

I opened the door and saw him struggling with an arrangement so large that there was no table that could accommodate it, and it had to sit on the floor. The card read "Love, Marlene." Well worth being ignored.

It was about this time that I joined a unique sorority: ever since the release of *The Last Picture Show*, *Playboy* magazine had tried to get me to pose nude by throwing money at me. First I was offered $5,000, then $10,000, then $50,000, to no avail. Then they figured out how to get me for free. My unwelcome Christmas present that year was my naked likeness in the magazine's year-end "Sex in Cinema" issue, also featuring Jane Fonda and Catherine Deneuve. Technology provided a method of making a frame enlargement from a 35-millimeter print of the movie that had been borrowed for a screening at the Playboy mansion. I called a lawyer and sued for the right to control my image, insisting that there was a difference between the legitimate press and a magazine like *Playboy*. The suit claimed that I was a young woman of "dignity, intelligence, modesty, and artistic and personal integrity"—a legally accurate if not quite apt self-description.

The case dragged on for five years. *Playboy* started out treating it like a nuisance suit, using their local lawyer in Los Angeles, who coincidentally had been my lawyer's professor at Stanford. When they realized that I was serious, they brought in the head of their Chicago law firm. My lawyer was looking through their files, and either they were pretty dumb or extremely honest because he found a smoking gun: a handwritten memo from Hugh Hefner to his secretary that said, "I've been stymied in every way to get pictures of Cybill Shepherd for the 'Sex in Cinema' issue. I'm screening *The Last Picture Show* tonight, so have [Mario] come up here with his magic machine."

Hef was willing to settle after that. But instead of asking for a shitload of money, I wanted a book that *Playboy* had under option, a novel by Paul Theroux called *Saint Jack* about an amiable Singapore pimp. Hefner came to my house, offering a formal apology and informal arrangements for a settlement. The standard Screen Actors Guild contract now includes a protective clause that prevents unauthorized use of movie frames for still photographs. It served as excellent protection for actors until the world of cyberspace, which is proving impossible to police. Not long ago, I discovered that anyone can pay fifty dollars and go to a Web site where my head is stuck on some other woman's naked body in the anatomically graphic poses favored by smut magazines. If I decided to sue, I'd have to do it country by country because there's no international law in this area, and the fabricated photos would just resurface in another form.

I WENT TO THE PETER BOGDANOVICH SCHOOL of Cinema. Peter didn't want to exercise, sweat, get dirty—he only liked to watch movies, and he watched with a curator's eye. When we went to a movie theater, he was always quick to tell the projectionist if a reel was out of focus. In our apartment, the focal point of the living room was a rebuilt 16-millimeter projector aimed at a blank wall. Several times a week we went to a studio screening room that smelled as if it hadn't been opened since Fatty Arbuckle was thin. We'd eat moo shu pork out of paper cartons while we watched *The Merry Widow*—the silent Erich von Stroheim version with Mae Murray and John Gilbert (and an extra named Clark Gable)—then the 1934 remake with Jeanette MacDonald and Maurice Chevalier, and the other Ernst Lubitsch musicals: *The Love Parade, Monte Carlo, One Hour with You.* When we moved to a house, the first thing we added was a screening room that had bright red carpets and plush white couches with ottomans, the walls covered with classic movie posters. The film department at UCLA would let us borrow silver nitrate prints of the golden oldies, even though it was illegal to screen them at home: the film is flammable and explosive if it breaks, and the law stipulated two projectionists and a double-insulated flameproof projection room. But screening the only 35-millimeter print of Ernst Lubitsch's *The Smiling Lieutenant* that existed at the time was like seeing the way God sees: a face in sharp close-up, scenery in the distance, and everything clear in between. The expression "silver screen" comes from the actual silver in the film itself, which shimmered. All of modern technology can't achieve that brilliance and depth of focus.

My endurance level didn't approach Peter's (often a triple feature), and I sometimes fell asleep during the third movie. I learned that all kinds of acting can work: the broad energy of James Cagney or the minimalism of Gary Cooper. The only important question is: do we believe the actor? Can we suspend disbelief? Movies demand a leap of faith from the audience, a willingness to forget that what it's seeing is fake. It was said that when Jimmy Stewart appeared on-screen, he annihilated disbelief.

I would ask Peter, "You sure you don't mind seeing this again? You've seen it twenty times." He would say, "I'm looking at it with new eyes." Every week he'd mark the *TV Guide* for the films I should watch. Anything directed by John Ford, Howard Hawkes, or Jean Renoir became required viewing. Living with Peter was like inhabiting these movies. We developed a private language, borrowing bits of dialogue, like "I close the iron door on you" (John Barrymore in *Twentieth Century*), or "Don't you think it's rather indecent of you to order me out after you've kissed me?" (Carole

Lombard in *My Man Godfrey*). And we weren't above quoting from *The Last Picture Show* ("Comb your hair, Sonny—you look like you smelled a wolf"). Sometimes when we were out, I'd stomp my feet and pound my fists, and people in the restaurant would think I had lost my mind, but Peter would crack up, knowing that I was doing one of Lombard's tantrums from *Twentieth Century*.

We were living in Bel Air at 212 Copa de Oro Drive, a Mediterranean-style house with a red-tiled roof that had belonged to a newlywed Clark Gable and his bride Kay Spreckels. I found that house in 1974, and Peter bought it with money borrowed from Warner Bros. against his next project. We moved in with only a mattress on the floor and filled the rooms with furniture by spending a whole day at a Beverly Hills store called Sloans. Each of us had a bedroom suite upstairs, connected by a large closet: after years of unlocked doors and a sister who pummeled me out of bed, I readily embraced Virginia Woolf's fine idea about a room of one's own. Peter's room had a niche in the wall for an antique Italian daybed covered with champagne-colored raw silk. Mine had a waterbed with a patchwork quilt we bought in Big Sur. Every wall was white and hung with Peter's father's paintings.

Peter and I were the couple *du jour* in Hollywood, but I often felt like an impostor among the real denizens of the film world, and I tended to be quiet in their company. When Larry McMurtry wrote *Lonesome Dove*, he sent me the galleys with an inscription that said, "You were the seed of so much of it. I started it fourteen years ago with Lorena's silence—the silence of a woman who won't give her voice and heart to the world because she had concluded that the world would not hear it or understand it or love it. I felt such a silence in you." People often acted as if my brain was blonde and watched rather than listened when I spoke, as if wondering where the ventriloquist's hand went.

Even my agent, Sue Mengers, seemed to perceive me that way. "When you go to a meeting, don't talk," she'd instruct. "Just wear a lot of makeup and do your hair." Sue was never known for her tact. She spoke very slowly to me, as if I needed extra time to process the information. Peter would get annoyed and tell her, "You don't have to talk to Cybill that way." She'd speed up to normal for a while, then decelerate and say, "I'm so sorry, I did it again."

My first real Hollywood party was at Sue's faux château in the Hollywood Hills, at the end of a series of hairpin turns on a thrillingly narrow road. We had to park in what seemed like another town and arrived somewhat breathless to see Gregory Peck straddling a chair, drunk as a skunk. I felt as if I had entered a parallel universe in which my idols turned into their evil twins. I didn't have the courage to start a conversation with anyone, and the only person who approached me was a producer who said, "So you're an actress. Who are you studying with?"

"Nobody," I answered.

"That's a mistake," said the producer with a sniff. "You'd better start soon because you'll need all the help you can get."

I put down my wineglass, fled outside, and was halfway to the car when Peter came to retrieve me.

"They're all phonies," I said. "They're all horrible."

"I know," he said, "but we can't leave."

When I did open my mouth, my irreverence sometimes backfired. Sue Mengers was hoping to foster the notion of my working with Dustin Hoffman, another of her clients, and she gave an intimate dinner for Peter and me, Dustin and his wife, Anne, and Sue's husband, Jean-Claude Tremont. Entering the small dining room, Dustin sat down just long enough to look up at me, my rather long torso extending well above his, and then pushed up on his arms, as if trying to make himself taller.

"Why don't you ask Sue if she has a couple of phone books?" I said with misguided humor.

Dustin looked as if he'd just been hit but didn't know how to fall down, and the evening never recovered. The Hoffmans made a flimsy excuse and left early.

Foolishly trying to mitigate that sin, I went to the set of *Marathon Man*, taking an inch-thick Beverly Hills phone book. I delivered it to Dustin, saying, "This is what I meant." He mumbled "thanks" and walked away. Perhaps this was one of those times when he stayed up for days to look appropriately scruffy and exhausted for a scene, prompting his costar, Laurence Olivier, to ask, "My dear boy, why don't you try acting?"

It would be understatement to say that I failed to impress Marlon Brando. On a warm summer night Peter and I drove the great acting coach Stella Adler to a party in her honor at Brando's home atop Mulholland Drive. There were Japanese lanterns strung through the trees, and I was seated on a garden bench next to Brando, but for once I was chattering away rather than deferring to the conversation of others. Brando was holding a beer bottle when he looked at me with unsubtle disgust.

"If this girl doesn't shut up," he said to no one in particular, "I'm going to hit her in the face with this bottle." I was too stunned for a moment to move. I couldn't believe that my idol had spoken to me in such a manner. I gathered my wits and fled to the other side of the patio. Later that evening, I noticed Brando motioning for me to come over toward him. I gave him a weak smile, and projecting his voice so everyone could hear, he said "Cybill, could you come over here and then walk away so I could watch you?" I did as he asked, but I wish I'd told him to flush his head down the toilet.

Years later, when I was doing the *Cybill* show, Marlon Brando was the only celebrity the writers knew they could malign with impunity. I'd say, "Just make it Brando, and I don't have a problem with it," so the joke would become, "One beesting, and I swell up like Marlon Brando."

PETER TOOK EVERY OPPORTUNITY TO SIT AT the feet of great filmmakers, and I usually got the big toe. In 1972 he readily agreed to interview Charlie Chaplin for a documentary, conducted at his home in Vevey, Switzerland, but Chaplin was in his dotage. At lunch, he suddenly stopped eating and said, "You know, my daughter Geraldine is very rich."

We'd been there four hours, and those were the first words I'd heard him speak. "Really?" I replied. "That must be nice for her." Then I went back to my soup.

One day Peter came home from a visit with Alfred Hitchcock, badly in need of black coffee and aspirin. Peter has little taste or tolerance for drink, but he had arrived at the great man's hotel suite to find him pouring whiskey sours. Although Peter tried unobtrusively to nurse the drink, Hitchcock kept noticing and chastising him in that sonorous voice, "You're not touching your glass."

By the time the two of them left for dinner together, Peter had a nice little buzz going. They were descending in the hotel elevator full of people when Hitchcock turned to him and said, "So there he was, sprawled on the floor, blood pouring from every orifice and seeping into the carpet." Peter reeled. He was a little drunk, but had he blacked out momentarily and missed the earlier part of this conversation? Everyone else in the elevator was rapt as Hitchcock went on, "The music that had been playing in the next room stopped, and I could hear a scratching sound." Just as the elevator reached the ground floor, Hitchcock said, "So I kneeled over him, asking, 'My God, man, what happened to you?' He grabbed my shirtfront, pulled me down and . . ."

Just then the elevator door opened in the lobby. The other people were hanging back, straining to hear the end of the story, but Hitchcock sailed past them, with Peter in tow, and began discussing the restaurant plans.

"But Hitch," Peter said, "what happened to your friend?"

"Oh, nothing," Hitchcock said, "that's just my elevator story."

In 1973, John Ford was to be given the Congressional Medal of Freedom, the first filmmaker so lauded. The public knew him as the director responsible for such classics as *The Grapes of Wrath*, *How Green Was My Valley*, and *The Searchers*. I knew him as a neighbor, living across the street, and as a flasher. By this time he was mostly confined to bed, dressed in a pajama top and a bedsheet that he liked to rearrange for shock value, often after drinking one of the two daily bottles of stout he was permitted. (Mary, his wife of fifty years, once told me, "Never believe anything you hear or read, and only half of what you see. And make sure the back of your skirt is clean because that's where they'll be looking.") On the night of the award ceremony, outside the hotel, Henry Fonda had to fight through the anti-Vietnam picketers led by his daughter. Cary Grant was standing on line ahead of us, and as we got to the reception table, he said to the ticket taker, "I'm terribly sorry, I've forgotten my invitation."

"Name, please," said the woman, consulting her master list without looking up.

"Cary Grant," he said.

The woman glanced up over half-glasses. "You don't look like Cary Grant," she said suspiciously.

"I know," he said apologetically, "no one does."

ORSON WELLES CAME TO COPA DE ORO FOR dinner one night and stayed two years, intermittently with an elegant actress of Hungarian and Croatian descent named Oya Kodar, who had perfectly formed eyebrows and spoke in a thick, high voice, like the way a child would imitate a snooty librarian. She seemed too remote and exotic to be a pal, but we shared the same sort of alliance with bossy, self-involved men. Once, when the four of us were eating in a Paris restaurant, Orson and Peter were completely excluding us from the conversation, so we set our menus on fire with the candle on the table. Fortunately we got their attention before burning the restaurant to the ground. Orson was always broke—despite the accolades, his films weren't profitable, and for years he had put all his money into his work. He never slept through the night, but he napped off and on around the clock, and I was instructed not to knock on the door of his room for any reason, day or night. Once he summoned me inside where he was playing with the cable TV box, channel-surfing by punching at a long row of numbered buttons.

"Come and look at this," he said, his heroic voice heavy with excitement. "It's the most brilliant show on television." The program that had elicited such praise was *Sesame Street*. His second favorite was *Kojak*. The most frequent noises emanating from his room were the gurgles of Big Bird and Telly Savalas saying "Who loves ya, baby?" But he also encouraged me to study opera, which I did for three years. Working with a voice coach, a drama coach, and a language coach, on top of having a movie career, nearly did me in, and Orson finally told me, "You have to choose or you're going to have a nervous breakdown. Opera or film." One of the reasons I chose the latter was that when I sang opera, people either stared as if they were watching Mount St. Helen erupt, or just laughed.

It was Orson too who helped me with the talk-show circuit, where I kept making wrongheaded attempts to be clever. It took me a long time to figure out that the host must score with the first big laugh at my expense, that I was supposed to be smart and cute and funny, but not smarter, not cuter, and certainly not funnier than Johnny/Jay/Dave/Mike/Merv. "All you have to do," Orson instructed, "is ignore the audience and have a conversation with the guy behind the desk." Carson could really bring out the risqué in me: on one occasion, he put on a pair of horns, got down on his hands and knees, and let me lasso him. Another time he knocked a cup of coffee over on his desk, and I said, "If you'd spilled it in your lap, I could have cleaned it up." On Leno I used my hands to approximate the position of breasts that are not surgically lifted. (They're so much more versatile with age—you can have them up, you can have them down, side to side, round and round, or you can swing them over your shoulder like a continental soldier.)

Letterman posed a different challenge. "Don't hug Dave too hard," warned his stage manager right before I was announced. (Same thing happened when Tony Bennett came on the *Cybill* show. Perhaps I have a reputation as a particularly effusive hugger?) Once when I was scheduled for his show but wasn't traveling directly to New York, I had the suit I planned to wear sent ahead. Dave hung it on the set, poking fun at it every night for a week as a kind of countdown before my appearance. When I heard about the stunt, I decided I'd be damned if I'd wear that outfit and instead came out wrapped in a bath towel. Years later, during another appearance on his show, Dave did pay up on a $100 bet that I couldn't lob a football into a canister after he'd missed it nine times. When we went down to the street with the former Super Bowl champ Joe Montana to see who could throw the ball through the window of a passing taxicab, I became Diana of the hunt. All those years of tossing a ball with my father paid off, and Dave was gracious in defeat, especially after I accidentally stomped his foot.

Since Peter worked more than either of us, Orson and I were often left in each other's company. One day we were drinking wine, sitting in the living room under a painting of Native American dancing. "You know," said Orson, looking up at the inspirational images, "there was a time when God was a woman." I told him I knew about Cybele from the Sistine Chapel, and he suggested I read *The Greek Myths* by Robert Graves, a kind of dictionary of religious stories throughout history. Reading that book cover to cover intensified my spiritual quest to learn more about the so-called Great Goddess.

Orson ate my leftovers off the plate in four-star restaurants, especially if he had insisted on my ordering something strange and previously unknown to me such as tripe (I had no idea it was intestinal matter) or whitebait (I didn't know the fish would come complete with heads and bones, curled into a position that looked like jumping). At home he would throw fits if we ran out of his favorite food.

"WHO ATE THE LAST FUDGSICLE?" Orson would bellow. Everyone knew that he'd eaten it, but we were too polite to say so. "That's just balls," he'd yell in a voice that sounded like God chastising Eve for eating that apple. "Everything you know is balls," he'd say. Then he'd make an omelette as an act of contrition, standing barefoot by the stove in a voluminous black kimono. One day in the laundry room I came across a pair of silk boxer shorts, three feet wide and custom-made on Savile Row, draped over the washing machine like the Shroud of Turin. He taught me how to cut and smoke fat, foot-long Monte Cristo A's, obtained from Cuba through European connections, holding the smoke in my mouth without inhaling and tossing out the last half, which he considered slightly bitter.

One afternoon I smelled smoke in the house and followed the smell to Orson's room, right below mine. Standing outside the door, I tapped timidly and called to him.

"Is everything all right?" I asked.

"I'm fine," he roared. "It's all taken care of. Go away."

I didn't know what "it" was until later. Orson had shoved a still-smoldering cigar into the pocket of a robe, which he dropped on a mat when he got in the shower. The cloth caught fire and burned into the rug before he realized the danger. The next day, as an apology, I received *The Victor Book of the Opera*, which he had inscribed with a play on an old nursery rhyme: "Ladybug, ladybug, fly away home, your house is on fire and your houseguest, a hibernating bear, is too." The illustration was of my house leaping with flames, the smoke smudged, he said, with his own spit.

In August of 1972, Peter and I were invited to meet Richard Nixon at a fund-raiser in San Clemente for the president's Hollywood supporters. Our disinclination toward Republican politics paled in comparison to our annoyance that *The Last Picture Show* was deemed too racy to be screened at 1600 Pennsylvania

Avenue, but nobody turns down an invitation to meet the president, even if it was Nixon. I ransacked my closet and came up with a full-length gown by Jean Patou that was as close to an American flag as a dress could be—a red-and-white-striped skirt with a blue bodice. The invitation had read, "Less than cocktail dress," but this was the president of the United States (even if it was Nixon). When we stopped to ask directions at a Shell station, the attendant simply pointed to the sky and the huge khaki green helicopters circling above an estate surrounded by chain-link fence. Granted admission, we felt like the Mel Brooks joke about going to a party where everyone is a tuxedo and you're a brown shoe. There were Clint Eastwood, Billy Graham, Henry Kissinger with Jill St. John, Debbie Reynolds, Glen Campbell, Charlton Heston, and Jim Brown. Peter introduced me to John Wayne, who mentioned his admiration for *The Last Picture Show*. "But I'll tell ya the truth," he said in his signature drawl, "I was a little embarrassed. I mean, my wife was there." Nixon gave a stuffy little speech paying homage to Wayne. "Whenever we want to run a picture at Camp David," he said, "I always say, 'Let's run a John Wayne picture.'" Wayne, who had a drink in his hand, probably not his first, raised his glass and said, "Keep those comin'."

An aide-de-camp informed us that the men should precede the women in the reception line on the grass, where the president was standing. When we came face-to-face with Nixon, I smiled and said, "I wore this dress especially for you, Mr. President."

"And you look lovely, my dear," he said. Then, directed at Peter, "You ought to put her in a picture."

"I did," Peter said. "It's one you haven't seen."

Nixon looked perplexed. "What's the name of that production?" he asked with great formality.

"The Last Picture Show," said Peter.

Musing over the title, Nixon said, "That's a black and white production, isn't it, the one that takes place in Texas?"

"That's right," Peter said, genuinely surprised.

"I saw that," said Nixon. "That's a remarkable picture." Then he turned to me and, touching my arm in a kindly manner, said, "And what part did you play, my dear?"

Nearly stuttering, I finally got out the word "Jacy." Peter, who was enjoying my discomfiture way too much, added, "She's the one who stripped on the diving board."

Nixon and I both turned crimson. He kept patting my arm lightly while still maintaining eye contact with Peter as he said, "Well, everyone gave a remarkable performance in that film. And of course, I remember you very well now, my dear."

Not long after, we were invited to visit the legendary director Jean Renoir, then in his eighties and living in Beverly Hills. Jean had repeated his father's predilection for angering his compatriots: the French threw rotten vegetables at the Impressionist exhibit where they first saw Auguste Renoir's paintings, and years later Jean Renoir's film *La Règle du Jeu (The Rules of the Game)* would be so severely panned that he would say he was either going to quit making films or leave France.

When we first entered his home, the only thing I could see was a luminous portrait of a young man in the woods holding a rifle (a painting that now hangs in the Los Angeles County Museum of Art). So distracted was I by this glorious work of art that I didn't even see Renoir himself until I heard a strange motorized sound and saw a sweet-looking old man being raised up to a standing position by an automated chair. He took a faltering step toward me, and I saw the bluest of eyes in a pale crinkly face, right out of the painting. His wife, Dido, who looked to be about thirty years younger, served white wine in short, very cold sterling silver cups that formed refreshing droplets of condensation, delightful in the heat of the summer day. We mentioned our visit to San Clemente, but naturally the talk turned to filmmaking. We were having an animated conversation with Dido, who had served as her husband's script supervisor, about the unfortunate necessity of dubbing. Suddenly the great man looked agitated, his pale face flushed, and he started rising out of his chair again. "I have the answer to Richard Nixon," he said excitedly. "Nixon is dubbed! And in a civilized time, like the thirteenth century, men would have been burned at the stake for less!"

IT IS FASCINATING TO WATCH, ALTHOUGH I could hardly do so without passionate self-interest, as a budding career becomes a meteor. I'm talking about Peter here, not myself. Equally fascinating is the chronicle of the roads not taken. (Orson said, "Your career is made more by what you don't do than by what you do.") Before *The Last Picture Show* had even opened, it was generating an expectant buzz in the industry, and Peter got a call from Robert Evans, then head of production at Paramount, which had just bought a book about the Mafia by Mario Puzo. Peter had no interest in directing a film about organized crime and its peculiar ethos of *la famiglia*. Ten years later, Evans was still chastising him for bad career choices.

"Hell, you even turned down *The Godfather*," said Evans.

"No, I didn't," said Peter.

"Yeah, you did," said Evans, recounting their conversation. But Peter was able to do some reciprocal reproaching because Evans's bad judgment had cost him his marriage. He had tried to recruit Peter once again, this time to direct *The Getaway* with Steve McQueen. Ali MacGraw, then Evans's wife, was to costar, but the part was written for a barefoot southern girl, a prototype of which just happened to be living with Peter. "Ali MacGraw can't play this," he insisted to Evans. "Isn't she from Bennington, Vermont?" McQueen didn't want me either (it's much harder for the leading man to make a move on the leading lady if she's the director's babe, since the director is omnipresent). Disagreeing with the casting, Peter turned down the assignment. MacGraw got the part, and McQueen got MacGraw.

When Evans began producing his own films, he asked Peter to direct a detective story in the Raymond Chandler tradition starring Jack Nicholson, with whom Peter had a friendly personal rivalry. (I'd made one date with Jack to spite Peter for going to a film expo with his ex-wife, which I took as a sign to the world that we didn't really exist as a couple. When Pe-

The not-so-happy couple... David Ford and I in 1978.

In 1978, I was presented to Queen Elizabeth. I turned my instructions about meeting her into a mnemonic verse: "Wear white gloves, don't chew gum, call her ma'am, which sounds like mum."

My second husband, Bruce Oppenheim, me, and Bruce Willis. What is it with me and guys named Bruce?

BELOW: He said, he said, she said, he said.
(*from left*) Jay Daniels, Bruce Willis, me, and Glenn Caron. (Scott Downie, Celebrity Photo Agency, Inc.)

LEFT: October 6, 1987:
The day my twins were
born, there was happy
news all around.
(Photograph by
Bettmann/Corbis; logo ©
New York Daily News, L.P.
Reprinted with permission)

BELOW: Of all the
Dubious Achievements
of 1985, leaving my
name off the cover has
got to be the worst.
(Courtesy *Esquire* Magazine)

Just checking to see if
everything is where it
should be. Here I am
with Madame Tussaud's
wax version of me.
(AP Wide World Photos/Adam
Nadel)

Four generations of women in my family: (*clockwise from top left*) me, my mother, my grandmother, my daughter Clementine.

BELOW: One of the reasons I bought my first house in Memphis was this beautiful dogwood. Here Clementine and I are enjoying it.

BELOW, RIGHT: My waterbabies: (*from left*) Zachariah, Clementine, and Ariel.

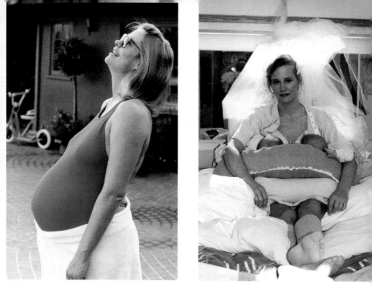

Portrait of the Artist as Behemoth: pregnant with Ariel and Zachariah.

ABOVE RIGHT: Nursing Ariel and Zachariah and, yes, I am wearing a wedding veil (it's for an episode of *Moonlighting*, okay?).

And in this corner, weighing in at . . . At the lake house.

"Oh, Miss Eula...?" "Yes, Mr. Quick." Don Johnson and I made the cover of *TV Guide* for *The Long Hot Summer* in 1985.

BELOW: With Ryan O'Neal on the set of *Chances Are.* (Photofest)

With Rosa Parks at the dedication of the National Civil Rights Museum, January 20, 1992.

"Nice work if you can get it." In bed *and* singing a duet with Tony Bennett. (*Cybill,* Courtesy of The Carsey-Werner Company, LLC/Michael Yarish)

With our future President in 1992: I found Bill Clinton a very attractive person. When I met him at a fundraiser, I said, "You'd better stand on the other side of the room. You don't need any more trouble."

Who says nursing ruins your breasts?

ter called and apologized, I canceled the date. Jack has never spoken to me since, except for "Hi" at a party.) Again Peter wanted to cast me in the femme fatale role opposite Nicholson, but Evans declared me too young. He wanted Faye Dunaway, so Peter said no to *Chinatown*.

I WAS BUSY MAKING MY OWN MISTAKES. THERE are whole chapters of my life that can be written with the postscript, "And the part went to . . ." The exalted director George Cukor had been acidly flattering about *The Last Picture Show*—he'd told Peter, "You're going to put us old-timers out of work." Cukor was the undisputed king of comedy for brainy, beautiful women, and I had practically memorized his oeuvre—Jean Harlow in *Dinner at Eight*, Katharine Hepburn in *The Philadelphia Story*, Judy Holiday in *Born Yesterday*. I was honored even to get an audition with him. But when I tried out for a small part in *Travels with My Aunt*, he said, "That was a really bad reading. Why don't you take it home and study it? You can come back and try again tomorrow." Peter and I spent two or three hours on it, and the next day I went to Cukor's office for another reading. I thought I didn't do half badly, considering that I hadn't slept all night, visions of the bungled lines prancing before my eyes. But Cukor put down the script, looked at me over horn-rimmed glasses and said, "I'm going to give you some good advice, and if you have any sense, you'll take it. You have no comedic talent. Never try it again." (The part went to . . . Cindy Williams, who became the latter half of *Laverne and Shirley*, and I developed an irrational hostility for her from which I never recovered.) A celebrated director had gone out of his way to be brutally discouraging, and I whimpered, worried, agonized, and almost believed him. But even though I've given up lots of times in my life, I usually only allow myself a week or two of sulk. Like the little engine that could, I get back on track. Ultimately no public or private humiliation has ever stopped me.

Orson Welles had given me the novella *Daisy Miller*, about a rich, spoiled, brash but naive young woman from Schenectady, New York, trying to infiltrate nineteenth-century European society. "Henry James wrote this for you," he said, slipping me a slim volume bound in faded red linen. "You act wonderfully on camera just like Daisy, but you overact in real life. And either Peter or I should direct it for you." Peter got the job, and he filmed the book almost verbatim—there were perhaps three words in the dialogue that James didn't write. Daisy chatters on, and on, and on, about her mother's dyspepsia, about her nettlesome little brother, about strangers met in railroad carriages. Her manner of conversation and free spirit are judged harshly—one character says of her, "I don't think she is capable of thought at all." Since people often felt the same of me, it seemed perfect typecasting. In 1972 I was doing essentially what Daisy did in 1865: pushing the limits of polite society and ruining her own reputation.

Cloris Leachman gave one of her extraordinarily compelling performances as Daisy's mother—permissive, whining, perpetually flustered—and Larry McMurtry's son James (in his first acting job) was the bratty little brother who drones on like a fly that won't be swatted away. The story is told completely from the point of view of Fredric Forsyth Winterbourne, the achingly correct young man who is infatuated with her but horrified by her defiance of curfews and convention. Peter had spoken to Jeff Bridges about casting Barry Brown (they had worked together in *Bad Company*), but no one realized that he was in the last stages of an addiction that would cause him to take his life just a few years later. He was glum and withdrawn, and his breakfast of champions consisted of beer, coffee, and Valium, a pattern that couldn't help but affect the shooting schedule. Twilight is frustratingly evanescent for a filmmaker—there are endless hours of preparation for a small window of opportunity—and Barry once staggered onto the set so drunk that we couldn't shoot the scene before we lost the lovely light. Since he was in practically every scene, replacing him would have necessitated trashing all the film that had been shot and starting from scratch. "If he reaches for another drink," Peter yelled to an assistant, "break his fucking arm or I'll shoot him."

As the filming dragged on into the heat of tourist-clogged Rome in August, Peter and I both became rather brooding and testy. *Daisy Miller* necessitated meticulous period details and locations in Italy evocative of the society that wealthy Americans wanted to invade, but it was to be Peter's first movie without Polly as set designer. The wardrobe was made by Tirelli of Rome, the penultimate movie costumer, and the only liberty taken with historical authenticity, at the suggestion of costume designer John Furness, was to move the time forward by five years so the women didn't have to wear such huge, exaggerated bustles. Fittings took eight hours, and I developed chronic back pain from the tight corsets of the period, which stretched all the way from the bust to the hip, creating a perpetual swayback. There were times when I had to stop and be unlaced or reach for the smelling salts to keep from passing out.

One day I fell asleep in my dressing room and showed up half an hour past my call. "You will never be late again," Peter screamed. "I don't care how big a star you become. Time is money in this business. It's not only expensive, but it's insulting to the rest of the cast and crew. Marilyn Monroe was fired from her last picture for being late." His tirade made an impression. In that scene, my eyes are puffy from crying, and I played the scene with exactly the right pervasive sadness. (Maybe he did it on purpose. You know how these auteur directors are.)

Despite the fact that this movie was a dream opportunity for us, Peter and I weren't having a lot of fun together, on or off the set. He was exhausted, often not feeling well, and he didn't want to leave the hotel. I wanted a playmate to make a midnight gelato run to the Piazza Navona. I wanted to make weekend excursions to cool Tuscan villages. I wanted to make love in Roman ruins. As always, I was better at acting out than talking out.

The perfect accomplice for hooky was a deputy producer my own age who had gotten his start working on Peter's movies as a gofer (go for coffee, go for errands . . .). Our friendship began during *The Last Picture Show*, and we had spent afternoons by the pool of our Texas motel, taking turns bouncing on the diving board and pretending to jump into the freezing water fully clothed. We shared a love of music and a childhood informed by alcohol: his father was a jazz guitarist who went off the wagon at John Ford's wake and died of a heart attack. The Producer had thinning brown hair, which never mattered to me (my first erotic fantasies were about Yul Brynner), and still had the carefree demeanor of a Southern California surfer: athletic and game for anything. We quickly became buddies, both of us pretending not to notice the powerful attraction because it was beyond inappropriate.

I had to go to New York to crown the new Model of the Year, and since Peter couldn't leave, he asked The Producer to accompany me, oblivious to any potential threat. We were making a quick turnaround, Rome to New York and back to Rome in less than twenty-four hours, so Charles Bluhdorn, who ran Gulf & Western, the parent company of Paramount, got his friend Edgar Bronfman, head of Seagram's, to lend us his private Gulfstream II. The jet was a libertine playground, all shag carpet and free-flowing champagne. We managed to behave on the flight west, but there was no way these two steam engines on the same track were not going to collide, about ten seconds after checking into the Waldorf-Astoria. When I had to go off to the pageant, I could barely walk.

I sent daisies, for obvious reasons, to The Producer's room, reminding him of our pact: *That was great, and that was all. We're not going to do this again.* However ... when the heating system of the Gulfstream sputtered and failed on our return flight, we rationalized that mile-high sex would be the most efficient way to keep each other nice and warm. Back in Rome, we had to cool way down, trying not to touch or even to look at each other for fear of being discovered. We would not be lovers again until the filming was over. But we were both screwing the boss, and I found the deceit, the subterfuge, and the recklessness thrilling. The blend of sex and lies was comfortable and familiar territory for me. Betrayal? Not in my vocabulary.

The budget for *Daisy Miller* was just over $2 million, a paltry sum considering the overseas locations and period costumes. Peter was proud of the work but doubtful of the box-office potential. "It doesn't feel like an audience picture," he'd say over the dailies. His mood was not enhanced when he screened the rough print for Paramount executives.

"It's okay," said Frank Yablans, the chief of production, with a shrug and little emotion.

"'Okay'?" Peter repeated, waiting for something more affirmative.

"What do you want from me?" said Yablans. "You're Babe Ruth, and you just bunted."

When the film came out in the spring of 1972, *Newsweek* raved and the *New York Times* called it "a triumph for all concerned." We were invited to screen *Daisy Miller* at the Harvard Hasty Pudding Club. (We later found out that the student who carried our bags was Joel Silver, who would produce all the *Die Hard* movies.) But the movie critic Rex Reed recommended, "Go back to your blue jeans, Cybill." That was almost laudatory compared to some reviews. At the start of production, Peter had been quoted in *Time* saying, "I thought that if Henry James had gone to all the trouble to write a good part for Cybill, I should shoot it." The *Time* film critic didn't agree: "Among all the flaws in this movie—the numbing literalness, the flagrant absence of subtlety—nothing is quite so wrong as Cybill Shepherd. Bogdanovich installed her in the lead as if she were some sort of electrical appliance being plugged into an outlet." I understand that reviewer is dead now. I had nothing to do with it.

Daisy Miller was a box-office bomb, but it was our relationship, not the film, that most critics seemed eager to review. I believe that good reviews can be more dangerous than bad ones because it's easier to believe them and stop striving. But there's no way that actors don't feel bad from the slings and arrows of outrageous fortune. Peter and I didn't have children, so our movies were our babies, and we were wounded by the reproach. We consoled each other by reading aloud from an anthology called *Lexicon of Musical Invective*, which detailed the critical assaults upon great composers. ("*An American in Paris* is nauseous claptrap, so dull, patchy, thin, vulgar, long-winded and inane, that the average movie audience would be bored by it." "Beethoven's Second Symphony is a crass monster, a hideously rising wounded dragon that refuses to expire, and though bleeding in the Finale, furiously beats about with its tail erect.") We flaunted our solidarity, brazenly leaving a press junket to make love in the next room. We were the first live-in lovers on the cover of a new magazine called *People*, and on the inside pages we bragged insufferably about how living together was sexier than being married. We were arrogant and smug, the message being: we're Cybill and Peter, and you're not. He was constantly given credit

for my career, as if he were Pygmalion sculpting
Galatea, or Svengali controlling Trilby's singing
through hypnotic powers. (I jokingly called him
"Sven," but he wasn't allowed to call me "Trilby.")

"Stop telling people you're so in love and so
happy," Cary Grant warned Peter.

"Why?" he asked.

"Because people are not in love and not happy,"
said Grant.

"I thought all the world loves a lover," said Peter.

"Don't kid yourself," said Grant.

It was around this time that I got a reassuring call
from Cary. "Now listen, Cybill, you're very intelligent
and I can see they're offering you really dumb parts,
but don't get discouraged. If I was still acting, you're
the kind of girl I'd like to work with. Whatever you do,
don't get depressed and start eating."

Peter had an aura of superiority about him and
could be rude. When people didn't understand something he considered basic, he would act as if they belonged in a day care center. Suddenly wealthier than
he'd ever imagined, he changed the way he dressed,
favoring brass-buttoned blazers and ascots, and drove a
two-toned Silver Cloud Rolls-Royce with red leather
upholstery. I bought him a quarter horse and a hand-
tooled Mexican saddle with his initials on a silver
horn; he bought me an Appaloosa jumper and a
Hermès saddle; both arrived, draped with red ribbon,
outside our house in a trailer on Christmas morning.
We were disgusting.

However I might be deceiving him in private, I carried professional allegiance to extremes. When I was
asked to present the 1972 Academy Award for Best

Supporting Actor, I thought I'd have a little fun. "The nominees are John Houseman for *Paper Moon*—I mean *The Paper Chase*—and Randy Quaid for *The Last Picture Show*—I mean *The Last Detail*." I was astonished when I heard two weak chuckles and the dead silence of thousands. Billy Wilder wrote in *Variety*, "Hollywood is now united in its hatred of Peter Bogdanovich and Cybill Shepherd."

I'VE ALWAYS BEEN INSPIRED BY A LINE FROM Goethe: "Whatever you can do, begin it. Boldness has genius, power and magic in it." With great qualms, I decided to invade another medium and record an album of standards called *Cybill Does It to Cole Porter*. Peter agreed to produce the album, and his assistant, once again, was The Producer, who was conveniently living in an apartment less than a mile from our house. Peter had the idea to send advance cassettes to Orson Welles, Cary Grant, Fred Astaire, and Frank Sinatra, asking for blurbs to be quoted on the jacket cover. The first three sent glowing, appreciative comments, and I was hoping for the same from Sinatra. I'd met him once after a performance at Caesar's Palace.

"I love you," I gushed.

He fixed his cerulean eyes on me. "I love you too, baby," he said.

But he sent a telegram after listening to the album: "Marvelous what some guys will do for a broad!" Peter tried to convince me we were just one typo short of a rave, that a misplaced exclamation point would have made the review read, "Marvelous! What some guys will do for a broad."

It was on the basis of this album that Peter convinced 20th Century-Fox to green-light our next collaboration, an original musical comedy called *At Long Last Love* that he wrote using Cole Porter songs, about a madcap but impoverished heiress who loves a millionaire playboy who loves a Broadway star who loves an Italian roué. In movie musicals, actors usually record the vocals in a studio long before the film is shot and then lip-sync to those tracks when filming, so the sound of their voices is perfected with millions of dollars of studio enhancement. Audiences are accustomed to hearing this kind of technical quality, which can't be duplicated in live performance. But Peter was more interested in spontaneity than perfection. Inspired by the 1930s Lubitsch musicals, when it was impossible to record voice and orchestra separately, he loved the subtle changes in tempo afforded by musicians following the actors. He asked the sound department at Fox to invent a process by which he could record the actors' voices live while we heard a pianist on the set through tiny receivers in our ears, the antennae wired through our hair. One night when we were filming in downtown L.A. the police got suspicious of this equipment and threatened to arrest Peter for unlawful broadcasting.

Today many people actually love *At Long Last Love*—presumably it inspired Woody Allen to do a musical called *Everyone Says I Love You*. But when it came out, it was almost universally ravaged. We had four weeks of rehearsal (Fred and Ginger had six), and the stress took its toll: two or three times a week, Burt Reynolds would start hyperventilating and had to breathe into a paper bag. The last day of shooting I slammed three fingers in various doors (I still have a scar in my thumbnail where a studio nurse punctured it with the end of a paper clip that had been held in a flame). I bounced bra-lessly through the movie in 1930s-style silk-satin gowns that wrinkled so badly, I couldn't sit down, so I spent the long shooting days propped up against an old-fashioned "leaning board."

Considering that this frothy cinematic cocktail was released in 1975, just as the country was reeling from a post-Watergate malaise combined with a serious recession, the timing could not have been worse. Though defending it in public, Peter and I privately referred to *At Long Last Love* as our debacle. There was a tremendous pressure from the studio to get the movie out in a hurry, and Peter felt he was talked into some bad editing choices, which he would spend $60,000 of his own money to correct. The film was one of the last to be shown before Radio City Music Hall closed its doors for years, prompting Orson Welles to chastise us, "You shut down the fucking Rockettes!" The film community was thrilled; they'd been waiting for us to fail. The movie critic Judith Crist called Peter before the picture was released and asked, "How is it?"

"Pretty good," said Peter.

"It better be," she said. "They're waiting for you with their knives out." When Gene Shalit reviewed the film on the *Today* show, he said, "In this movie Cybill Shepherd appears as if she cannot walk or talk, much less sing." Then he held up a sign that read BOMB and ended with "produced, written, directed, and ruined by Peter Bogdanovich." Vincent Canby at the *New York Times*, who'd had such kind words about me in *Daisy Miller*, wrote that "casting Cybil [*sic*]

Shepherd in a musical comedy is like entering a horse in a cat show." Another critic, again reviewing the relationship, called Peter "an eager foil for Cybill Shepherd, his well-publicized but untalented girlfriend." I was crushed, humiliated, asking myself: *Is it possible I am talentless?* There's an expression that goes, "If three people tell you you're dead, lie down already." But I kept thinking: *It's not how many times you get knocked down but how many times you get back up.*

To that end, I met with the producer David Merrick and the director Jack Clayton, determined to have them cast me as another Daisy, opposite Robert Redford in *The Great Gatsby*. But when they asked for a screen test, I haughtily refused. "Can't they see I'm perfect?" I asked my agent. (And the part went to . . . Mia Farrow.) I passed on a chance to do Agatha Christie's *Death on the Nile*, since I would have spent most of the film as a corpse. (The part went to . . . Lois Chiles.) Certain actresses would become my nemesis: When John Schlesinger declared me too old and not vulnerable enough for *The Day of the Locusts*, the part went to . . . Karen Black. And she got the part I was hoping to play in *Family Plot*, which turned out to be Alfred Hitchcock's final film.

I was also hoping to play the fictionalized Norma Shearer role in *The Last Tycoon*, a roman à clef about Irving Thalberg, which Harold Pinter had adapted from the final novel of F. Scott Fitzgerald. The producer, Sam Spiegel, and the director, Elia Kazan, asked to meet me at a Beverly Hills hangout called the Bistro Gardens. It was mid-afternoon (possibly they'd heard about my appetite and didn't want to spring for lunch?) so the restaurant was almost empty, save for the waiters rattling cutlery as they set up tables for the dinner service. I knew that Kazan was a major Hollywood player, that he had cofounded the Actors Studio (birthplace of "the Method"). He introduced James Dean to the movie-going public in *East of Eden*, exposed union corruption in *On the Waterfront*, and assailed anti-Semitism in *Gentlemen's Agreement*. I also knew of his controversial testimony before the House Un-American Activities Committee and his part in the Hollywood blacklisting. When he named colleagues who were suspected of being Communists, Stella Adler said that he committed matricide and patricide. But the luxury of turning down jobs based on political beliefs is something most actors can't afford.

Kazan was quiet during our meeting, but Spiegel talked about working in Nazi Germany in the early 1930s and using the pseudonym S. P. Eagle when he first came to this country, thinking it sounded classy and American. He kept looking at the red and blue scarf double-wrapped around my neck, as if it were making him itchy, and finally said, "Honey, take that thing off."

"I can't," I said with what I thought was amusing drama, clutching my throat, "I have a hideous scar." Kazan perked up and exchanged a glance with Spiegel—if the scene had been a cartoon, the caption would have read: "How can she talk with her foot in her mouth?" (The part went to . . . Ingrid Boulting.)

I went around serenading myself with a childhood rhyme that I would repeat with a certain self-absorption for years to come: "Nobody loves me, everybody hates me, guess I'll go eat worms. Big fat juicy ones, little tiny skinny ones. Boy how they're gonna squirm." After my notices for _At Long Last Love_, it took granite ovaries to call the great jazz saxophonist Stan Getz and ask him to collaborate on an album called _Mad About the Boy_, named for the Cole Porter standard. The Producer produced the album. We were afraid to have Peter's name anywhere near it, for fear of enflaming the critics, but the three of us financed it, putting up $10,000 each. Getz came on to me, and when I declined, he snarled, "It's your fault if I go back to being a junkie and a juicehead," ignoring me for the rest of the session. The album remained in limbo for four years, as I personally shopped it around and got turned down at the major record labels. (There's nothing like rejection right in your face to keep you humble.) Miraculously, a few jazz critics actually heard it and liked it (being compared in the _Los Angeles Times_ to Lee Wiley and Ella Fitzgerald is about as good as it gets). Eventually the album was released by a small company called Inner City Records, which went bankrupt a few years later. The company's lawyer ended up with rights to the musical catalog, changed the name of my album to _Cybill Getz Better_, and informed me that the copies I requested would cost me an additional $10,000. I suggested he change the title to _Cybill Getz Screwed_.

With Peter's approval, I had decided to rent a room of my own, a tiny studio in a tall tower on the oceanfront in Santa Monica. It was decorated with photographs of Buster Keaton, a shrine to his comic genius complete with burning candles, and I had every surface except the floor covered with smoky mirrors. One drawer of my bureau was filled with naughty gifts from Peter intended to enliven our sex life—motorized

erotic gadgetry, books about tapping the lower
for full sexual awakening, crotchless panties from F
erick's of Hollywood. (The toys were okay, but I'd just
as soon go into the vegetable department of a store to
find playthings, although the moral majority is probably working on legislation outlawing cucumbers.) Peter called the apartment the Love Pavilion (there was
no place to sit except the king-size bed), and together
we sang the lines about "our little den of iniquity" from
a Rodgers and Hart lyric: "For a girlie and boy, a radio's
got so much class, and so's a ceiling made of glass."

I don't know if Peter assumed he was the only
"boy," but I was pretty sure I wasn't the only "girlie" in
his life. My dance instructor on *At Long Last Love* had
told me about one of his flings. I was horrified,
shocked, angered, and ultimately relieved. He never
asked what went on in my apartment beyond his
ken—we were still operating under our policy of mutual nondisclosure, and the apartment made it easier
for me to see The Producer. But shuttling between
two lovers did not preclude my taking a third, or
fourth, or fifth. Perhaps my infidelity was a dysfunctional way of hedging my bets so I wasn't as vulnerable
as my mother, assuring I'd never be left by the man I
loved. What was so unsatisfying about the relationship
with Peter that I needed to do this? Was I trying to re-
claim some control over the man who represented all
the power, all the money, just as my grandfather had?
Peter had given me sexual license, but he surely did
not imagine that I would dare extracurricular activities
quite so recklessly close to home, practically using his
Rolodex as a personal dating service.

The Director was someone whose work Peter and

craggy-faced man more than … senior who tended to wear long … thick gold ID bracelet and was … …ious actress. We were on the same Ho… …y circuit, making the occasional foursome for … …er.

Peter was out of town when The Director called, and while we were talking, I somehow ended up on the bathroom floor with the telephone cord looped around me twice. When he asked what I was doing, I embroidered the truth into something more provocative.

"I'm lying in an empty bathtub," I said. "I often do that when I'm on the phone."

He responded with a well-timed laugh and the appropriate question. "What do you wear while lying in the empty bathtub?"

"What does one usually wear in the tub?" I answered.

"Interesting," he said. "I never knew you were this crazy."

I mentioned the shrine to Buster Keaton at my beach apartment. "I'd love to see it," he said. "Will Peter be upset if I take you to dinner?"

"Surely not with you," I said.

We arranged to meet at the apartment. "You smell incredible," he said when I opened the door. "What is that scent?"

"Why, honey, it's magnolia oil," I replied in my best southern drawl. As he stepped past me, he jingled the change in his pocket distractedly and squirted his mouth with Binaca breath freshener. When I saw him looking for a place to sit, I ran to the balcony for a wooden stool, then changed my mind. "Let's go to the pier," I said. "It'll be an adventure."

The Santa Monica pier was a faded relic of the Roaring Twenties, with a few seafood shanties, some rundown souvenir stands, and a wonderful carousel, closed on this chilly, foggy night. I was peering through the locked gates at its painted stallions when I heard change jingling again. It seemed to be The Director's version of clearing his throat.

"Are you ready to go back?" he asked.

No, I wanted to walk all the way out to the end of the pier, deserted except for a few fishermen, who avoided eye contact. He walked along with me, grudgingly admiring my hitch-kicks over several garbage cans. As we got back to his car, he looked at me with a cold, self-assured expression. "If this was a scene," he said, "I'd rewrite it."

"How?" I asked.

"Oh, I'd have to sit at my typewriter," he said. "That's where the juices start flowing. I rent a house out in Malibu. It's the only place in Los Angeles where I can breathe. Why don't we go out there? You don't have to worry. It'll be perfectly all right." I didn't know if he was reassuring me that he had no designs on me, that he wouldn't overstep the boundaries of his friendship with Peter, or that we wouldn't get caught. I didn't know which I wanted. But if you have to ask, maybe you shouldn't do it.

The beach house was so close to the ocean that it vibrated with each breaker, and a depressing dampness filled the rooms and every surface, even the toilet seat. "Will you excuse me a minute?" he said rather formally. He was gone more than a half hour, performing, I assumed, some preseduction toilette. (I heard a Binaca spritz at least once.)

We went for a walk on the beach while he smoked a loosely rolled joint, getting red-eyed and more withdrawn. Then we sat on the sofa making excruciating small talk until he finally said, "It's getting late. I'd better take you home."

He phoned the next afternoon. "I called my psychiatrist today," he said. "We're just friends now—I finished my analysis three years ago—and I mentioned the situation with you. He thought that I was confused and guilty and that it would probably be healthy to indulge my impulses." There was a lingering pause. "What kind of time did you have last night?"

"Horrible," I admitted.

"Me too," he said. "I wanted you, but I had no idea how you felt. I thought you found me unattractive, and I was afraid of being rejected."

I reassured him that he was Everywoman's idea of Adonis, and moved on to another card in the Rolodex.

Peter and I were good friends of the director John Cassavetes and his wife, the actress Gena Rowlands. John was one of the world's great flirts, but when I phoned him at his office one day, I couldn't get him to play.

"How are you?" I asked, an obvious siren call.

"Why are you calling me here?" he said with irritation. "What are you doing?"

Good question. I didn't know what I was doing. I no longer believed that sexual desire meant love, but I was still convinced that I was out of control, therefore not culpable. I was using men and being used. (There is no coldheartedness toward someone else in

which the cold heart is not also hurt.) As long as I
didn't get caught, I believed I was okay. I had learned
early on that love is not about what you feel, but what
you can get if you act lovingly, as I had with my
grandfather. Men were supposed to want me, but I
wasn't supposed to want them. When I disconnected
from my mother's moral stance, which was based on
the idea that my only value to the culture was sexual
but I wasn't supposed to enjoy it, I lost the protective,
parental voice in my head, the voice that says: *Cybill,
what are you doing?*

It took years to gain some understanding of my des-
perate sexuality. I had to believe in myself as a person
with value beyond the sexual, a person with boundaries, a person who can say yes when she means yes
and no when she means no and know the difference.
Up until then, I'd been trying to save my life the only
way I knew how: lying.

CHAPTER SEVEN

"I Need a Cybill Shepherd Type"

AN OLD HOLLYWOOD JOKE (OFTEN REPEATED with the substitution of different names) lists the five stages of an actor's career. First: Who is Dustin Hoffman? Second: Get me Dustin Hoffman. Third: Get me a Dustin Hoffman type. Fourth: Get me a young Dustin Hoffman. Fifth: Who is Dustin Hoffman?

In 1975, when I was twenty-five years old, my agent, Sue Mengers, got a call from a young director named Martin Scorsese who was casting a movie called *Taxi Driver.*

"I need a Cybill Shepherd type," he said.

"How about the real thing?" she asked.

I had to beg Sue to be truthful with me when we first worked together, and after that she was unfailingly, unflinchingly honest. "Just suck up to Marty," she instructed when Scorsese agreed to see me (invoking memories of Moma's suggestion to "love up on Da-dee's neck"). "Be a nice, sweet, innocent girl.

Smile and look pretty. Don't talk a lot, don't make jokes, and don't tell him he needs to sit on a phone book."

When I read the script that was sent over by messenger to my hotel in New York, I threw it across the room, trying to hit the wastebasket. The violence was so relentless, and my character, a political drone named Betsy, was such a cipher, that I couldn't imagine breathing any life into her. My anxiety was palpable—what's a Cybill Shepherd type anyway? With my little pilot light of insecurity, fanned by a few years' worth of scathing reviews, I thought: *Maybe I'm not even good enough to play my own type*. But I admired all of Scorsese's films—*Mean Streets* was a searing portrait of small-time hoods in Little Italy, and the evocative *Alice Doesn't Live Here Anymore* had resulted in an Academy Award for Ellen Burstyn, my mother in *The Last Picture Show*.

In person, Scorsese was energetic to the point of manic—he talked as if his life depended on maintaining a certain velocity. One of the people he talked about was the talented young actress he was hoping to cast in the role of the child prostitute Iris.

"This girl Jodie Foster is so young, I don't know if her mother will let her do it," he said. "You know the nature of the material. But she's so good. And she looks just like you when you were fourteen."

Concomitant to the talks about *Taxi Driver*, Peter was planning our next project, entitled *Nickelodeon*, which would reunite him with Ryan O'Neal. Their friendship was improbable—Ryan was an enthusiastic participant in the recreational drug scene of Hollywood, while Peter rarely considered fogging his brain with even a cocktail. Ryan often greeted Peter by kissing him on the lips and grabbing him by the balls, and he never considered their camaraderie an impediment to chasing me—on the contrary, he had a reputation for pursuing the girlfriends of all his friends. He pinned me against a wall at one of Sue Mengers's parties, ran his fingers through my hair, and whispered, "Let's fuck." I giggled and slugged him in the solar plexus.

One day I answered the phone to find Ryan on the other end calling Peter, who wasn't home. "And how are you?" he inquired, all Irish charm. I'd just come from a dance class and told him that I was getting into shape. Carbohydrates had been my chief form of consolation after the debacle of *At Long Last Love*, and although Peter still liked me nice and round, I wasn't sure about Martin Scorsese.

"You'll have to stop eating to lose weight," said Ryan, his charm suddenly dissipating. "I couldn't believe Peter putting you in nothing but white for *At Long Last Love*. You looked like a beached beluga. And everybody's starting to wonder if he's lost it. The sound of that flop is still echoing through the Hollywood hills."

Most other "friends" had been more tactful than to repeat such gossip to my face. I started to cry. "Look," he said, both guilty and triumphant, "we're supposed to work together. I'll come pick you up, we'll drive to my house at the beach and talk."

Red lights and warning buzzers should have been going off—STAND AWAY FROM THE DOOR, NOT A THROUGH STREET, TOXIC IF INGESTED—but I didn't see or hear them. Since Ryan had just indicated he found me unappealingly fat, and since establishing some bond of friendship seemed a good preamble to working together, I agreed. Ryan barely acknowledged me when I got into his Porsche and almost knocked down the exit gate in his impatience to leave, giving me a filthy look as I buckled my seat belt. I couldn't figure out if he was trying to keep me off balance by shifting his mood without warning. There was no possibility of conversation—he was singing along to loud acid rock on the radio—and he left the motor running with the music blaring when he pulled into a 7-Eleven. I could see him sharing some laughs with the counterman as he paid for a six-pack of Coors.

Pulling up to his house off the Pacific Coast Highway in Malibu, he touched a button on the dashboard and the garage door opened, revealing a wooden floor with a rich varnish like a gymnasium. I turned to comment on such unexpected elegance, but he had already vanished inside, leaving the door open behind him. I'd been in this house for a party once, had already seen the pool table, the stereo equipment, the brass-framed movie mementos ("To Ryan, with deep and sincerest affection, William Holden"), but then I was with Peter, and I'd stayed downstairs.

"Ever seen my bedroom?" he asked. "C'mon upstairs. The view is fabulous." WRONG WAY, NO OUTLET, DANGEROUS CURVES—I still didn't see the signs.

Climbing the stairs, we entered a bachelor pad, decorated in earth tones with a fur spread on the bed—the real thing, I think. Suddenly there was a clatter of bottles coming from the bathroom. Ryan ran in and emerged a moment later, with a pretty girl in tow. She was wearing a cheap cotton shift and rubber gloves. "This is Sarah," he said familiarly. "She's doing a little tidying up, but she's going to come back later. Now beat it, honey," he said, giving her behind a playful slap. As soon as she left, he turned to me and said, "I don't know why I let her in here—she has no idea what she's doing." I didn't know what she was doing either, but I had clearly interrupted something.

Gesturing toward a couch, he said, "Have a seat," but he stood near the window with its spectacular view of the surf, pointing out the various celebrity homes up and down the beach. "I can see everything that _____ does," he said, naming a well-known actor, "and believe me, he's weird." Then he came to the sofa, standing over me. "You know, you could be really good if you had the right parts," he said. "Something has happened to Peter. He has to get back on track, and you've got more to do with it than anyone." As he talked, he periodically used both hands to cup his balls, which were right at my eye level, a gesture that, at the time, I didn't know as checking his package.

The whole scene was starting to give me the creeps. I stood up, saying that it was getting late and I needed to get back. He stopped me by putting his arms around my shoulder, drawing me close to his chest, and making little moans of satisfaction as we swayed back and forth, one of his hands on my neck and the other at the small of my back. I started to pull away and felt his muscles resist, stop me for an instant and then relax. I excused myself to use the bathroom, and when I came out, he was looking at his watch—another mood shift.

"I'd better be going too," he said irritably. "I'm supposed to pick my son up by six."

On the way home, he put a Vivaldi cassette in the car's tape deck. "If you like this," I said in a friendly tone, "I can turn you on to some music that makes this sound like shit."

He snapped his head around. "How can you say this is shit?" he snarled.

"I didn't mean that," I said hastily, seeing that I had insulted his tastes and not wanting to provoke him. "I just meant that there's some beautiful Beethoven I'd like to play for you. . . ."

"I know about Beethoven," he said, then popped out the Vivaldi and turned on the radio full blast, although it could barely be heard through the whoosh from the open sunroof. The Vivaldi turned out to be part of the soundtrack for Ryan's next film, *Barry Lyndon*, and after I'd seen it, I sent him a copy of the Beethoven Piano Concerto no. 4 with the inscription, "This is a fitting tribute to your superb performance." He never responded.

Both *Nickelodeon* and *Taxi Driver* were to be made for Columbia Pictures, whose president, David Begelman, announced that I had to choose between the two. It was a tough decision—Peter had written a part especially for me, incorporating my myopia into the character, which gave me an excuse to do a lot of pratfalls. But we were still in a public relations abyss—one of the kinder assessments at the time labeled me "a no-talent dame with nice boobs and a toothpaste smile and all the star quality of a dead hamster." We both knew that anything we did together in this vitriolic atmosphere was doomed. And not working with Ryan

O'Neal was the consolation prize. It was a crushing disappointment to give up *Nickelodeon*. The part went to . . . Jane Hitchcock, who'd modeled with me in New York. And Begelman got busted for embezzling money from the studio.

In 1975, Robert De Niro still had a youthful, almost preppy quality, the antithesis of his character in *Taxi Driver*, the psychotic Vietnam veteran Travis Bickle. We used the same technique of scrawling microscopic notes on the script, covering every inch of the page, but I'd never seen an actor immerse himself in a role at De Niro's level of intensity. He actually got a hack license, and during the preproduction phase, when he was still filming *1900* in Italy with Bernardo Bertolucci, he would leave Rome on a Friday, fly to New York, and drive a cab for the weekend. He went to an army base in northern Italy to tape-record the voices of some soldiers from an area in the Midwest that he wanted to use for Travis Bickle's accent. Once we started filming, he stayed in character all the time. Waiting for the cameras to be set up for our "date" in Child's Coffee Shop (airless in hundred-degree heat and perfumed by years of lard for deep-fat frying), he stared at me with a goofy but menacing half grin so disorienting that I called over the hairdresser to change the dynamic to a less threatening threesome.

Scorsese, who was given to wearing white straw fedoras with colorful hatbands, used the sights and sounds of New York City like a big palette of colors to create a mood, and he dealt with the limited budget by shooting at night with a minimal crew and high-speed film, as if for an underground movie. He liked his actors to improvise and videotaped our efforts with a handheld black and white camera during rehearsals in his St. Regis hotel suite, inserting the bits of dialogue that worked best into the script. De Niro is a master at underplaying, doing little and having it be effective. That's part of what makes it so terrifying when Travis Bickle does go off the deep end. The first day of shooting, I remarked to Scorsese that De Niro epitomized Hitchcock's advice to actors: Don't put a lot of scribble on your face. "I think I should try to match that," I said, and it became my pact with Scorsese.

"Do less," he would say. Then, "Now do even less." And then, "Now do even less than that."

One day, De Niro and I were walking up Fifth Avenue together at the end of the day.

"Do you want to get some barbecue?" he asked, fixing me with a sexy half-smile.

In approximately an hour, I was expecting The Producer on my doorstep, after an absence of three or four weeks, and I wasn't about to blow off what I knew would be a torrid reunion, not for this intense, inscrutable man who still seemed to be vaguely in character. "I can't," I said. "I have someone, a friend, in town."

"Oh," he said, "is Peter here?"

"Not Peter."

He grew rather quiet, walked me to the door of my apartment, and said good night. Other than as Travis Bickle, that was the last time he spoke to me during the filming.

At the end of the shoot, I had a special taxi key chain made and inscribed for Scorsese—it cost the larger part of my salary. I was so grateful for the opportunity, but it wasn't until twenty years later when the film came out on video disk that I could fast-forward quickly enough through the savage finale and realize that I'd been given an extraordinary last scene. Of course, I remembered shooting it, but wasn't sure that it made the final cut: I'm a wimp about movie violence, even though I know it's really chicken blood or Max Factor Technicolor Blood Number 5. Recently, I saw those final rearview mirror shots of Travis and Betsy, who has unknowingly gotten in his cab. At the end of her last ride, she leans through the window and starts to apologize to Travis. She appears to realize there's no point and dejectedly asks, "How much was it?" I feel a subtext between Cybill Shepherd and Robert De Niro, almost as if I'm saying, "I'm sorry I didn't give you a tumble," and he's saying, "You better believe you're sorry, baby. You can't imagine what you missed."

It wasn't until the rerelease of that film that I was credited with a performance of any merit—at the time I was still the no-talent dame with big boobs too closely associated with Peter Bogdanovich. Julia Phillips, one of the film's producers, declared in *You'll Never Eat Lunch in This Town Again* that the only reason the Italian Scorsese had cast me was my big ass.

OVER THE PAST SEVERAL YEARS, A SERIES OF strokes had disabled and silenced my grandfather. Still physically capable of speech, he mostly sat in a chair seeming rather docile and lost, as if he didn't know quite where he belonged, until he was summoned elsewhere, like the dinner table. Moma took him to

Romania for monkey-gland injections, which, to the surprise of no one else in the family, did nothing to help. I'd gone home to see him propped up for their fiftieth wedding anniversary party. Failing in memory and strength, he spent the last year of his life in the Rosewood Nursing Home and died in the fall of 1975.

My reaction was curiously impersonal and detached, more an acknowledgment of a milestone than a true sense of sorrow. I thought, in all naïveté, that Da-Dee had ceased to have any power over me or my direction in life. His funeral was to be the first I ever attended, not counting the time that our dog Freckles unsuccessfully tackled a car on Highland Park Place, a far more traumatic event in my life. I didn't even want to go home, but my mother insisted, and it would have been unseemly to take Peter. He had not seen my mother since her insults at the premiere of *Picture Show*, and Peter is nothing if not grudge holding. The Producer volunteered to come along, and his twisted humor got me through the day—we exchanged irreverent glances about the wavering vibrato of the buxom redhead singing the gospel that Moma loved, along with the absolute latest in dying offered by the Memphis Memorial Gardens. There were three panels of automated curtains: the first opened to reveal the coffin to the immediate family; the second revealed the coffin to the larger group of mourners; the third revealed the family to the mourners. I stared at the folded freckled hands of the man in the open coffin, the only part of him that looked as elegant as in life, his once vibrant face shriveled and masked with makeup, his ungainly ears oddly flattened against his head by the mortician, and I thought I might throw up.

My grandfather's last words, according to my brother, were, "Don't let the hens getcha." He had never placed much faith in Moma's business acumen, and I remember more than one occasion when she'd say, "Cybill, darlin', rush to the bank with this cash. I've just bounced a check, and I don't want Da-Dee to find out." Trying to ensure that my grandmother would never get control of Shobe, Inc., he named the bank as trustee, but Moma fought his posthumous bully pulpit in court for six years and won the right to run the firm herself. For the following twenty years, she used the company letterhead for all her correspondence, simply writing "Mrs." in front of her husband's engraved name.

A few months after my grandfather's funeral, I was alone with Peter at Copa de Oro. It would be the first time we listened to my album *Mad About the Boy* together. Peter had already heard it and wanted to be free to give me notes, so he requested that The Producer not be present. That night I was talking to a friend on the phone when I heard a strange click on the line. Immediately I had the thought that someone was in the house. (We'd had two intruders there: an overzealous fan who walked through the gate behind a delivery truck, with a picture of me in his wallet, and an escapee from a mental institution who ran through the halls screaming, "Where am I?") I quickly dialed the emergency number for the Bel Air Patrol, then went and got Peter from his office, and we locked ourselves upstairs, me wishing I'd been willed part of Da-Dee's arsenal. When the security police arrived, they searched room by room, suddenly yelling from the basement: "We've got somebody. Says he knows you."

My heart nearly stopped when two security men in gray uniforms brought The Producer upstairs, slumping, with a firm grip on each of his arms. He had his own set of keys to everything in our lives and had let himself in. "It's okay," Peter said, "we know him." Once we declined to press charges and the cops left, The Producer gave us an explanation about being there—he had wanted to hear Peter's unexpurgated comments about the Getz album, and he adamantly denied being the telephone eavesdropper. I was sure that Peter would find out about our secret past, but he seemed to accept the theory that The Producer had been temporarily wiggy and stressed out too.

But I was growing weary of amorous subterfuge that smacked of my teenage years and remorseful about my duplicity. Having sex with another man's business associate is pretty much beyond the pale. And living with a lie is a prescription for going crazy. Chekhov wrote that the quickest way to reduce the stature of a man is to lie to him. I had done that with both Peter and The Producer.

Feeling the stress, I started grinding my teeth at night until my doctor prescribed Valium. I was dreaming about a clean slate, starting fresh, not lying. In a moment of unprecedented candor, I sat with The Producer in a Westwood coffee shop and told him it was over. He had been such a significant presence in my life—maybe not the creative partnership I had with Peter, nor the irresistible flame of Elvis, but an enduring passion. We used up half of the thin folded napkins in the metal dispenser as surrogate Kleenex.

It would be so easy to dismiss the next decade of my life as the lost years, defined by unremarkable or irredeemable projects. There was a movie called *Special Delivery* with Bo Svenson, who introduced himself to me by knocking at my dressing-room door and dropping his pants. I couldn't even get Michael Caine to kiss me as an adulterous sex kitten in *Silver Bears*. The first time I saw him coming across the ornate lobby of the lakeside hotel in Lugano, Switzerland, he seemed to glow from within—here was a real movie star. But shooting our love scenes, his mouth clamped shut, and a damp line of perspiration formed on his upper lip. The lack of heat was so obvious that the director, Ivan Passer, came to me privately and asked if I couldn't warm things up.

"He won't kiss me," I protested.

"Well, you know what to do," said Passer. Actually, I didn't. But once the production moved to London, Caine's attitude changed: he was frisky, enthusiastic, inspired.

"Am I imagining it, or is the difference apparent?" I asked Passer.

"Sure," he said, "Shakira's in town." It seemed that Caine was a more passionate leading man when he could look past the camera and see his own wife on the set. But *Silver Bears* suffered the fate of being Columbia's "other" movie, released in 1978 at the same time as *Close Encounters of the Third Kind*. Almost no promotional efforts or finances were put into it, and the film disappeared.

There would have been no problem playing love scenes with the cameraman, since we were acting them out privately. All my resolve about fidelity didn't amount to a hill of beans. I saw, I wanted, I took. In my long career of sleeping with charming cads, he was among the charmingest and caddiest, a married rogue with long black hair and a goatee who liked to drive his Mercedes at a hundred miles an hour. During one lusty encounter, he sucked my chin so hard that the next day, I looked like a bruised peach, and when he viewed me through the camera lens, he started to laugh. When we were scheduled to shoot some footage in Las Vegas, I made sure I got to the location early so we could have some time together. The first night I came down to meet some of the movie people for dinner and saw him already sitting at the table, nuzzling another blonde. I could hardly justify outrage that a married man was not only cheating with me but *on* me. For several days, I lay around my room at Caesar's Palace nursing a broken heart, writing self-pitying poems and listening to a constant odd hum that turned out to be the lights on the building's facade. As much as I liked to believe, even announce, that I could have a relationship that would be purely physical, not emotional, I got hooked. Miserable and looking for distraction, I went to see Sinatra perform and found him strangely wooden and listless. I found out that he had chartered a plane to bring his mother out to Vegas—the same plane that had been used for the shooting of *Silver Bears* the previous day—and it had crashed into the side of a mountain.

Since I knew I had a lot more to learn about acting, I sought advice from Orson Welles. "I don't know which direction to take," I said. "I may have an offer to do a revival of the play *The Philadelphia Story* in New York, or I have a definite offer from the Tidewater Dinner Theater in Norfolk, Virginia, to do *A Shot in the Dark,* or I could go study with Stella Adler in New York."

"Do not take acting classes," he said. "When you walk through the door, you will be envied and despised because you are already more famous than most of them will ever be. Learn by doing theater, and do it anywhere but Los Angeles or New York. Just make sure that you talk loud enough so that people in the last row can understand what you're saying. Nobody will support you, but it will be the most important thing you ever do. It will give you an opportunity to fall on your face. The audience will teach you what you need to know."

The only person who thought this was a good idea was Gena Rowlands. "Oh, Cyb," she said, "it's easy, and you're going to have the time of your life." Everyone else acted as if there might be the need for an intervention, including Peter. (Stella Adler actually supported the theater plan, with a caveat. "No more ingenues," she said. "Play what you haven't lived. It will help you with your life.") I went to Virginia, reprising Julie Harris's murderous role in *A Shot in the Dark*. That's when I really fell in love with acting. What I discovered is that film is more a medium for the director and the editor, but in the theater, the writer and the actor have more control. The preparation is intense, but once the performance starts, there's no one saying, "Cut," or "That was a little over the top, Cybill, take it down a peg." Every night, from the entrance stage left to the final curtain, there is a full dramatic arc to follow. After opening night I felt: Not only do I have wings, but I can fly.

In 1978 Peter was still depressed about the failure of *Nickelodeon*, thinking that his career was going to hell in a handbasket, even without me. He was set to direct

Saint Jack, the book whose rights I'd won as part of the settlement in my suit against *Playboy*. There was never a part in it for me, but I thought it was an unusual story and even wrote a first-draft script.

I was starting to feel an impetus for another kind of production, but Peter had always rejected the notion of his ever having another child. If I had been asked even a year before whether I wanted children, I would have said no. I was afraid it would keep me from doing what I wanted to do in my life. But at the age of twenty-eight, I began longing intensely for a baby.

The last time I'd broached the subject with Peter, we had just made love. "Please don't bring that up again," he said with mood-killing finality, grabbing a robe at the end of the bed and sitting down at his desk with his back toward me. Part-time single fatherhood was one long unending battle for Peter, and pushing the issue probably meant unconsciously scripting the end of our relationship.

Sensing a last hurrah, a few months later I joined him on location for *Saint Jack*. I flew to London and then on to Singapore, where we stayed at the fabled Raffles Hotel—romantic in a slightly seedy way, cooled by ceiling fans reportedly invented for the hotel in the late 1900s by the Hunter Fan Company of Memphis, Tennessee, which had given me one of my first modeling jobs. One night we were sitting in the lounge drinking potent Singapore slings when I realized that the fans were no longer spinning, but the room was.

There was a small part in the film played by a beautiful young Asian actress named Monika Subramaniam, who lowered her eyes when she met me and lit up like Las Vegas when she saw Peter. I didn't confront him. He didn't have to confess. I just knew. Our relationship was limping to an end anyway. This didn't help.

$\mathcal{T}$WO THINGS HAVE ALWAYS SAVED MY LIFE: reading and singing. Books and music have comforted me, informed me, helped me define myself. It's impossible to overstate their importance to my mental health, spiritual sustenance, and survival on the planet. The difference, of course, is that while reading is private, personal, unexamined, with no need to explain or justify, singing is quite the opposite. I put my voice out there to be examined, reviewed, sometimes reviled, as I've done since childhood, when my parents would ask me to sing for company and I always felt that people seemed a little disappointed. But I always come back to it. Every song has at least one character—and I don't need a movie studio or TV network to finance it. Cabaret is an opportunity to tell stories around a fire. From an early age, long before the benefit of therapy, I have felt my heart healed by singing. But it takes the most courage of all. For the performer it's like being stripped naked, and for the audience it's like being in the performer's living room—really torturous if you don't like the person. I've had some mean things said about my voice. No matter: even if I felt that my singing was utterly unappreciated, it would remain a necessary component of my life.

I was feeling disconnected from Peter, even though nothing had been articulated between us, and I had no movie or TV offers. So I went to New York and sang on

Sundays at a glorified hamburger joint in Greenwich Village called the Cookery. The rest of the week belonged to the extraordinary blues artist and fellow Memphian Alberta Hunter, who had learned the music that played on the gramophone in the St. Louis brothel where she went to work as a ladies' maid when she was eleven years old. She wrote Bessie Smith's first hit "Down-Hearted Blues" ("I've got the world in a jug and the stopper right here in my hand, and if you want me pretty papa, you better come under my command."). Her performance was so moving, so dignified, so authoritative. Music is about the pauses as much as the notes, and even her breathing between the phrases was powerful. Alberta called me "Memphis" and always greeted me with tremendous warmth, which was more than the audience did. I stood at a microphone in front of a small room, singing over the sounds of conversation and cutlery banging against crockery. Nobody wanted to hear me—one woman approached the stage and asked quite loudly, "Where's the rest room, honey?"

During the two weeks of my engagement, I slept in a tiny room at the Pierre Hotel with three different men in quick succession: one was the sexy young waiter at the Cookery, who roamed the room in a figure eight moaning "Woe is me. I've been in love with you my whole life, and now I can't get it up." Two was an agent I met, a married father of five. (I know, I know.) Three was Charles Grodin. My *Heartbreak Kid* costar, who I had found distant, humorless, and unappealing, called when he heard about me performing and shocked me by making me laugh. Either he got funny or I finally had a sense of humor. We went to dinner at a dive not listed in any guidebook, the sort of dark and clandestine place that is the culinary equivalent of the No-Tell Motel. Our one-night stand never went beyond the morning after, when I found out that he was living with someone else.

Suddenly, and rudely, my life as a sexual libertine caught up with me. The only protection I'd ever been taught was abstinence, based on an archaic morality. Condoms had become antiques—at that time there were no sexually transmitted diseases that couldn't be treated out of a prescription bottle. When I moved to Los Angeles with Peter, I had been on the Pill since I was sixteen. When I was twenty-seven, I had a notoriously gallivanting Copper–7 IUD, which eventually got "lost" and X rays were required to locate and retrieve it. By the time I was in New York, I was using a diaphragm. But it was not fail-safe.

Even a woman who feels passionately that abortion should be safe and legal does not terminate a pregnancy with an easy heart. For me it was testimony to another kind of failure, like going back to the sexually secretive dungeon of high school. I checked into a clinic under a false name on a Saturday when there were no other patients and vomited from the anesthesia by myself in the recovery room. I told no one what I was doing.

The female body gearing up for pregnancy is a hormonal roller coaster. The hips automatically tilt forward; the body has more blood and fluid. (When I later became pregnant with twins, I needed a retainer because my bottom teeth started moving around.) The aftermath of my abortion was like hitting the wall. Along with the feeling of relief was a nagging wonder: will I get another chance? Regardless of how important and correct the choice was at the time, a woman always wonders about the child she didn't choose to bring to life.

Women will always end unwanted pregnancies, safely when they can, unsafely when it's the only option, and several hundred thousand die every year as a result. I've marched for the right to choose, and I know, deep in my bones, that pregnancy as punishment is bad for both women and children.

I knew I had done the right thing. But I was feeling the emptiness of sex with men who didn't matter, feeling like I didn't matter to them either. I actually felt like a hooker when the owner of the Cookery paid me for singing by saying, "Here, baby," and stuffing some crumpled twenty-dollar bills in my hand. Like a wounded animal, I called my mother, who listened, mostly silent, as I poured out my unhappiness. I heard my voice rise and soften like a little girl through sniffles and sobs. Finally my mother spoke, strong and reassuring. "Cybill," she said, "come home." She had gone through her own miserable and lonely post-divorce odyssey, finally carving out a busy, optimistic life. At fifty-three, she met a charming and high-spirited widower named Mondo Micci (which is pronounced "Mickey" in Memphis), a former Golden Gloves champion who used to climb up the fire escape at the Peabody Hotel to sneak into the rooftop dances there. For the first time in her life, she was being protected and cared for by someone else, making it so much easier for her to protect and care for me.

I'M ALWAYS PRESSING MY NOSE TO THE AIR-plane window as I fly into Memphis, searching for the first sign of the Mississippi, and I try to make out old channels in the river that look like imperfectly healed wounds in the earth. The markings of the land have become as familiar over the years as the lines in my own palms. I can even identify individual streets and buildings, the landmarks of my childhood, from a great height.

One of those buildings feels like my foster child. A musician named Hillsman Wright was involved in an effort to save from demolition the grand old Orpheum Theater at Beale Street and Main, the ornate movie palace of my childhood dreams, where I'd seen *The Ten Commandments* and *Gone With the Wind*. He took me backstage, up rickety staircases, and across catwalks dating from its days on the vaudeville circuit, and he played Bach on a monster Wurlitzer pipe organ as it rose up from the orchestra pit. That was all I needed to get involved in the fund-raising campaign, making a public service announcement and eventually singing Hoagy Carmichael's "Memphis in June" at the Orpheum's fiftieth-anniversary celebration.

One night I went with my brother to Blues Alley, a smoky club on Front Street near the riverbank. Leaning against the bar was a burly, dark-haired man whom I first mistook for the cameraman, the English cad who broke my heart. This was David Ford, who was twenty-five years old (three years younger than I), and still living with his parents in the suburb of White Haven and working as the manager of the parts department at a Mercedes repair shop near the airport to pay for classes at the University of Memphis. I sent him one of those nakedly undisguised C'mon-a-my-house looks that are possible between strangers in nightclubs, and before the evening had ended, I knew we were destined to be lovers. I thought: *Maybe I can find happiness in Memphis with a regular guy*.

Thus began an interesting confluence of events, as my mother and I were both dating others but living under the same roof. While David and I were necking on the living room couch, I'd hear a car pull in the driveway, idling for too long until the motor shut off, when Mother would come inside with a satisfied smile. The first time David and I made love, we had to wait until my mother was asleep before we raced to my brother's bedroom. After all those years, I was still sneaking around.

Before urban renewal almost renewed Beale Street out of existence, most white folks went there in the wee small hours after too many martinis, observing a tradition known as Midnight Rambles. Back then, Beale Street was mainly whorehouses, pawn shops, and saloons like Pee Wee's, where in 1912 William Christopher Handy first put the notes on paper for a song he called "Memphis Blues." No one had ever used the word *blues* in a song title before, and as a result, in the 1970s Congress proclaimed Handy "Father of the Blues" and declared Memphis "Home of the Blues."

David Ford became my companion in the search for my musical roots. He introduced me to Ma Rainey II who, from a wheelchair, could whoop up "Got My Mojo Working" better than anybody. I also got to know Furry Lewis, another Memphis legend. Though his recording career had ended in the thirties, he'd had an amazing career revival in the sixties, opening for the Rolling Stones and making frequent appearances on the *Tonight Show*. During the lean years in between, he had been employed as a street sweeper for the Memphis sanitation department. His slide guitar technique, sweet voice, and songwriting skills were backed up by a dignified but wicked sense of humor. One time we visited his home where he sat on the side of his bed playing guitar, singing, and talking. He wore thick Coke-bottle spectacles to compensate for cataracts, and kept a saucer on the top of his glass. In between sips of Ten High Whiskey he said, "I can't see too good and I want to be sure there's nothin' in there but the High."

I was privileged to get to know and work with many more great Memphis musicians: Lee Baker, Jimmy Crosthwaite, Jim Dickenson, Little Laura Dukes, Prince Gabe, Honeymoon Garner, L. T. Lewis, Harold Mabern, Don McMinn, Jamil Nasser, Calvin Newborn, Sid Selvidge, Bob Talley, William Thais, and Mose Vinson. Grandma Dixie Davis would so inspire me with her barrel-house version of Handy's "Beale Street Blues" that I would sing it for twenty years and finally record it in 1998 on my CD *Talk Memphis to Me*.

When you hear the blues in Memphis, the musicians kind of sit back on the melody, playing a little behind the beat so that if the leader holds a phrase out for an extra measure they can follow with a kind of *fa-lop*. That's what makes it funky. That's what makes it Memphis. As Lee Baker used to say, "even the Memphis Symphony plays behind the beat."

In 1978 I recorded *Vanilla*, my third album of standards, featuring the renowned jazz pianist Phineas Newborn, Jr. The producer was tenor saxman Fred

Ford (he had howled like a dog on Big Mama Thornton's recording of "Hound Dog"). He was surrounded by his Beale Street USA Orchestra, usually twenty pieces but, as he said, "mortified down to twelve for this occasion."

In 1978 I was quite optimistic about my first TV movie. *A Guide for the Married Woman* was a followup to *A Guide for the Married Man*, a clever romp about the art of adultery. David managed to take some time off and accompany me to Los Angeles, staying at my apartment. I sent David and a bad toothache to the dentist who treated Peter and me, and the two of them happened to cross paths in the office. The dentist mentioned that the shaggy-haired fellow who'd just left was an out-of-town referral from me, and Peter figured it out. When I drove to Copa de Oro to see Peter, he confronted me with his suspicions. I admitted to the affair and in a fury he threw a heavy crystal ashtray across the room. It was a final gesture of disillusionment at the end of our grand plans. There was a visible dent where it shattered on the tile floor.

We did have one last phone call. Feeling bad about the ashtray-throwing scene and knowing that both of us were in Los Angeles, I tried to reach out to him and called to ask if it was okay to come over and talk. I didn't know that his latest squeeze, Monika, was also in residence and that he was hosting a party for a dozen of our mutual friends.

"It's really not a good time," he said with genuine discomfort in his voice. Later he would say that he wanted to make everyone else disappear. Although he'd never told me, I think he wanted to give our relationship another chance. But I was calling to repair, not renew. Our reparations would be postponed, but once made, they have endured to this day. Peter remains one of my only truly intimate friends, and I think the main reason for our abiding friendship is that I never took him to court to get money. When I moved out, I said, "Send me whatever you think is mine," and he sent rugs, books, his father's paintings. There were no lawyers to extend the period of discontent. And we say "I love you" to each other as much now as when we were a couple.

The best thing about *A Guide for the Married Woman* turned out to be the way my hair looked. Next, in the summer of 1978, I was cast in a remake of the witty forty-year-old Hitchcock classic *The Lady Vanishes*, shooting at Pinewood Studios outside London and in the Austrian Alps. I was cast as a "madcap heiress" working with a *Life* photographer played by Elliott Gould to solve the disappearance of Angela Lansbury on a train. Though I'd played madcap before, this time I got the wardrobe right: a bias-cut white silk satin dress worthy of Carole Lombard. (The costume department made nine identical copies.) In one scene I was supposed to run alongside a vintage steam engine on fist-size sharp gray rocks, wearing high heels. I had sprained my ankle playing basketball in high school, so the director Anthony Page agreed to let me do it in high-tops, shooting me from the knees up and earning the eternal gratitude of my ligaments. Angela and I sang Gershwin together while waiting for scenes to be set up. But Gould was mercurial, seemingly detached from the process and easily miffed. One day we were told about some glitch in production.

"*Oy vey*," I said with a weary sigh.

"Don't ever use that expression again!" snapped Gould. "You have no right." (Years later I would tell this story to the Jewish producer of *Moonlighting*, Glenn Caron, who said, "That's ridiculous," and immediately wrote me an "*Oy vey*" scene.)

I didn't want to be away from David, but he knew that if he took any more time off from his job, he'd be fired, so his arrival in Europe, unemployed, was a rather emphatic declaration of love and commitment. The only discordant note in our reunion was a bell-hop at the hotel asking him "Where shall I put your bags, Mr. Shepherd?"—a portent of things to come. We stayed near Pinewood at a three-hundred-year-old inn called something like the Crocked Bull, with ceilings so low that we had to bend over to climb the stairs. There was no central heating, and I had to report to the set in the frigid predawn, so David lovingly got up with me and filled the tub with the hottest water. When we made love, I had the primal, mystical, earliest awareness of conception.

Not long ago, that child remarked, "I wish I'd been wanted." Extracting the knife from my heart, I convinced her that nothing could be further from the truth. Just because a pregnancy is unplanned doesn't mean a child is unwelcome. My children were wanted, which is the most important message of pro-choice, for to be wanted is a child's surest protection against being abandoned or abused. David and I decided to live in Memphis (naively, I thought it would be possible to have a career while bringing up my child in the place that felt like home, a feeling that eludes even native Californians). And we decided to marry, despite my lack of enthusiasm for the institution, because in my hometown, wedding bells are the socially acceptable antecedent to impending parenthood. When Michael Carreras, the film's executive producer, heard there was to be a wedding, he asked if we'd like to be married in the Anglican church and signed an affidavit stipulating that we'd been staying with him in the parish to satisfy the residency requirements. But I had to fill out a lot of paperwork for the rector at St. Peter's of Wynchecombe. He wore pince-nez over almost colorless eyes that indicated years of study in musty church archives, and had no discernible sense of humor.

"How old are you?" the vicar asked.

"Twenty-eight," I said.

"A spinster," he noted.

"I am not," I said, heartily offended.

"Miss," he said sternly, "if you're over eighteen and unmarried, you're a spinster."

The wedding took place just before we left for the States. I recited the standard wedding vows about "honoring," eliminating the "obeying" part, but in private I made a heartfelt pledge to David. "I will never lie to you," I promised. "I will never cheat on you. I will always be honest with you. Just don't ask me any questions if you don't want to hear the answers. And don't leave me alone." I didn't have any illusions about happily ever after, and left to my own devices, I didn't trust myself to be faithful. My wedding gown was a boldly printed red and black dress that was the best thing I had in my suitcase. I didn't have a mother or a father there, but I had a producer and director:

Michael Carreras walked me down the aisle, and Anthony Page was best man. But I was so violently nauseated, it was all I could do to keep from tossing my cookies at the altar (although my queasiness about marriage might have had something to do with my equilibrium), and I literally ran from the magnificent poached salmon at the wedding lunch, held in an old vicarage owned by Anthony's sister. For months, the only food that stayed down was avocados and digestive biscuits. And we lied to my grandmother about the date of the wedding.

There was a glorious Victorian house for sale in a historic district of downtown Memphis, but Bob Sanderson, the real estate agent who was a friend of my mother, kept intoning in a solemn voice, "Dead in bed, you'll be dead in bed." So we chose (and I paid for) a modest 1928 bungalow on Court Street, half a block from the apartment where my mother had lived as a baby. One of the two bedrooms had a deck shaded by a beautiful old dogwood, but what sold me was the huge wooden swing, big as a bed, on the front porch. My mother never forgave Bob for letting me pay the asking price. He said $75,000, and I said okay. I figured if I paid the full freight, they'd have to sell it to me. (The owners of another house I wanted had reneged on the deal when a better offer came along. As Kipling said, "There is no promise of God or man that goes north of ten thousand bucks.") And I went to the dealership where my grandfather bought a new white Cadillac El Dorado every year (my family had made a religion of white automobiles) and got myself a silver Caddy.

David and I attended childbirth classes given by

two certified nurse-midwives: Peg Burke, a former nun who had served in Vietnam during the war, and Linda Wheeler, who had worked for Vista. Their attitude was: even though there is no such thing as a "normal" birth, every woman should have the freedom and dignity of being prepared. They gave me an extensive reading list that included *Childbirth Without Fear* by Grantly Dick-Read. Nearing the age of thirty, I had heard next to nothing about menopause until I read these books, some of which reduced the process to a one-liner: you dry up and you take hormones. (I decided I'd skip that stage.)

I gained forty-five pounds during my first pregnancy (even though I kept missing my mouth whenever I ate because my swollen belly kept me at some distance from the table), and just to keep me company, my husband, David, gained fifty. But our mutual leviathan state was not a deterrent to a satisfying sex life, proving once and for all that size has nothing to do with eroticism. Relatively late in my third trimester, I was given permission to fly to London for the premiere of *The Lady Vanishes*, my doctor figuring that I'd literally be in good hands, since it was a benefit for the Royal College of Obstetrics and Gynaecology. But none of my maternity clothes were worthy of a premiere, let alone a royal one. A kindly saleswoman gave me the name of a shop in Palm Beach that catered to very wealthy, very large women. I was sent a fire-engine red dress festooned with red feathers and beads. I looked like a transvestite Santa Claus. I turned my instructions about meeting the queen into a little mnemonic verse (wear white gloves, don't chew gum, call her Ma'am, which sounds like Mum), and I should have charged admission to the comic routine of a gigantic me trying to curtsy while towering over the petite and porcelain-skinned monarch.

Guided by the midwives, David and I had made a list of things to take to the hospital: nuts, raisins, cheese, lollipops, a thermos, a plastic rolling pin, and a sock with a tennis ball for back labor, lotion for back rubs, Chapstick, breath freshener, tape recorder, guitar, change for the vending machines, and a prewashed flannel baby bonnet. As I was packing the bag, we had a fight. I have no idea why. I couldn't sleep, so I got up and cleaned the whole house. As I was dusting the bookcase, my water broke. There were no contractions, so we were told to go to the hospital. Room 518 had been reconfigured into a birthing center. Peg, Linda, and David took turns breathing with me, rubbing my shoulders, feeding me ice cubes, and keeping me as comfortable as possible. David tried to distract me by sticking an empty diaper box on his head and playing the guitar. But twenty-seven hours later I was exhausted but not fully dilated. I was given the synthetic hormone Pitocin to stimulate contractions. It felt like being electrocuted. I couldn't handle any more pain and pleaded for drugs. My epidural lasted for forty-three minutes and then it started to wear off.

"I'm ready for more, please," I announced.

"You can have more," Peg said. "It's your decision, but if you do, you might not be able to push the baby out when the time comes, and if that happens we'll need forceps."

"When is this motherfucker going to be born," I growled.

She looked at the clock, which said 6:11 P.M. "Seven o'clock," she said.

My darling Clementine arrived at 6:59 P.M., weighing eight pounds, two ounces. After the hardest work of my life, I was starving, and David brought me an enormous stack of blueberry pancakes with double bacon on the side.

When she was christened six weeks later at Calvary Episcopal, I wore Birkenstocks. My mother and grandmother complained, but I told them Jesus wore sandals and would have understood.

I'd never seen anyone nursing a baby until I was pregnant myself, at my first meeting with the La Leche League, an international network of women dedicated to promoting and sharing information about breast-feeding. I called the instructor for advice all the time, especially when I started to travel. Some doctor in a strange city would tell me I couldn't nurse if I was taking a certain antibiotic for strep throat, but the La Leche leader would check the most updated list of medicines and assure me that Clementine would suffer no ill effects. It was a wonderful way to start parenting, a bonding experience that my own mother had been denied because of a breast infection, although she was horrified that I nursed in public places.

"I just hope you don't embarrass the family," she said. "How long do you intend to do this?"

"I think Clementine should be weaned by the time she's in first grade," I said.

"Sarcasm does not become you," she harrumphed.

"And of course you know you'll lose your bustline. You'll probably need one of those breast deductions."

The first appearance I made after Clementine's birth, when she was six months, was an album-signing for *Vanilla*, and just as I was chatting up the disc jockey of a local radio station, I started to feel the pins and needles that signaled my milk letting down. I was still wearing pregnancy clothes, and the sticky fluid seeped through the synthetic red knit material of my pantsuit jacket, making a rapidly expanding wet circle. I grabbed an album and held it in front of me until I could stop the leakage by pressing my wrists against my nipples.

I was still about twenty pounds overweight when I tried out for an Albert Finney film called *Wolfen*, having been told that the director wanted "a Lauren Bacall type." I wore high heels thinking I'd look thinner. (I had to look it up to know that the part went to . . . Diane Venora.) Instead, I got to do *The Return*, not quite the worst movie ever made but close. The plot, such as it was, concerned aliens who come to Earth and inhabit cows. Raymond Burr played my father, Martin Landau was a scientist, and Jan-Michael Vincent was my love interest—a rather sad group of actors, all of us trying to resurrect our diminished careers. Burr read his lines off a TelePrompTer. To simulate the spaceships coming to Earth, there was a helicopter rigged with lights that created a dust bowl as it hovered above us, so noisy you couldn't even hear yourself scream. I did the scene once, then walked over to the prop man and asked to borrow his walkie-talkie.

"We're going to try this one more time, Cybill," the director said through static.

"I don't think so," I said. It was just too scary. (A short while later, the actor Vic Morrow and two young children would be killed in a helicopter accident on a movie set, and the director, John Landis, would face criminal charges. He was ultimately acquitted.)

That same night I had to be tied up in Bronson Cave near Griffith Park, surrounded by gas torches. The prop man kept trying to light them, and the gas kept blowing the match out. I could hear the sound of the gas getting louder in the one next to me— whoooooosh, then a sudden explosion, like the gas grill years before, and I couldn't get loose. Ever since then, I have had an extreme aversion to being tied up.

The Return was eminently forgettable in every way, though I'll always remember it just because I had the largest breasts and wore the tightest jeans of my career. (The fashion of the time dictated that jeans were supposed to be so snug that you had to lie flat in bed and lift your hips up to close the zipper.) I was still expressing breast milk while I was working outside the house so that it wouldn't dry up, so I could continue nursing Clementine. First I bought a breast pump at the drugstore, a fiendish device worthy of the Spanish Inquisition, with a lever that clamped down and sucked my nipple into an elongated clear plastic tube, a perfect realization of the expression "a tit in the wringer." The La Leche League had taught me that the best breast pump is the human hand anyway, so I gave up the mechanics and stood over the sink, squeezing milk out like Elsie the Cow. When I'd ask the teamsters for yet another roll of paper towels to mop up the floor of my trailer, they'd groan, "Must be milking time again." I'd long since given up the Los Angeles apartment, so I stayed at a motel in Santa Monica and took the baby for walks in Ocean Park with all the local loonies, like the guy who wore a cowboy hat and a black ski mask.

It turned out that one of the most valuable experiences of my life was not being able to get a job in television or movies. The shrunken celebrity that I hauled around was getting old in an industry where you are only as good as whatever you did twenty minutes ago, and failure begets failure just as surely as success begets success. So I went back to the theater. I did *Vanities* in St. Louis, staying in a high-rise Holiday Inn where the windows were sealed shut and it rained incessantly, so it seemed to be dark all the time. David was petulant and distracted. One night we went to Toronto, where I'd been asked to sing on a talk show. It was a far piece down the road for a one-night stand, but I wasn't exactly in high demand. Returning through Customs, a Royal Canadian Mountie found a tiny reliquary pebble of hashish in David's guitar case and made a big deal about it. I was strip-searched, and not gently, by a Mountie-ette, but my interrogation was conducted by a man.

"How much do you make a year?" he asked.

"None of your fucking business," I said.

"We've just arrested your husband," he said menacingly, "and we're trying to decide whether to charge him or not."

It was probably the wrong time to stand on a principle of constitutional rights as an American citizen, so I told him my income. He seemed disappointed, which, under the circumstances, worked in my favor. Perhaps he felt I could ill afford to miss a performance. "Consider this your warning," he said, and let us go.

When I did *The Seven-Year Itch* at Granny's Dinner Theater in Dallas, I was so nervous that I read the entire New Testament in the suite reserved for the "talent," where the previous tenant, Robert Morse, had left a pair of Jockey shorts under the bed. Opening night I imagined Jesus floating in his robes in the fifth row of the theater. But I didn't know why my costar, Joey Bishop, seemed so miserable. During a performance at the end of our first week, he said his lines, then cursed under his breath, just loud enough for me to hear, "Fuck you, you piece-of-shit bitch." I was so shocked that I forgot my next line, and during the long silence I wondered what monumental atrocity I had committed. Later that night I asked another actress about the incident.

"I've had that happen," she said knowingly. "It's a matter of one-upmanship, showing you who's boss. If it happens again, stop, turn to him, and say loud enough for the audience to hear, 'Excuse me, what did you say?' That will shut him up."

Joey pulled his "asshole-piece-of-shit" act on me the next night, so I followed my colleague's advice and asked him, pointedly and out loud, to repeat what he'd said. He froze, got momentarily lost, glared at me, and continued with his scripted lines. That night, he went to the theater manager and said he was having trouble working with me—I'd become too difficult. Luckily, it was a limited run.

David showed promise as a jazz guitarist and had played with my band when I did cabaret at Reno Sweeney's. But the dynamics changed when I was booked for a week at a New York club called Marty's, sandwiched between appearances by Mel Tormé and

Tony Bennett, which finally made me think that my singing was giving someone besides me some pleasure. I hired a new musical director who selected his own musicians, and he wouldn't have taken the job if told he had to work with my amateur husband. I had a sense of dread when I told David he was out, and his disappointment surely added to the tension and resentment in our marriage. I've often wondered if the power imbalance in my marriage was a reaction to, even a reversal of, my relationship with Peter. Perhaps it was my turn to be in charge.

In our newly purchased mini–motor home, David and I drove from Memphis to New York, swatting mosquitoes the size of mice and plying Clementine with Cutter as we camped out in the national parks of the Shenandoah and Blue Ridge Mountains (they seemed to be covered with snow, but in fact they were thick with dogwood blossoms). The day before my opening, I was diagnosed with bronchitis. "Don't say a word you're not paid for," instructed the ear/nose/throat specialist who wrote "SILENCE" on his prescription pad, and I had to shut down for two nights. I was certainly craving some spousal support, but David went out both nights—he said he wanted to see the music scene in New York with my musical director, who was temporarily sidelined because of me. One night after I'd recovered enough to perform, one of the musicians asked, "Can I borrow your bathroom?" It wasn't until Richard Pryor nearly burned himself alive that I realized the musician had been freebasing cocaine, which explained why his tempo was way too fast. I'd had half a beer (the only time in my life when I performed under the influence of *any* substance), which made me a little mellow. Rhythmically, we were on two different planets.

Most photographs of family occasions from Clementine's childhood include a dignified woman with burnished copper skin, silver hair pulled back in a French knot, and a thousand-kilowatt smile. This is Myrtle Gray Boone, who worked as a housekeeper for both my mother and grandmother. When Clemmie was born, I didn't want a trained baby nurse. I wanted Myrtle, mother of thirteen children, grandmother to thirty-two, an indomitable presence in my family for as long as I could remember. (Moma said she'd be the best nanny in the world but railed against the generous salary I offered and warned that I'd "spoil" Myrtle if I paid her a penny more than a hundred dollars a week.) Myrtle could quote Robert Louis Stevenson and hum Bach. Had she lived at another time, she could have been an ambassador instead of a domestic. When I asked her to go on the road with me, she said no at first, then called me back the next day and said she'd changed her mind. "Everybody else always gets to travel," she said. "Now it's my turn." But while we were in New York, we got the news that Myrtle's mother in Memphis had died. Tears streaming down our faces, David and I put Myrtle in a cab bound for the airport and promised to follow the next day in the motor home. We were still crying when we returned to our room, though I didn't know that he was crying about something else.

I'm an expert liar, and sometimes I recognize when people are lying to me. I'd felt a funny twinge of doubt those two nights David was out when I was sick, and I checked out his story, obliquely, with my musical director, who didn't know enough to cover for him. I didn't have the heart or the stomach to confront him for several days. But now I did.

His words came out in soggy clumps. "Remember that actress who did *Vanities* with you in St. Louis?" he said. "She's in New York. And I've been with her."

I've heard such moments described as a body blow. But hearing David's confession was more like watching an egg fall and shatter in slow motion. I went to Clementine's rented crib, lowered the slotted side panel and picked her up, needing to feel the warmth of her body. Only when I saw that her pajamas were wet did I realize I was still crying.

"Are we getting divorced?" I asked.

"I don't know," said David, sitting on the bed with his head in his hands.

"How can I ever trust you again?" I asked.

"I don't even know why I told you," he said.

"I know why," I said. "You want me to feel as bad as you do. People don't like it when they do something rotten—it makes them feel terrible. And you think this is as much my fault as yours."

We slept fitfully that night, lashed to opposite sides of the bed. In the morning, we drove back to Memphis for the funeral, spending one night in the camper to save money. I lay awake, drinking beer and listening to Billie Holiday sing "Good morning, heartache, You old gloomy sight, Good morning heartache, Thought we'd said good-bye last night. . . ." I'd never really appreciated the raw pain in her voice. Now she was singing for me.

I'm told that marriages survive infidelity, but neither David nor I had the tools. We tried to reconcile

for almost a year, but the damage had been done, and
not just because of his affair. In the early stages of our
relationship, I must have seemed like a big blonde tro-
phy, followed shortly by the realization that life with
me could be a drag—the long and odd hours on location, the lack of privacy, the subtly dismissive treatment of the celebrity spouse by that partner's
entourage. Everyone deferred to my needs, wants,
schedules. I began to lose respect for David as I
watched him squander this chance to develop his musical talent. He had the time and opportunity, but not
the discipline. As Clementine got older, David told
her that he hadn't wanted the divorce, and I think that
was true, that he wanted to be forgiven, which explained his initially bitter and vindictive behavior
about division of property: he demanded half of all my
earnings. (Two words sum up divorce: how much?)
But my lawyer made a suggestion. "Get a legal pad,"
he said. "Tell David you're not promising anything,
but make a list of everything he wants." He backed
down, managing to extract some measure of revenge
years later by selling a story about me to the tabloid
press. I paid for him to move out to California and go
to bartending school so he could be near Clementine,
and to his credit, he has never tried to use our daughter as a pawn or bargaining chip.

IN 1980 MY AGENT DIDN'T EXACTLY HAVE ME
on speed dial, inundated with offers of work, so I leapt
when he told me about a chance to read for Sidney
Lumet, who was directing a film called *Just Tell Me
What You Want*. I wasn't making much money to sup-

port my child, so it was a big deal to pay for my own plane ticket to California, leaving Clementine with her father. It was my first trip to Los Angeles since our marriage had dissolved, and we were still navigating a contentious divorce. When I got to the Beverly Hills Hotel, I was so lonely that I sent flowers to my room, spending even more money I didn't have. I called someone I thought was still my friend: The Producer. I didn't know how to have a friendship with a man without being sexual, and we ended up in my hotel bed. The next day, he disappeared, never phoning or returning my call. (Actually, he returned the call years later, when he heard I was writing a book and asked me to sing in a show he was producing for the Atlanta Olympics. "I know I treated you badly that time," he said, "and I wanted you to know why. I had just gotten involved with the woman who's now my wife.")

When I showed up at the Universal lot and greeted Lumet, I got the feeling he wasn't expecting me. "What are you doing these days?" he asked solicitously. When I mentioned reading for his film, he looked somewhat stricken. "Didn't your agent tell you?" he said. "The role's been cast." It was the last time that agent had the opportunity to screw up on my account, although even the satisfaction of firing him didn't make up for the expense of plane, hotel, and flowers. (The part went to . . . Ali MacGraw.)

There are skewed friendships in Hollywood. People assume every phone call has a hidden agenda of exacting a favor or trawling for work, and usually they're right. I felt uncomfortable contacting anyone from my old Hollywood crowd, and a call to my former agent Sue Mengers proved that my instinct was correct.

"Honey," she said, "I can't get work for the ladies I already represent. Besides, you've been gone so long, you might as well be dead."

The near dead, it turned out, are offered the straw hat circuit. I had auditioned for the Broadway production of *Lunch Hour*, reading for the playwright, Jean Kerr. (The part went to . . . Gilda Radner.) A few months later, I was having lunch with a producer at Sardi's. A call came through for him, and a telephone was brought to the table (in the dark ages before cell phones). "I'm sitting here with Cybill Shepherd," he said. Ten minutes later I was offered a part in the national tour of *Lunch Hour*.

We toured from Colorado to Michigan to Maine—everywhere but New York and Los Angeles, just as Orson had advised me to do. At the Cape Cod Playhouse, I was honored to put on my makeup in the dressing room used by Gertrude Lawrence, even if there was water oozing from the walls. But I absorbed much of what I know about comedy from the audience, which is the ultimate teacher. I learned not to work too hard at being funny, not to imitate myself from the night before, to try to make each performance as if it were the first time I'd ever done it. Somewhere between Detroit and Denver, I got funny. And I mastered a most important theatrical adage: always check your props. There's a famous story about Stella Adler being onstage one night and reaching for a gun that the prop department had forgotten to put out. She pointed her forefinger and said, "Bang," convincing everyone in the audience that she had a gun. *Lunch Hour* called for me to eat deviled eggs, made by the prop people in each theater. In Denver the eggs were perfect. In Detroit they were so dry, I almost choked. In Falmouth, Massachusetts, I threw myself on the mercy of the stagehands.

"Can y'all help me out?" I begged. "It's really important to get enough moisture in the egg yolk or I can't say my lines."

"Sure thing, Miss Shepherd," they said, and at the next performance, I picked up the egg to see the yellow part wobbling—a liquid yolk. I remembered the old actors' rule: use it. If you're miserable because you have to pee or your costar has skunk breath or the egg tastes terrible, use it, and I developed a repertoire of broad faces, burps, drools, and dribbles. Acting is about specificity. One moment is: *I'm happy to have the egg in my mouth*; the next moment is: *I don't know about this*; and the next is: *I'm going to hurl*. Most of the time, the audience loved it, although there was an entire mountain range in the Poconos where not a single person in a sold-out theater laughed. I learned that you can never get too full of yourself as an actor—every night there are different ways to fail and to triumph.

I became friends with one of my costars, getting together for a bite to eat or a glass of wine, and during our rehearsals in New York I was thrilled to be invited for tea one day to the home of his mother. But the thrill was brief. "You know," she said dismissively as she poured from a silver teapot, "you're really not one of us."

When the tour was over, The Costar and I drove to the Chesapeake Bay to visit his friends in their sprawling ranch house. Though we had become lovers, we quickly progressed to the imperfect phase of the relationship, what one friend calls the "congealed fat in the frying pan" stage. That night the four of us had Maryland crab cakes for dinner, and The Costar had quite a lot of vodka. We went into the guest room where we would be sleeping and he came on to me. I was revolted by his alcoholic reek and, pulling away from him, said, "Fuck you, I don't have to fuck you." I stormed into the kitchen, thinking I would find the car keys and leave, when he appeared behind me. "Don't even think about going anywhere," he said, "because I have the keys right here in my pocket." Then he ripped off the delicate gold necklace that he'd given me, saying, "That doesn't mean anything anymore." Then he shoved me to the ground. I got up, ran down the hall, and banged on his friends' bedroom door. "I'll take care of it," said the husband, grabbing a robe and trudging down the hall with a weary sense of familiarity. "It's better if The Costar just drinks beer."

I sat with the wife until The Costar got quiet and fell asleep. We got up the next morning and drove in strained silence to Knoxville to see my friend Jane Howard as planned. Finally I said, "You knocked me down."

"You fell down," he snarled. As soon as we got to Tennessee, I told him the relationship was over. No man I'd had sex with had ever made me fear for my physical safety before, and I didn't want it to happen again. It took me many years to feel safe enough to spend the night with a man again.

I hadn't seen Peter Bogdanovich since he threw the crystal ashtray at me, but after my marriage ended, he began calling me every few months, taking blame for the end of our relationship, telling me he finally understood that I had been serious about wanting a child. When Peter called over the Christmas holiday of 1980, I had just spent several weeks writing, longhand on legal pads, a screenplay for a book called *September, September* by Shelby Foote, a haunting story about three white racists from Mississippi who kidnap the only grandson of one of America's first black millionaires. I told Peter that I'd like to option it but couldn't afford it. "Let me lend you the money," he said, and sent me a generous check that allowed me to option the novel. Foote, whom I met at a Memphis wine-and-cheese party, had spent twenty years writing *The Civil War: A Narrative* and looked like a Rebel general himself. When I told him I'd love to play the white-trash woman in the trio of kidnappers, he said in his honeyed Mississippi drawl, "Mah dear, you're fahhhhhhh too young for the part."

I had stayed in touch with Larry McMurtry ever since *The Last Picture Show*, and our bond was really secured when he visited the set of *Daisy Miller* (his son played my brother) and sat with me in the lobby of the Hotel Trois Coronnes, rubbing my feet and reading aloud the gruesome "Crazy Jane" love poems by Yeats. He was, physically, one of the least attractive men imaginable, but as a friend he was everything I wanted: a renaissance cowboy, an earthy intellectual, a Pulitzer Prize winner who could take pleasure in a dive that served two-dollar tacos. He became my touchstone in life, and for a brief time our collaboration became sexual.

Our friendship never faltered because we became sexual or because we stopped. Larry always managed to come see me, in Los Angeles or Memphis or just about anywhere else I was working. He was always flying off to a remote corner of the maritime Alps or driving through the Ozarks in a U-Haul truck, buying up private libraries for his bookstores in Washington, D.C., and in Texas. I didn't even have to give Myrtle a menu—I'd just say, "Larry will be here about four o'clock," and she'd say, "I'll get the catfish." He felt he had to spend all his money to keep his creative edge, and he never entered my house without gifts, not just for me but for Clementine and Myrtle. (Myrtle is in the dedication of his novel *The Evening Star*, the follow-up to *Terms of Endearment*.) In between visits he kept up a steady correspondence—long, literate, ardent letters usually typed (with mistakes *xxxxxxxx*'ed out) on the same kind of cheap yellow paper he used for his books and scripts:

> *Interestingly enough, since I'm a somewhat analytical man and have analyzed plenty of relationships, I feel no impulse to analyze us. I trust my affinities and I like the quality of our companionship very much, without needing to examine the components. . . .*
>
> *You have brought joy and fragrance to my life. Your human fragrance is as complex as your new perfume: partly dry, light, of the brain; partly wet, deep, of the heart and loins. . . .*
>
> *Of course, when you love someone very much, you have a natural fear that they will stop loving you. It's part of what makes the whole business of need-desire-attachment-freedom-dependence so complicated. Love is so easily bruised and ruined, or, even more often,*

simply worn out and lost in the repetitiousness of life. I
often have these fears where you are concerned, and
yet mostly I have a deep trust in us. . . .

You're a very wonderful woman; you'll compel
the love of many men. As long as you can learn to
roughly distinguish those who mean you well from
those who mean you ill, that's as it should be—there
would be something wrong in nature if men didn't
love and want you. Only learn not to get yourself hurt.
I know you have learned now that actions speak
louder than words. What men do is important, not
what they say.

Larry called me "the lost zygote" of my family and
was always encouraging me to expand my horizons.
In 1981 it was his idea that I apply for entrance to the
women directors' program of the American Film In-
stitute, and as part of my application for admission, I
submitted my script for *September, September*. Partly
to assuage my disappointment when AFI rejected
me, Larry agreed to work with me on the script, and
on the strength of his name, we were given a development deal at Carson Productions, which operated
under the auspices of Columbia Pictures. After working on it for almost a year, we were granted a meeting
with Columbia chief Craig Baumgarten. The moment we entered his office, he said, "This is a hateful
story that no one would want to see, and we wouldn't
dream of making it." We did get the go-ahead from
Turner Broadcasting, although not with the director
Stanley Kubrick, as Shelby Foote had hoped. (He declined with a nice handwritten note that ended,

"Please say hello to the General.") When I finally went with Larry to see Shelby Foote in 1991, ten years after our first meeting, he opened the door to his house, looked at me, and said, "You're old enough now."

CHAPTER EIGHT

"The Cybill Sandwich"

IN 1980 I ARRIVED IN NEW YORK, FINALLY
ready to take acting classes with Stella Adler and the
Actors Studio. I got a call from a Los Angeles casting
director named Robin Lippen, offering me a guest appearance on the TV show *Fantasy Island*. To say that I
was underwhelmed doesn't begin to describe my
qualms about this nadir of my career. I wasn't even the
lead guest star, and I didn't get to arrive on the island
as Tattoo shouted "The plane! The plane!" to Mr.
Roarke.

"Oh, Cybill, you should not be represented at a big
agency," Robin said. "They'll want to cast Goldie
Hawn or Sally Field—clients who are going to make
more money. If you do this role, you'll get five thousand dollars and a plane ticket, and while you're out
here, I will set up meetings for you with the top independent agents, who will turn your career around."

It was a great piece of advice, and with little to lose

I accepted her offer. I checked into the Sheraton Universal, which I referred to as the Universal Sheraton because it sounded more important, and eventually met with an elfin and enthusiastic agent named David Shapira. The first job he got me was for a TV pilot called *Masquerade* produced by Aaron Spelling and distinguished by more takeoffs and landings of jets than any other pilot in the history of television.

My second job was starring in the series *The Yellow Rose*. I was to play the widowed owner of a large Texas ranch, and Sam Elliott was the illegitimate son of my much older dead husband. I was called back to read four times, the last time to see if Sam and I had the right chemistry. When I walked into the production office, sitting on the couch, and waiting to read for the same part was Priscilla Presley. Hard to imagine a worse sign: There was, first of all, my history with Elvis, and I had no idea if she knew about it. It was like a marquee had been set up, flashing: "One of you will not get the part." Both of us were uncomfortable, but we smiled and exchanged pleasantries.

Shapira called with good news/bad news. "You got the part," he said, "but you've been fucked." Sometime before, I'd gone up for another NBC pilot about race car drivers. I didn't get the part, but my agent at the time had agreed to a fee of $1,000 an episode. Even though other actors on *Yellow Rose* were demanding and getting much more, the network knew what it could get me for.

The bargain-basement salary was maddening, but it was enough to put a down payment on a town house in Studio Village, with what I referred to as a view overlooking the Los Angeles River, which was nothing more than a giant concrete chute created by the U.S. Army Corps of Engineers. Most of the time there was just a trickle so insignificant that kids would skateboard through, but a heavy rain could create a giant flow of rushing water. Beyond was a lovely field of wildflowers, my own Tuscan landscape, dotted by the soundstages of what was called the Mary Tyler Moore studio. I spent many afternoons looking longingly across the L.A. River wondering if I'd ever get a chance to work there. The loveliness of the setting paled when I learned that the condominium complex had been the site of two grisly murders by bludgeoning, including the mistress of Alfred Bloomingdale, whose friendship with Ronald and Nancy Reagan had been the stuff of tabloid headlines, sometimes alongside headlines about me.

Sam Elliott and I were asked to come to New York to take part in the network's announcement of new fall programming. But when we went to meet the producers for lunch at the "21" Club, I was refused admittance because I was wearing running shoes, a New Balance model that cost $150. I went down the street and paid $11 for black rubber flats, then made a grand show of sitting in the restaurant's reception area to change, daintily doing a striptease with my socks. No sneakers allowed? *Watch me.*

Exteriors for the series were shot in Lancaster, California, north of Los Angeles—wide open country meant to approximate Texas, with a panorama ranging from snow-capped mountains to the Mojave Desert. Sam seemed to grow ever more despondent as the show sank into soap opera territory, a conspicuous imitation of the runaway hit *Dallas*, involving the kind of weekly intrigue, deception, and lust that couldn't possibly take up the time of real ranchers or else we'd all be vegetarians. (Larry McMurtry wrote to me, "There were not a few steals from *Hud*, I observed. The cook and the boy seem a little Patricia Neal and Brandon de Wilde–ish.") Sam had signed on to do a TV series that was a western, while I had signed on to do a TV series that was a *job*. I had few complaints: it was the first long-term work I'd ever had, and I was getting paid to ride a horse. I talked to the show wranglers and got involved in choosing my own championship roper named Red that I could guide with my knees.

Two weekends a month, the wranglers went out to practice their roping technique at Castaic Lake Arena and invited me to come along. Quarter horses are the fastest horseflesh on the planet for one quarter of a mile—they can outrun any thoroughbred at Santa Anita for that distance—and I could feel their power like g-force in my chest. The horse is backed up into a box with no door, a bell rings, and the horse and steer are released at the same time into the rodeo ring. The horse's job is to line up the rider so he or she can swing and throw the rope, jerk the slack, and tighten the noose around the steer's horns or neck. When you tie off the rope on the saddle horn, the horse stops, and the steer gets yanked to the ground. The most important rule, I was told, is: keep your thumb up when you're tying off. Anyone who tried to teach me to rope had fingers missing, having gotten them tangled in the rope when the horse stopped but the steer kept moving.

A dedicated actor wants to do as much of the stunt, safely, as possible to "sell" it to the audience, making it believable and giving the director the ability to edit in the expert. A movie set is really a construction site, an inherently dangerous place, with jagged pieces of wood and nails everywhere and huge sources of illumination called "nine-lights" tottering on skinny retractable rods. One day I was inside a corral, having done my side of the scene on horseback, but the director asked me to mount my horse to do the other side of the scene for the other actors (a professional courtesy called "off camera"). Horses can "shy" or panic because of the ways their eyes are placed, with a blind spot in the middle, so objects can appear to jump. I love them, but they have a brain the size of an orange in a two-thousand-pound body.

I'll never know what frightened Red, but he backed up and caught an electrical cord from a nine-light between his right rear shoe and hoof. It fell forward, bouncing and sparking, and he took off, dragging it around the ring. There was no dismounting, and no one could approach—the camera crew went running for their lives when faced with a runaway horse.

I used a technique learned in my horse-crazed childhood called "pulley rein," gradually slowing the animal down to increasingly smaller circles, until R.L. Tolbert, the stunt coordinator, could get close enough to gently take the reins and let me dismount. That was the last time I was ever "off camera" on the back of a horse. From then on, it was a ladder for me.

R.L. was a former rodeo champ with thick silver hair that formed a widow's peak. He was a wonderful reference source about cowboys. He made gentle fun of the hat I wore for the show, which did not meet his standards. A proper cowboy's hat has profound, immutable requirements, and much of the unwritten code is about brims. When you put the hat on a table, you lay it crown down so the brim isn't misaligned. Your hat must never blow off (this constitutes a huge loss of face among peers). When you remove it, there had better be a deep red impression in your forehead, and hat hair is a badge of pride. I was apparently walking around with a scandalously loose, battered-brim hat, and he helped me pick out a proper one.

One weekend he invited me to the rodeo at Santa Barbara. On a shining Saturday afternoon, we drove up the Pacific coast in his big white pickup truck (it was the first time I ever saw a date spit tobacco into a cup). When I see water, I want to swim, and I don't go anywhere without a bathing suit in my bag. R.L. didn't have one. "But I know a beach," he said, "where we don't need them." I learned where the term *redneck* comes from: R.L. had a burnished tan on his neck and hands, but the rest of his body was fish-belly white. At the rodeo we bought big cups of 7-UP, drank them halfway down, and then filled them back up with Jack Daniel's. When I started getting sleepy, he instructed, "You have to keep drinking so your blood alcohol doesn't go down." By the time we arrived at a crummy little beach motel, I was ready to test out R.L.'s private stunt work.

Ever restless, I soon moved on to another stuntman. It was his idea that I learn Formula Ford race car driving—I think he liked the idea of Miss Teenage Memphis chewing up the track with the big boys. I took a three-day course at Riverside to qualify for the Toyota Grand Prix, then remembered that I was the mother of a small child, so I never actually competed. But the training served one good purpose: I never again needed to drive fast for the thrill of it.

The Stuntman was an energetic, imaginative lover. And in my sexual odyssey, this was the experience that confirmed something enlightened women know but men never quite believe: size doesn't matter. There are all kinds of places inside a woman that a man can move a small penis, and he knew how to find them. One night, in a playful mood, we were talking about sexual fantasies, and I admitted that I'd imagined being with two men.

"I'd like to make that one come true for you," he said with a twinkle.

"Don't be crazy," I countered. "Do you have any idea how much the *National Enquirer* would pay for that story?"

But he had a proposal: his close friend, another stuntman of guaranteed discretion. "If you ever meet again," he promised, "there will see no indication that it ever happened." I was intrigued, excited, and quite scared. An hour before the friend was to arrive, I said I couldn't go through with it. The Stuntman said, "You don't want to back out now. Have a little snort of coke."

There's a real argument to be made that if you need controlled substances to make something acceptable, maybe you shouldn't be doing it. In the 1970s there was a sense of self-righteousness about drug taking, a supposition that it would be enlightening, that artists needed to expand their minds. In the "me decade" of the 1980s, everyone I knew was still getting high with some regularity. At parties there were sugar bowls full of cocaine (not yet considered addictive), and nonparticipants were regarded as weird. I was hardly a doper—on the contrary, I'd always been the safety monitor in my crowd, the one who insisted on buckling up seat belts and warned about the perils of cigarettes.

"The Cybill sandwich" turned out to be a positive sexual experience. Having all the pleasure points being attended to simultaneously rather than sequentially made me feel adored, emancipated, and more relaxed about sex. Years later, an episode of *Moonlighting* called for a chain-saw fight, and the fellow hired to train me turned out to be the *ménage* partner. True to his word, he was circumspect and discreet. "Cybill," he said warmly, extending his hand, "I haven't seen you in a few years." He didn't even linger over the word *seen*.

The Stuntman started acting overly involved in my career, presenting me with too many ideas for merchandising tie-ins with *The Yellow Rose*, like my name on a map of Texas that he wanted to sell. He had the same obsession with ladylike hands as my grandfather, even to the point of offering to polish my nails. (This turned out to be surprisingly erotic. He brought three color choices, and it took hours.) One night while he was out, I was waiting at his house, talking on the phone to my gynecologist. We were admitting that we were attracted to each other when he was married and I was with Peter, and I told him I'd been close to having an orgasm when he put in my IUD. (I know, I know.) The next day, The Stuntman accused me of being depraved. "That's revolting," he said angrily, "to get off with your gynecologist." There was no way he could have known that secret, and I discovered that he was recording every phone call made to or from his house. I think his paranoia had more to do with his drug connections than with spying on me, but it was an alarm that signaled the beginning of the end of that relationship.

Perfect opening (you should pardon the expression) for The Gynecologist. He was an attractive, divorced man, and any sense of impropriety did not override my life motto: Why not? He lived in a contemporary palace high in the canyons with a collection of modern art and a teenage son who hated me on sight, baring his teeth like a cat when he spoke to me. One night the doctor and I were eating steaks he had grilled on the barbecue. Suddenly his face went pale, his shoulders went up, and he wasn't making any noise. Running into the boy's room, I yelled, "Come quickly, I think your father's choking!"

He looked up without even feigned interest and said, "Give me a fucking break."

"Listen, you little worm," I screamed, "you may hate me, but unless you want to inherit the Hockneys tonight, get your ass in here and help me do Heimlich!" The doctor survived, but the affair didn't.

My hairdresser on *The Yellow Rose* was a lively woman who raised turkeys on her farm—"all natural," she told me, "none of those chemicals and hormones and poisons and shit"—and she offered me one for Thanksgiving. On our last day of shooting before the holiday, she told me, "I brought you a beautiful bird. It's out in my truck." Peeking over the back door, I saw what appeared to be a small hatbox. *That couldn't be it*, I thought. Then I heard the squawk. It was alive but packed so it couldn't move, like something out of *Box-*

ing Helena. Undaunted, I called around to various restaurants, asking euphemistically, "Where can I have this taken care of?" and finally, someone suggested Chinatown.

My friend Jane Howard was visiting for the holiday, and we walked around the crowded streets looking for a shop with dead poultry hanging in the windows. We hadn't heard another peep out of that turkey—I think it had conceded its fate. An accommodating butcher took the box from my hands with little fanfare and, five minutes later, handed me a parcel wrapped in brown paper, no longer moving. The turkey was cooked by my housekeeper, who brought it to the table, according to her family tradition, with its two claws crossed upright. And it was tough as shoe leather. Give me a Butterball shot full of chemicals any day.

It was extraordinary for me to be working on a studio lot like the ones where the movies I'd watched with Peter were shot, and the day I found out for sure that *Yellow Rose* would not be picked up for another season, I went over to the Warner Bros. Burbank studios and walked around the set sobbing. Movie camp was over, and I thought I'd never work again—not an irrational thought considering the sobering statistic that something like 90 percent of the Screen Actors Guild members are unemployed.

When you bump into people you haven't seen for a while in Hollywood, they seldom ask the mechanical "How are you?" They ask, and they really want to know, "What are you doing now?" I had no answer.

CHAPTER NINE

"TV's Sexiest Spitfire"

GLENN GORDON CARON SAYS THAT HALFWAY through the pilot of *Moonlighting* he realized he was writing the character Maddie Hayes as Cybill Shepherd. He asked if there was any way he could get a meeting with me. When my agent sent me those fifty pages, I immediately recognized the part I'd been hankering to do for a long time. For years I'd studied the screwball comedies directed by Howard Hawks, especially *Twentieth Century* (1934), *Bringing Up Baby* (1938), and *His Girl Friday* (1940). These films glorified Carole Lombard, Katharine Hepburn, and Rosalind Russell—they talked fast and acted sexy, smart, and funny.

Glenn was only thirty but no wunderkind. He'd done a couple of failed pilots, and his main credit was for *Remington Steele*. I was invited to meet him and his colleague Jay Daniel at a restaurant in the San Fernando Valley. Glenn was boyish, charming, portly, clearly excited by the presence of Maddie Hayes incarnate and not afraid to show it—he later said that his negotiating strength had been hampered when his chin hit the table and his tongue hit the floor. He remarked that he'd seen me in a movie wearing "that dress" (the bias-cut satin from *The Lady Vanishes*). The first thing I said to Glenn after hello was "I know what this is—it's a Hawksian comedy." He had no idea what I was talking about, so I suggested we screen my three favorites to see how overlapping dialogue was handled by the "masters," and he agreed. We talked about the way the *Moonlighting* script played with my image as a spoiled bitch, although Glenn claimed to have been largely unaware of my reputation as the "most clobbered actress in Hollywood." There wasn't an actor in the world who hadn't been in an ill-suited movie, he said. I'd just had more than my share.

City of Angels is run, none too efficiently, by a character named David Addison, whose creed is "Live fast, die young, leave clean underwear," and who convinces Maddie to become his partner, renaming the agency Blue Moon after the shampoo for which she was a well-known spokeswoman in her modeling days. Addison is described as an emotional adolescent, cocky and sexually aggressive, whose humor and puerile charm ameliorate his obnoxious behavior and language. Apparently there were three thousand men who saw themselves with those attributes because that's how many actors answered the casting call. Chemistry between actors is either there or it isn't. I'm not sure you can act chemistry on-screen any more than you can in real life when your well-intentioned cousin sets you up on a blind date with a troglodyte. I thought it was imperative that the chemistry between Maddie and David be genuine, since the show was driven by snappy, overlapping banter and palpable sexual tension. I had casting approval, and when the pile of résumés from David-wannabes was winnowed down to a lean half-dozen, I went to meet them.

ABC's offices were located in a tall glass tower in Century City, and the casting sessions took place in a long conference room with a wall of shuttered windows. Several candidates came and went, but nothing especially magical was happening. By midafternoon, I was weary, picking at bits of tuna and lettuce from the salads that had been brought in for lunch, when Bruce Willis entered the room.

He was, I would later learn, five years younger than I, wearing an army fatigue jacket, several earrings, and what looked to be the compensatory three-day beard of a man with a receding hairline, the rest of his hair punkishly cut and moussed. There was a careless, desultory way he walked around the perimeter of the big table, keeping his distance from me and sauntering over to Glenn and Jay. His eyes were crinkled and his lips pressed into a mocking smile, a composite that was to become the signature David Addison smirk.

Bruce had been earning a living as a bartender in New York, sharing a walk-up in Hell's Kitchen with large rats while playing mostly uncredited bit parts, like "courtroom observer" in Paul Newman's legal drama *The Verdict* or "diner customer" in a Frank Sinatra movie, *The First Deadly Sin*, and he had just been turned down for a role in *Desperately Seeking Susan* that went to Aidan Quinn. Unlike the other actors who'd auditioned, he didn't especially flatter me;

in fact, he actually avoided eye contact, directing most of his vaguely smart-ass male-bonding comments to Glenn, like "Just got off my shift at the bar." But there was definite chemistry between us, and it escaped no one—the temperature in the room jumped about twenty degrees. After he'd left, I leaned over and murmured, as much to myself as to Glenn, "He's the one."

"Are you sure?" he responded. Glenn knew it would require Herculean effort to convince the ABC brass that this quirky, attitudinous guy with negligible professional experience and rather unconventional looks was perfectly cast for a prime-time hit on their network, which was then third place in the ratings. The suits saw him playing "heavies," declared he was "not leading man material" and asked me to read with better-known actors. The part was actually offered to a clean-cut actor named Robert Hayes, who turned it down in favor of I don't know what. The only way Bruce Willis would be considered was if I agreed to do a screen test with him. With the camera rolling just as we were about to do the scene, he looked at me with perfect satisfaction and said, "I can't concentrate. You're too beautiful." The suits were convinced.

The week before we shot the pilot, Glenn, Bruce, and I watched *His Girl Friday* and *Bringing Up Baby*, as I had suggested. They were the gold standard for the overlapping dialogue we were going to use in *Moonlighting*. When we showed up on Stage 20 at 20th Century-Fox for the first time, it felt as if both of us were playing roles that were custom-fit by a meticulous tailor. The first time my face is seen is in a montage of photographs on the wall: real *Vogue* and *Glamour* magazines, Cover Girl and Clairol ads from my modeling days. Maddie Hayes would be the ultimate bitch goddess who gets her comeuppance, with a nemesis who engenders conflicting feelings of outrage and attraction. The character of David Addison was bearable, even likable, precisely because he just loved being a jerk, as, I was to discover, did Bruce Willis.

In the pilot's climactic scene, we were being chased by a diamond thief onto the roof of the historic Eastern building in downtown Los Angeles, where I was suspended from the minute hand of a clockface twenty-five feet above the fourteenth floor. I'm a gung-ho girl, and I declared that I wanted to do enough of the stunt so the audience believed it was really me. Half a dozen crew members were lined up single file on the narrow plywood platform of a steel scaffold that was swaying in the Santa Ana winds. The hairdresser was terrified of heights and had declared in the lobby, "I'm going to have to do your hair down here," but my makeup man, Norman Leavitt, gamely came up to the roof, passing powder puffs and lipstick stuck into a Kleenex box out to me from his precarious perch. The director of photography, Michael Margulies, was communicating via miked headphones to the four camera crews. Suddenly I panicked, and grabbing two handfuls of Michael's brown leather jacket from behind, I screamed, "I can't do this! I can't do this!" But he couldn't hear me. When he felt the tug, he turned around and said, "Did you say something?"

"No, I'm okay." And, having momentarily vented, I was.

For two weeks of shooting, Bruce was upbeat, light-hearted, fun. But it wasn't long before his mood darkened, particularly during visits from his girlfriend, the former wife of Geraldo Rivera, who sat in the wings with her arms crossed, looking as if she had smelled something bad. ("She disapproves of me doing television," he confided one day.) Her visits became less frequent, eventually ending altogether, but he remained cranky and aloof. Almost automatically, we had off-camera spats just before our scripted ones, but they seemed like a harmless way of working up to the emotion of the scene. It did not escape me that the growing attraction between Maddie and David mirrored what was developing between the actors who portrayed them. After one particularly heated rehearsal, I walked off the set with him and said, "Are we going to do something about this or what?"

He looked startled but not unpleasantly so, and then squinted his familiar half smile. "Why don't I come over to your place tonight?" he said.

There was a bottle of Gentleman Jim in his hand when he knocked on the door of my apartment, and it wasn't long before we were passionately sucking face. "Maybe we shouldn't do this," I said, feeling ambivalent and aware of the potential complications. "We might be working together a long time." But we were quickly too far gone in a lusty missionary embrace, leaning halfway back on a La-Z-Boy lounger that tilted almost to the point of toppling over.

Suddenly he stopped, arched his back, and looked at me with lines creasing his forehead. "Maybe you're right," he said, grabbing the wide arm of the chair for support as he pushed off and stood up. Rearranging himself as well as his remaining clothes, he announced, "I think I'll go to the bathroom." When he returned, he picked his jacket up from the floor where it had landed, mumbled something about getting a good night's sleep, and was gone. Maybe Bruce liked the chase better than the catch. Maybe he preferred the character to the real woman. We never did finish what we started in private, but anytime we had a kissing scene, he stuck a big camel tongue halfway down my throat.

For the pilot of *Moonlighting*, my hair was sleek and unteased. Before every scene, I'd bend forward and brush it out, but Glenn and Jay said that took too long, so for some of the later episodes, my hair was teased and sprayed into an effusive helmet that looked like a wig. Unsolicited, Bruce commented that my hair was "dippy," which I assumed to be a derisive colloquialism from his New Jersey boyhood. No one had taken such an interest in my hair since my mother obsessed about my darkening blonde tresses. Certainly L'Oréal thought enough of me for all those commercials in which I purred, "I'm worth it." And Bruce was on thin ice: his own bare scalp was filled in with greasy dark cosmetic pencils for the camera. After one too many sarcastic remarks, I snapped, "At least I have some hair." Turns out he did too, just not on his head. Bruce liked to moon the crew, and I got so tired of seeing his hairy ass that I finally said, "Could you give me some warning so I don't have to look at it every time?"

I averted my eyes from the lively procession of young women in and out of Bruce's motor home, until he met Demi Moore and settled into some version of monogamy. (I can attest to the fact that she taught him how to kiss.) But I was hardly in a position to judge anyone else's personal life. A cousin was getting married in Memphis, and I had no prospects of an interesting escort for the wedding. (If the tabloids had only known the headline they were missing: FORMER BEAUTY QUEEN DATELESS.) I asked a friend to set me up and her suggestion turned out to be a broad-shouldered, six-foot-four cycling champ who'd missed qualifying for the Olympics by a millisecond. He picked me up wearing Clark Kent glasses and a tailored tuxedo jacket over a tartan kilt, complete with sporran, the furry pouch that substitutes for a pants pocket. (What are men supposed to be carrying around in there anyway?) He had impeccable manners, spoke with ease about a variety of subjects from sports to feminism, and it wasn't long before I discovered that real Scotsmen don't wear anything under their kilts. But I was thirty-five and he was eighteen.

If the ages had been reversed, our romance wouldn't have caused so much as a ripple of censure. As it was, we were a perfect sexual match. We ignored public opinion and defied our families by continuing to see each other for the duration of my stay and on subsequent visits. When he picked me up at my mother's house for a bike ride wearing the kind of cyclist shorts that hug the thighs and leave little to the imagination, Mother took me aside and chided, "Cybill, he's nasty in those pants." After a few months of long-distance romance, he left his job in the family business and followed me to Los Angeles. He rented his own apartment, but I couldn't prevent Clementine from developing a five-year-old's crush on him, getting into my makeup and doing a pretty good imitation of a mini–femme fatale when she knew he was coming over. His affluent father stepped up the campaign to separate us by implying that I was a gold digger, even offering to retire if his son came back to run the company, and finally issued an ultimatum: the business or the blonde. It was up to me to decide, my young lover said, and I couldn't ask him to stay. I didn't want to get into another situation where I was supporting a man, I had no interest in marriage, I couldn't even promise fidelity. I suppose I was really waiting for some grand gesture from him, something along the lines of "I don't care what my family says, you're the only woman in the world for me." Asking me what to do was tantamount to telling me he wasn't ready to commit. I relinquished any hold.

I left home at 5 A.M. each day. *Moonlighting* scripts were close to a hundred pages, half again as long as the average one-hour television series. Almost from the moment the cameras started rolling, we were behind schedule, sometimes completing as few as sixteen episodes per season and never achieving the standard twenty-two. It became customary to make up time with a "tow shot": loading a car onto a trailer and pulling it. Since we were just sitting in the car, there was no need to rehearse or "block" our places during the scene. We literally cut up the pages of script and taped the scraps to the dashboard—no time to memorize. The only respite was when the writers gave long speeches of "exposition" to guest stars, but Bruce and I were so exhausted that while we listened we often looked as if we were sleeping with our eyes open. Some of our highly touted innovations—like "breaking the fourth wall" and speaking directly to the camera in a prologue or a postscript—were born of necessity, to fill time, since we spoke the dialogue so quickly.

At $1.5 million per episode, *Moonlighting* was reportedly the most expensive show on television at the time. But it was one of the first in-house productions at a network, one of the rare hits for ABC (still in third place), and nobody was going to tell Glenn Caron how to run his show. His reputation, an image that he enjoyed and cultivated, was that he thrived on deadlines. In a *Time* magazine article that called the show "ABC's classiest hit and biggest headache," he blustered, "It sounds pompous, but maybe it's irresponsible to bring a television show in on time and on budget every week and have it be on nothing." (There was a private joke in an episode that featured a tabloid parody called *The National Pit* with a headline claiming: "Dr. Caron Discovers Antidote for Stress.") He often went to the studio before dawn to write a new scene, handing us pages of dialogue when we showed up later that morning. The writing was inspired and edgy, and I'll take last-minute changes that good any day. But the routine was grueling. We'd start on Monday at 7 A.M. and work until 9 P.M. Union rules stipulated the length of time actors need to break before reporting back to work, and we had to be paid an extra $1,000 if we didn't get a twelve-hour turnaround—it's called a "forced call." To avoid that expensive penalty to the producers, we'd start on Tuesday at 9 A.M. and go until 11 P.M. Then on Wednesday we'd start at 11 A.M. and go until 1 or 2 in the morning. And I'm not a night person. Plus there was a different director every week because the previous week's director was in the editing room. It took me ten long years to make my comeback and only one to feel trapped by my success.

As soon as I found out we were to do a mammoth

food fight, I went directly to Glenn's office and asked him if Bruce and I could get hit in the face with pies. Glenn laughed and told me that if I wanted to be hit in the face with a pie I would have to ask Bruce myself, which I did. Bruce chuckled for a minute and then asked, "Who's going to throw the pie?" I suggested someone neutral like our stunt coordinator, Chris Howel, and Bruce agreed. He and I clocked in a twenty-two-hour day for that food fight with the reward at the end being a refreshing pie in the face, accurately heaved by Chris. It was one of the finest moments for all involved.

$\mathcal{B}$URNOUT IS A GIVEN IN SERIES TELEVISION, but it doesn't come with a warning label, and my experience is that it doesn't bring out the best in people. I'd recover a little less each weekend until finally I never recovered, feeling the kind of fatigue that depletes every resource, including civility. Once when we were filming at the Ambassador Hotel, a woman in the lobby approached me for an autograph at just the wrong moment and I snapped. "Leave me alone," I said dismissively, and when she looked rightfully aghast, I countered, "I have a right to be a bitch." I really lost it at the end of one fourteen-hour day when I was called down to a basement on the old 20th Century-Fox lot for looping: redoing dialogue that hasn't been recorded clearly or doesn't have the right inflection of voice. The sound engineer was late, and I finally said, "Get another sound man." Then for an hour the buck-toothed associate producer gave me line readings on how to improve my performance

("Do it faster, now do it slower, really be angry, now a little less angry"). It was a manipulative power trip to make me jump through hoops. I was furious, and thrashing my arms in lieu of tearing out my hair, my hand came smashing down on the script stand, sending it crumpling to the floor.

I was almost sleepwalking. Once you reach that level of fatigue, it doesn't matter how much money you're making. The whole crew is affected, but they don't have expectations of physical perfection imposed on them as the on-camera people do, and it's worse for women. The face that stares back from the mirror at 5 A.M. under that kind of strain is not a pretty sight. I developed the clenched look of a soldier with post-traumatic stress disorder. But I was held to a much more stringent standard of beauty than Bruce, with two or three hours in hair and makeup every day compared to his fifteen minutes. I was blamed if I looked exhausted, whereas squinty eyes and a two-day stubble only added to David Addison's rakish allure. I insisted on wearing outfits with cinched waists: I have an old-fashioned hourglass figure, with broad shoulders and a big butt, and if my waist isn't accentuated, I tend to look like a Green Bay Packer. Our characters often wore sunglasses to look cool—a special design with flat rather than curved lenses that didn't reflect the set lights—that had the added benefit of covering dark circles. Gerald Finnerman, the director of photography, very kindly had a special sliding filter made for the lens of the camera, so when it panned from Bruce to me, the heavier diffusion was slid into place to make me look "prettier."

Angela Lansbury, my esteemed colleague from *The*

Lady Vanishes, was starring in *Murder, She Wrote*, and I asked her to dinner, seeking wise counsel from someone with a similar daily grind. "There's no way to survive an hour television format unless there are some ground rules," she said. "I come in at six A.M. and I leave at six P.M. Period. And I never start the season with fewer than eight scripts." But when I went to Glenn with this supplication, he just laughed.

"You might as well forget that," he said, "because it'll never happen."

At the beginning of our second season, Orson Welles agreed to introduce an episode called "The Dream Sequence Always Rings Twice"—an astonishing favor to me, rarer than a returned phone call in Hollywood. Standing on a set rigged to look like his office, he cautioned viewers not to be alarmed (an homage to his 1938 Mercury Theater broadcast of *The War of the Worlds* when, as a Halloween prank, he described a Martian invasion so vividly that thousands of listeners panicked). Approximately twelve minutes later, he explained, the picture would change from color to black and white. I was working at another location the day the scene was shot, and I kept thinking: *I have to go see Orson*, but I waited too long, eerily like Marlene Dietrich's character in Orson's classic film *Touch of Evil*: Marlene runs after Orson to say goodbye but arrives too late and finds him floating faceup, dead in the water. Two weeks after he did his *Moonlighting* bit, Orson died in his own office, slumped over a typewriter, and was buried in a Spanish bullfighters' graveyard. The episode, which was dedicated to him, unfolded from conflicting points of view like *Rashomon* (also reflecting what was happening on the set), switching between bad-David-good-Maddie and good-David-bad-Maddie, giving Bruce vintage ribald innuendo ("We would see more of each other, then all of each other") and me variations on Mae West's signature "When I'm good, I'm good, but when I'm bad, I'm better."

After a long professional drought, I reveled in the reviews and ratings for *Moonlighting*, lapping up my new designation as "TV's sexiest spitfire" in an "ouch-she's-hot comeback." (Perhaps most satisfying was Peter's report of a call from Cary Grant saying, "You were right about her all along.") But our first year on the air, the Emmy nominating committee lumped the show into the comedy category with sitcoms, which are, by definition, joke-driven. The competition was *Family Ties*, *Cheers*, *Kate & Allie*, *Night Court*, and *The Cosby Show* (which won). *Moonlighting* didn't get any nominations until 1986, when we were reclassified as a drama, "leading the pack" with sixteen nominations. It was a huge disappointment that we only won one—for editing.

You can get pushed over the edge of exhaustion on a crappy job too, but when the material is good and the people are passionate about it, everyone tends to be in even more denial, making excuses for their bad behavior. You tell yourself: *This is so clever, so classy, so valuable, that it's worth the sacrifice*, and meanwhile a little voice inside your head is screaming for sleep, sanity, salvation. In scientific studies, too many rats in a cage will attack and eat one another alive, even if they have enough food. It's an apt metaphor for the *Moonlighting* set, and we were all under pressure. Bruce Willis had never experienced anything close to this kind of success, and his reaction to it exacerbated the situation. The man whose high school yearbook recorded that his ambition was "to become deliriously happy, or a professional harp player" was suddenly rich beyond imagination. He bought a black Mercedes and a 1966 Corvette. I understood the heady mix of fame, money, groupies, and feel-good treats. I'd already been there and back, but Bruce was on his maiden voyage. The first time I experienced sudden success, I had my insufferable moments too.

There was a real cultural difference between a guy from "Joisey" and a girl from Memphis. In the South, what is considered acceptable behavior has at least a patina of courtesy and formality. That kind of ingrained etiquette has both positive and negative aspects: you may not know what someone really thinks of you, and there's a lot of "Honey child this" and "Darlin' that" covering up savage feelings, but on the surface it's Sunday-school gracious. The roots of my steel-magnolia temperament run deep, and I always try to alleviate tension with humor. I had my fan photo made into a dartboard and sent one to Bruce and one to Glen, complete with darts and a poem: "I'm giving you my picture, I hope you'll treat it nice, you can hang it in the attic to scare away mice."

I indulged in regular therapeutic massage to help cope with the stress of the shooting schedule, during which I could feel body and soul coming back together. One day my masseuse opened her big canvas bag and pulled out a tape called *Woman's Spirit*, a guided meditation with one's female ancestors. Lying on the backseat of my limousine on the way to the studio, I would listen to the tape and imagine myself in a field, holding my mother's hand, who was holding her mother's hand, who was holding her mother's hand, going back to a time of safety and peace. I was searching for a spiritual anchor, I needed to make God a holy and forgiving mother.

Despite massage, I developed debilitating headaches and a back stiff enough to build condominiums. A friend recommended a chiropractor who was known to make house calls and "set calls" for actors. When Bruce Oppenheim came to treat me during a late shoot, it was close to midnight and there was hardly room for his table in my trailer. I'd never had chiropractic work, but he had such strong hands and worked so quickly that I didn't have time to get nervous. The disappearance of my headaches made me an instant believer, and his twisted sense of humor made me laugh. I started having "adjustments" about once a month, and with my skewed sense of boundaries, it didn't seem to matter if I was dating a healthcare professional who was treating me. He didn't seem to be troubled by it either.

With the first serious money of my life, I bought a house at the end of a cul-de-sac in the Encino hills, framed by two stone lions. I removed the previous owner's expensive bad taste, and replaced it with my own expensive bad taste. Mother always said, "All your taste is in your mouth, girl." Behind sliding glass doors was a pool lined with small gold tiles that made me feel like I was swimming in liquid gold. Bruce brought me tea and melon in bed at the crack of dawn, then biked with me a dozen miles to the studio. Right before we left, I'd have a can of Mountain Dew plus a cup of coffee, so I felt like I had been shot out of a cannon. A teamster would drive me and the bike back at the end of the day, and Bruce often cooked dinner while I spent a little time with my daughter. He let me know that he'd never really considered having children of his own, but his relationship with seven-year-old Clementine was warm and affectionate. We already felt like a family.

Even though I was bone weary, I well knew the lesson about striking while the iron was hot—and I had lived through some cool-iron times—so I spent a springtime hiatus from *Moonlighting* doing a television remake of *The Long Hot Summer,* based on a short story called "The Hamlet" by William Faulkner. I wanted to play the role originated by Joanne Woodward but was pronounced "too pretty" (although hardly prettier than Don Johnson, the hot star of *Miami Vice,* who was playing the Paul Newman role). Such distinctions seemed unfathomable anyway when they gave the part to Judith Ivey, a lovely-looking actress who was deemed more serious, after making her do four screen tests and telling her she wasn't pretty enough. I was cast as the libidinous daughter-in-law originally played by Lee Remick.

The opulent homestead of the fictitious Varner family in "Frenchman's Bend, Mississippi" was replicated by the Oak Alley Plantation in Thibodaux, Louisiana. It had an unpaved road lined by stately two-hundred-year-old live oaks draped with Spanish moss, leading up to the white-columned mansion. Its several caretaker cabins with screened porches had been converted to guest houses. A high levee with a gravel road on top separated the house and the river, and I walked there every chance I got.

On a job with such a large ensemble cast, there's lots of time to sit around, which means more time to read. One afternoon while waiting on the screen porch of one of the converted caretakers' cabins, the book I chose would have an enormous impact on the direction of my life. It was *Outrageous Acts & Everyday Rebellion* by Gloria Steinem. Although I had called myself a feminist for fifteen years, I realized I had not committed a single Outrageous Act in any public way to support women's reproductive freedom or any other civil rights issue. It was also around this time I became aware that Congress had disallowed funding for abortions for poor women. Pregnancy as punishment because you're poor? It was one of those big moments in life when you say, "Hold on a minute, missy, that ain't right!" Determined finally to become part of the solution, I called *Ms.* magazine and asked to speak to Gloria Steinem, the magazine's founder, whom I had met briefly at a party in Manhattan a few years earlier. She took my call immediately, and without wasting time, I asked what I could do to help the cause.

"There's a political action committee I'm involved with called Voters for Choice," she began. "They're in need of a strong, morally committed spokesperson. Would you consider that?"

"Yes," I said without hesitation. I was finally on my way toward exorcising the demon of political inaction and apathy that had been brewing since my childhood when I had been surrounded by the racism of the segregated south. But once I started speaking out, there was no stopping me. I marched on Washington for reproductive freedom and women's equality, I spoke at fund-raisers for pro-choice candidates like Ann Richards (governor of Texas), Barbara Boxer (senator from California), and Bill Clinton (president of the United States of America). I marched again on Washington for gay and lesbian rights, I helped dedicate the Civil Rights Museum in Memphis, and was called to testify before a House subcommittee on the U.S. approval for RU-486. To this day, I believe that any excuse to discriminate against any group of human beings violates their civil rights. Regardless of their skin color, religion, sex, or sexual preference, all people must be treated equally. To do otherwise is un-American. Because of my advocacy for these basic civil rights, Gloria Allred, my longtime friend and fighter for feminist issues, asked me to seriously consider running for president of the United States in the year 2000.

But let's go back to the fun and games on the set of *The Long Hot Summer*. Don Johnson and I were aware of an intense attraction the minute we met. When ten journalists arrived for a press junket wanting to photograph the steamy scenes between us, they were astonished to hear that in the four-hour miniseries, there were none. I told the director and the producer, both separately and together, "You're crazy if you don't write at least one scene for Don and me." Unfortunately, it was assumed that I was trying to pad my part. Just because we were forbidden to explore our flirtation on-screen didn't mean we couldn't follow up on it in private. One night, as I relaxed on the screen porch of my little cabin, I heard a man's voice purr, "Ohhh, Miss Eula" (my character's name).

I responded, "Why, Mr. Ben Quick" (Don's character's name). "What are you doing here?"

"I'd just like to pay my respects, ma'am."

I opened the screen door a wedge. "Why don't you come on in and sit a spell."

We lasted a nanosecond on the porch and then rapidly progressed to my bed. It was like wolfing down a candy bar when you're starving—fast, furious, intense—and it was all over in five minutes. Somehow we never got around to another five minutes, since "Mr. Quick" moved on to one of the hairdressers, who thereafter acted as if I had bad breath.

The gracious and genial Jason Robards, who was playing the family patriarch, was well loved by the crew, but Don was not a favorite. He told too many of them too often how they could do their jobs better. A palpable tension seemed to arise when he walked on the set and disappeared when he left. Everyone was in awe of Ava Gardner, who was playing the mistress of the domineering Will Varner. We hadn't done our one scene together yet and nobody had bothered to introduce us. One night while we were shooting out in the middle of a swamp, the air-conditioning in my tiny trailer kept breaking down, and I decided to walk over to her trailer to say hi and introduce myself. I had just raised my hand to knock when the door flew open and slammed against the side of her trailer. Fortunately, I had leaped back into the darkness in the nick of time. I froze and watched, unseen in the shadows. Her hair was in rollers, and she was swaying, holding a bottle of white wine by the neck. Suddenly, she began screaming, "JASONNNNNNNNN!" I hightailed it out of there, but later that night, as the crew was setting up the dramatic fire finale and we were taking our places, I dared to approach her again.

One night Orson
Welles almost burned
the house down. To
atone, he sent the
Victor Book of Opera,
with this inscription.

Lady bug, lady bug
fly away home —
Your house is on fire
(and your house-guest —
a hibernating bear —
is on fire too)

he sends you
much love!
always
Orson

With my
bodyguard at
Sun Recording
Studios: Elvis never
had a problem
with two girls.

"Don't hate me because I'm beautiful." Morgan Fairchild and I on the set of *Cybill* after one of my infamous food fights. (*Cybill*, Courtesy of The Carsey-Werner Company, LLC/Michael Yarish)

ABOVE: Art imitates life. On the set of *Cybill* with Tom Wopat, Tim Matheson, and Alan Rosenberg, my television ex-husband, my boyfriend, and my other ex-husband, respectively.

(*Cybill*, Courtesy of The Carsey-Werner Company, LLC/Michael Yarish)

With Gloria Steinem, Marlo Thomas, and Whoopi Goldberg
marching on Washington in 1989 to protect women's
reproductive freedom.

With Christine Baranski on the set of *Cybill*. What did I do?

I always listen to wise women like my friend Cybill
Ann Richards

With former Texas governor Ann Richards. How about a Shepherd/Richards ticket in 2004?

At home in Encino with my kids and our two dogs.
(From left) Zachariah; me; our German Shepherd, Kim;
Clementine; our pug, Petunia; and Ariel.

I've been singing for so long that I'm finally getting good. Here I am onstage at the Rainbow and Stars in New York City, September 1998.
(Rahav "Cosi" Alfasi)

"I told ya I love ya, now get out." One of my standards at the Orpheum Theater in Memphis, Tennessee.
(Peggy B. Strickland/ Angel Hill Studio)

Here I am with Alicia Witt and Christine Baranski on the set of *Cybill*. Don't they realize I'm Glinda the *Good* Witch?
(*Cybill*, Courtesy of The Carsey-Werner Company, LLC/Michael Yarish)

"Only God, my dear, could love you for yourself alone and not your yellow hair."

(Ken Regan / Camera 5)

"Ms. Gardner, I am thrilled to be working with you." It took her a while to focus on me. Then she belched out a slurpy, "SHADDDUPP!"

The next day, around the motel pool, she seemed alert and agreeable, throwing her glorious neck back with a rich and lustful laugh. I took one more risk. "Ms. Gardner," I said, extending a tentative handshake, "I'm Cybill Shepherd."

"Oh, hello!" She beamed, flashing that profoundly sexy Ava Gardner smile. "It's so nice to meet you." The previous night had never happened.

Almost immediately I could tell that *The Long Hot Summer* was going to be a stinker. In one scene I actually begged not to have a close-up, and they agreed. The miniseries was so bad it was appropriately dismissed as "irredeemable, paltry and barren" by the *Washington Post* TV critic Tom Shales, who noted of my performance, "She seems playfully aware that the movie is garbage." It was shown on CBS opposite *Moonlighting*. *Moonlighting* won the time slot.

IN JANUARY 1987 I WAS GETTING DRESSED FOR the Golden Globe Awards, and my dress didn't fit. There was no mistaking the reason. The stomach pooches out more quickly in a second pregnancy because the muscles have been pregnant before. By the time I scheduled a doctor's appointment, a test was a formality—I was so violently nauseated I couldn't eat.

When the obstetrician got the results back from the lab, she called me. "Either you're further along in your pregnancy than you thought," she said, "or you're having twins."

I dismissed this possibility, even though my grandmother's sister and their grandmother had had twins.

It was recommended that I see a specialist for an early ultrasound. Two hours before the time of my appointment I was supposed to drink eight glasses of water (a full bladder lifts the uterus into a good position for a sonogram). I forgot and didn't start chugging on a big bottle of water until I was in the car on the way to the appointment, so when the doctor moved the probe over my abdomen, his face registered concern: he saw two amniotic sacs but he could detect only one heartbeat. I tried not to panic as I lay on the table in an ungainly position, pushing images of dead babies out of my head, while we waited for the water to do its thing. When the doctor came back to make another pass, his face brightened. A second heart was beating in syncopated rhythm with its sibling.

When I called Bruce at his office, I started with, "Honey, I want you to sit down."

"Why?" he said.

"Just do it," I insisted. "We're having twins." There was no response at first, then a slow "Whaaaaaaaaaaaaaaa—"

"It could be worse," I interrupted. "It could be triplets."

A twin pregnancy is considered high risk for any woman, let alone one closing in on forty, and I had to see three different OB-GYNs before I found one who didn't make me feel doomed, reading me a riot act list of all the horrible things that could happen. I called Peg Burke, one of the midwives who had attended Clementine's birth eight years earlier.

"The rate of cesareans in Southern California is

twenty-five percent," she said sympathetically. "Lotsa luck."

"There's got to be one doctor in Los Angeles who'll give me a chance for a natural delivery," I said. "Isn't there a nurse-midwife I can call?"

She suggested Nancy Boles, head of the midwifery program at the University of Southern California Medical School. I told her I understood that I needed to have a doctor present, but I wanted the same kind of midwife support I'd had when my first child was born.

"Yeah, I know," she said, the voice of resignation, "even though I've delivered two thousand sets of twins myself." I asked her to recommend a doctor, and she mentioned Jeffrey Phelan, who had recently published an article about a technique called "version," in which the doctor turns the unborn child into the proper position for birth. He had won Nancy's heart when she heard that he made his male medical students get up in the stirrups to see how their female patients felt during a pelvic exam.

People can be really dumb about a twin pregnancy. No woman who's given birth would ever say chirpily, "That's the way to do it: get it over with all at once." Dr. Phelan had a more experienced take. "I wish twin pregnancies on my enemies," he told me sympathetically, acknowledging the difficulty of dealing with twice the hormones, twice the heartburn, twice the discomfort, twice the nausea, twice the risk. I was not going to be a radiant bride.

I have a photograph of my mother and stepfather, Mondo (they had married eight years earlier), holding a shotgun at my wedding to Bruce, who made a happy adjustment in his thinking about parenthood. A rabbi pronounced us man and wife in the shortest cere-mony possible that was still legal. My gown was an an-tique ceremonial silk kimono, cream-colored with gold and orange fans. It was a wedding gift from my friend Kaori Turner (her mother had worn it), who also procured a black kimono for Bruce and a pink one for Clementine. The dining room of our house had been made into a Japanese tearoom, with rice-paper walls and tatami flooring. No shoes, which have always seemed a form of bondage to me, and no rings—I've never been big on jewelry.

Helicopters were circling over the house, trying to get a shot of us or celebrity guests. (There were none, just twenty close friends.) My father couldn't be in the same room as my mother, my sister didn't want to travel, and my brother and I weren't talking to each other because we had a dispute about money. The photo exclusive went to David Hume Kennerly, who was one of Bruce's friends and had won a Pulitzer for his Vietnam War coverage and had been the White House photographer during the Ford administration. A tiered white cake with a porcelain bride and groom and two baby carriages followed a steak dinner—ironic, since I had just been fired as a spokesperson for the Beef Council because a journalist wrote that I was trying to eat less red meat. (My mother, who knew me to lick the steak platter before I washed it, had ex-claimed, "Are they crazy?" and threatened to write the council a letter. But my attorney later told me that the real reason was because I was pregnant before I was married, a highly publicized fact.) I was asleep by seven o'clock. The next morning, I reported back to the set, and Bruce went into his office, working underneath an eight-by-ten glossy of me from my days as his patient, inscribed, "Dear Bruce, I've seldom had such a laying on of hands. Love and thanks, Cybill."

My pregnancy further widened the chasm between me and the producers, who reacted as if the news was a thoughtless inconvenience. Other television actresses had been allowed to work real-life pregnancies into plotlines and production schedules. When I suggested a similar approach to Glenn Caron, his response was a tepid, "Well, you don't leave me much choice." Despite the fact that I developed gestational diabetes and was forbidden to work during my last trimester, I occasionally went to the studio against doctor's orders. But Glenn continued to act as if I were personally, purposefully screwing him over (and would later claim that my pregnancy had destroyed *Moonlighting*). He attempted to accommodate the situation by having Maddie meet a short, stocky man on a train and marry him three days later. When I strongly voiced my objection that the character we had created in Maddie would never do such a thing, Glenn said words to the effect of "Just shut up and do your job, you're not producing this show."

I had doctor appointments every few days to ensure that the twins, whose welfare was compromised by the diabetes, were healthy and developing on schedule.

Eight-year-old Clementine, who had been begging for siblings, announced that she wanted to be present for their arrival. My midwife put together a slide show of some of her other births to prepare Clem for the noises Mommy would make, the presence of blood, and the fact that I would be in pain. After only two slides, Clementine put up her hand and said, "I don't want to see anymore, Mommy. Just call me when the babies are cleaned up."

Soon thereafter, she announced, "I've changed my mind. I've decided I don't really want a brother and sister."

"Well, what should we do when they're born?" I asked calmly. "Should we throw them out the window?"

She frowned. "Nobody ever asked me about this, you know," she said.

A few weeks later, she came to me with a proud plan. "When we get home from the hospital," she said brightly, "I'd like to put the babies in the washing machine."

"Really, honey?" I asked. "Why?"

"Because," she said, "I'd like to see them go around and around and around."

By my third trimester, I was so huge I began to resemble Marlon Brando. I could no longer get up off my futon on the floor, so I had a large platform built at the height of a normal bed. I still had to crawl to the edge and then push myself up. One early morning, I was awakened by an earthquake and in terror I stood straight up and jumped off the platform, running to see if Clementine was okay. She was, but my groin was not. I felt like I was walking around carrying two bowling balls between my legs. Every night I prayed, "Please God, let me get over *this* pain before I go into labor."

A few weeks before my October due date, Mother and Mondo drove out to California in a motor home. Every night, we'd sit in the yard taking a moon bath, soaking up the beams and watching the waxing crescent get fatter and brighter. The moon affects all bodies of water, I figured, and my babies were floating in their own private pool. On October 6, 1987, the moon went full at 12:03 A.M. My water broke at 12:08. I listened to a tape of Kathleen Battle singing "Ave Maria" as Mother, Mondo, Bruce, and I drove to the brand-new California Medical Center downtown.

Molly Ariel and Cyrus Zachariah were born thirteen hours later, both named for their great-grandparents but known by their middle names, with a hyphenated Shepherd-Oppenheim. But those thirteen hours were harrowing.

In transit down the birth canal, Ariel had pushed Zach out of the way (a very determined female from the get-go), and he turned sideways. Something, probably his foot, lodged up under my ribs and felt like it was pulling me apart one bone at a time. At this point, I began begging for drugs and screaming, "Kill me! Kill me! Cut the babies out!" A few moments later, and before any drugs could be given, Ariel was born (five pounds, eleven ounces) followed by Zachariah (seven pounds, two ounces).

My entourage took over almost a whole floor of the hospital—Bruce, Mother, Mondo, Clementine, Myrtle, the midwife, three nurses, and a bodyguard. (I had forgotten to include the doctor's name on a list of people to be allowed admittance, and he had trouble getting in to see me.) I guess this was the most famous I've ever been. There were two photos on the front page of the New York *Daily News*, accompanying the headline: "ROBERT BORK LOSES/CYBILL'S TWINS DOING GREAT." This was great news all around. Not only were the twins healthy and happy, but the antichoice Supreme Court nominee had been defeated. The paparazzi had been waiting at the front door of the hospital since before the babies were born, and every day the guard caught someone who managed to sneak through with a camera. I knew that the best way to get photographers to stop swarming around me was not to try to run from them, but Bruce was afraid of flashes going off in the sensitive eyes of our newborns. We arranged for his brother to leave the hospital with a nurse in a blond wig, holding two Cabbage Patch dolls, while we attempted a more private exit out back. No one was fooled, and Bruce and I almost crashed into a lamppost when one photographer jumped on the hood of our car—a small risk, he probably considered, since photos of the babies were said to fetch up to $100,000.

Going from one to three children felt like going from one to ten; the effort and responsibility involved in parenthood increases exponentially. Before going back to work, I bought a forty-foot motor home, with plenty of room for the twins and their paraphernalia, including Bruce Willis's gift of a teeter-totter and Glenn Caron's two giant pandas. Beloved Myrtle kept insisting that she could handle the nannying single-handedly (she'd had thirteen children herself), but I didn't want to put that much of a burden on her, and finding capable, trustworthy people for child care is the challenge of every working mother. I hired one woman who seemed to have impeccable credentials, only to discover that she kept a bottle of rum in her purse. Another simply disappeared and was apprehended a few weeks later in Scottsdale, Arizona, wandering nude with pictures of Ariel and Zack in her hand, saying she was looking for her babies.

$\mathcal{T}$HE YEAR 1988 BEGAN PROPITIOUSLY WITH A ceremony in which I was given a star on the Hollywood Walk of Fame, and it only cost me $4,322. Bruce Willis sent a telegram saying, "Sorry I can't be there, but one of us has to work." During this season of *Moonlighting* my dissatisfaction grew with the inimical atmosphere and changes in the way my character was written. Not only was she a virago, but she was starting to act bipolar. In an episode called "Yours Very Deadly," Maddie urges a female client to continue a correspondence with someone who has been sending the woman threatening letters. Maddie actually goes to this man's apartment, unarmed, pounding on the door, even though she knows him to be deaf and believes him to be a murderer. "No sane person would encourage a woman to engage with a harasser," I told Glenn, "and people who have experienced some fame are particularly sensitive to the dangers. I know that, and as a former model, Maddie Hayes would know it too." But Glenn was adamant that we keep to the story, and I gave it my best shot: the character acts bipolar, but with conviction. The next episode, "All Creatures Great and Small," dropped the little bomb that Maddie is an atheist. So. Not only is she a cold bitch but she doesn't believe in God. My character could go no lower: a feminist atheist.

Or so I thought. When Glenn came to talk to me about his idea for an episode called "Atomic Shakespeare" that would satirize *The Taming of the Shrew,* my first question was "Who's going to play the shrew?" I was serious when I suggested some contemporary gender bending, making David Addison the termagant. Glenn was not amused. When I read the script, I found that my Elizabethan character was to be bound, gagged, and married off against her will while a whole town cheered, as part of her husband's bet with her father. Kate aka Maddie aka Cybill was made to be an impossibly unsympathetic character so that Petruchio aka David aka Bruce could score. I was certainly aware that *Moonlighting* was entertainment, not a political treatise, as I was aware that some women are aroused by bondage. Maddie was definitely not turned on. In this case, binding and gagging was a symbol of violence against women—even Shakespeare didn't tame his shrew with ropes.

"Atomic Shakespeare" won more awards than any other episode, including Emmys for directing, editing, and costume design. I wore a sleeveless black velvet evening gown and Day-Glo orange high-tops to the ceremony, fully intending to change into pumps. It's a long ride to the Pasadena Civic Auditorium, and I had time to consider the prospect of an evening in pain. As my limousine pulled up to the curb, the driver said, "I'll wait for you to change your shoes."

"You can open the door now," I said. "I'm ready." I knew what I was doing—it was my personal rebellion against the tyranny of high heels—but people reacted as if I were naked. Actually, I felt that half the women there were cheering "Right on, sister," and half were muttering "You bitch." To this day, people are always checking out what I've got on my feet and seem disappointed if I'm in anything fancier than sneakers.

Bruce Willis was nominated again that year, but I was not. I went to the ceremony thinking: *I'll be okay as long as he doesn't win.* (Nice team spirit.) He won. I smiled and applauded. I understand that many actors have done good work for years and not gotten awards for it, but this felt like a slap in the face, as if he were the motor that drove the show, as if I were dispensable.

In the episode "Big Man on Mulberry Street," when David Addison's former brother-in-law dies, he goes to New York, and Maddie, in a show of support, crashes the funeral. In a moving scene, David recalls marrying his pregnant girlfriend and hoping that he won't end up in a blue Sunoco uniform with DAVE stitched over the pocket, then trying to keep the marriage going after his wife miscarries, only to come home one day to find the census taker on top of her, "getting all kinds of pertinent information that isn't on the form." When David's ex-wife admits that this infidelity was not with another man but with a woman, Maddie's reaction to this jaw-dropping news was cut. Even if the intent was to showcase Bruce, it would not have lessened the impact of his performance to see Maddie's reaction, and it hurt my character because it didn't show her humanity. The mutual sovereignty of the characters, the conflict between fully realized equals, was compromised. When I registered my complaint, Glenn told me I hadn't played the scene very well. The unspoken message was that I was a bitch; the salt in the wound was the news that I was a bad actress.

"Big Man on Mulberry Street" also had a musical number beautifully choreographed by Stanley Donen, the legendary director of *Singing in the Rain*, with a soundtrack by Billy Joel. It was supposed to be Maddie's dream, but to me it looked a lot more like David's fantasy. Glenn said that he wasn't interested in my opinion, and when I approached Donen with my reservations, I saw him go absolutely cold, almost as if he'd been prepared for my being impossible. As I left the set after a rehearsal, I was so frustrated that I picked up a director's chair and threw it at the wall. The tabloids reported that I had heaved the chair at Glenn. (If I had wanted to hit him, I wouldn't have missed.)

The distinctive door slamming that became a leit-motif of the show was something I learned from Ernst Lubitsch movies, and studio carpenters had to rebuild the Blue Moon Agency doors every season because we slammed them so hard. But one of my most painful memories revolved around the door slamming in "Symphony in Knocked Flat." The script called for Maddie to arrive at work and slam her way through the office in a rage because she had a boring date the night before. I didn't think that a boring date the night before was enough motivation for a hysterical tirade, and I ignored the stage direction, playing the scene more thoughtfully. I got away with it that time, but my next scene that required rage brought Glenn and Jay down to the set. We did it over and over, each time Glenn repeating, "That's not angry enough. Do it again." I felt so humiliated and upset that I began forgetting the lines I had known perfectly well when we started.

I watched the "Symphony" episode again recently and came away proud that I had followed my instincts and underplayed those two scenes. Though I still cringe at the thought of Glenn's and Jay's bullying,

I'm so glad I defended the integrity of my character, Maddie, in the face of public embarrassment. That episode represents truly wonderful work on everyone's part. And besides, how many people get to work with The Temptations and perform "Psychedelic Shack," like I did in the prologue to that episode?

Bruce became disenchanted with the classic David Addison smarminess, sometimes throwing a script across the room and calling it shit. Actors make a mistake when they act superior to the material. Good acting is like a tennis match. But somewhere along the way it felt like Bruce disconnected from what I was doing. It seemed as if he had already figured out all the moves, and it was far less exciting when the match between us was over.

One April day in 1988, I arrived for work fifteen minutes late to find an all points bulletin out for me. An assistant director approached my car as I drove onto the lot and said, "Cybill, don't bother getting out." Then he told the driver, "Take her right to Glenn's office." I felt like an intractable student summoned to the principal after sliding down the school banister—a bad acid flashback, and I'd never even taken acid. Jay Daniel and several people I didn't recognize were sitting in Glenn's office; Glenn was standing in front of his pinball machine and his jukebox loaded with 1960s rock and roll and every song by Tammy Wynette.

"You don't give a fuck about your work," he screamed the moment I walked in the door. "Your standards are down, and your ideas are crap." I could hardly respond, his rage was so vehement. And while he screamed, Jay sat silent, not uttering a word in my defense.

A few weeks later, when we came to the end of the shooting season, I wrote Glenn a letter. "I want to do everything in my control to help the show," I wrote. "But I need you to know that for me to work effectively, it is absolutely necessary to avoid another performance like the one you gave when I was summoned to your office several weeks ago to hear your diatribe—all in the presence of complete strangers. I have enormous respect for the work you have done and for the show you have created, but I do not respect that behavior and I will not willingly be subjected to the kind of abuse that you unleashed at that meeting. I take my share of responsibility for some of the problems we have had in the past and will do everything I can to correct those problems."

During the hiatus I made a film called *Chances Are*, a fantasy about a woman who remains devoted to the memory of her dead husband and falls in love with him again, reincarnated in the form of Robert Downey Jr. The producer was a pal of Ryan O'Neal and lobbied for him to play the family friend who's really been in love with my character all along. Considering our history, Ryan was the last person I wanted to work with. "Casting him is a great way to ruin this movie," I warned. But everybody else kept turning down the role, so we got him by default. (Turned out I was wrong. He was terrific.) I had avoided a love scene with him in real life, but I couldn't stop my nervous laughter when I had to kiss him on-camera. The director, Emile Ardolino, took me aside and whispered, "Could you please stop giggling? It's upsetting Ryan." Not an unreasonable request, and I stopped laughing by thinking of deaths in the family and biting my upper lip.

I thought the script would have been improved by dispensing with the reincarnation storyline and exploring a romance seldom seen on film between an older woman and a younger man, a relationship I've often played out in real life. The first day of rehearsal, Downey didn't show up or respond to phone calls. Somebody from the production office got the manager of his hotel to open the door of his room and found him in bed with a woman, sleeping off a bad night. It was apparent that he had substance abuse problems, and he was told that if he was ever late again, he would be fired. A monitor in the guise of a "trainer" was hired to keep him out of trouble for the remainder of the shooting schedule. I relished the experience of working with Emile Ardolino. As a director he pushed me beyond what I had thought of as my "dramatic limits" as an actor. Some years later, Emile stopped returning my phone calls. This is a common occurrence in Hollywood but hardly what I would have expected from Emile. About six months later, a mutual friend called and told me the sad truth: "Emile died of AIDS today." Now, whenever I cry as an actor part of my motivation is always the thought of Emile and missing him.

When production started on the new season of *Moonlighting*, I received a "personal and confidential" letter from the lawyers for Capital Cities/ABC, Inc., as did Bruce Willis. Attached was a list of "guidelines" regarding production, stating the network's right to cancel episodes or the series if the guidelines were not strictly followed. (Bruce and I would be responsible for the loss of revenue in such an event.) The normal day onstage, the memo stated, was from

7 A.M. to 7 P.M., but night work was at the producer's discretion. The production company would make every effort to deliver scripts one day in advance of shooting, but the script was nevertheless to be learned. The producers were to maintain a written record of the actors' work pattern during each day of production, including the time elapsed after being called to the set, which was not to exceed five minutes. Bathroom breaks were also limited to five minutes.

My lawyer responded to this demeaning memo by reminding ABC that I already had a contract governing my services; that nowhere in my agreement was the network given the right to impose additional terms and conditions, particularly those more suitable to a reform school; that I resented any attempt to impute to me responsibility for their cost overruns; and that such insinuations were defamatory, injurious to my reputation, and the cause of severe emotional distress.

One more letter arrived from ABC. Dispensing with the legalese, the gist of it was "Yeah, yeah, yeah." And with such posturing, the tempest was over.

In the fall of 1988, Glenn Caron left the show, stating that it was him or me and he didn't think the network would choose him. What had begun as an alliance between Glenn and me, as well as a newcomer named Bruce Willis, had turned into Glenn and Bruce against Cybill. Not only David Addison but Bruce Willis had become Glenn's alter ego and I became the troublemaker, the difficult one out to get them (whatever part I had in creating this I will forever regret). Recently, the pilot of *Moonlighting* was released on DVD. The disc includes almost nonstop commentary on the making of the series by the cre-

ator, Glenn Caron, and the star, Bruce Willis. Need-
less to say, I was not thrilled to be excluded, but now
there can be no doubt that there had been and still is a
boys' club to which I'm not invited. Glenn describes
himself and Bruce as being virtually the same. They
have similar backgrounds, the same things disgust
them, and the same things make them laugh. The
only thing that really matters is that a whole new audience is enjoying *Moonlighting* on DVD as well as
nightly on the Bravo network. And I'm really proud of
the good work we did together. In any case, Jay Daniel
took over as executive producer, and Roger Director,
already working on the show, was promoted to head
writer. (He later wrote the roman à clef *A Place to Fall*,
about a neurotic, petulant actor, and Bruce Willis
threatened to punch him out.) The show lasted for
two more years, and Peter Bogdanovich made a mem-
orable guest appearance in an episode about all the
men in Maddie's past. But with the success of the *Die
Hard* movies, it became clear that Bruce was ready to
move on, that he had outgrown *Moonlighting*. He was
so disdainful of the material that he often hadn't bothered to read it before arriving on the set. He was impatient about any time I spent in the trailer with the
twins, although he increasingly wanted to leave early
himself. I put up a punching bag on the set, suggesting that we hit it instead of each other. One day, when
filming threatened to delay his early getaway, the
whole set started to vibrate from Bruce's pummeling.
Thank God for that bag.

One day, as nursing time for the twins approached,
I asked to be released for a twenty-five-minute break.
The first assistant director kept delaying it, so after

about an hour, my motor-home driver turned on the walkie-talkie so that the whole set could hear the two screaming infants and announced "Cybill, it's time!" After that, I was free to go.

The final episode surely echoed the sentiments of viewers. "Can you really blame the audience?" a silhouetted producer asks Maddie and David. "A case of poison ivy is more fun than watching you two lately."

I was breaking up with two Bruces at once—Bruce Willis and Bruce Oppenheim. I will always regret that I never got to raise kids beyond the age of two with their fathers present. Children don't know from incompatibility. They only want Mom and Dad to live together in love with each other and with them. When Bruce got angry, he shouted, and when I got angry, I ran away. I'd never heard my parents have an argument. I observed their brawls and mutually cold, silent treatment. I had no sense of two people being able to negotiate conflict and come to a reasonable compromise. Operating under a veil of exhaustion and frustration from work, I gave up on my marriage.

Bruce and I were forced to work with a court-appointed counselor, both of us legitimately afraid that divorce would mean seeing the children a lot less. Our separation was the catalyst for what was surely long overdue therapy for me. I wheeled a big rolling rack of baggage into the therapist's office and took out one suitcase at a time, asking, "Is this because I'm an asshole?"

Not long after the separation, I was walking on the treadmill and watching MTV. A video came on of a song by Martha Venessa Sharron, Ronald Lee Miller, and Kenny Hirsch called "If I Could." The lyrics moved me instantly to tears: "If I could, I'd teach you all the things I never learned / And help you cross all those bridges that I burned." I started weeping so profusely that I had to push the emergency button on the treadmill to keep from falling down.

CHAPTER TEN

"I'm Cybill Shepherd. You Know, the Movie Star?"

I WAS TERRIFIED ABOUT MY PROSPECTS WHEN *Moonlighting* ended, and it didn't help to hear Joan Rivers dismiss me on her talk show as the head of the "Fucking Lucky Club." It seemed like my luck was running out. I spent several years doing projects of no particular consequence, playing a collection of wives, nurses, bitches, and sociopaths.

The 1990 TV movie *Which Way Home* was based on a true story about a nurse who rescues five orphans from a refugee camp, substituting Thailand for Cambodia. I asked my doctor for something to help me sleep on the long flight over, and he gave me Halcion, a potent narcotic that can erase short-term memory. When I arrived, somebody had to tell me where I was and why I was there. But I have distinct memories of a location shoot fraught with water problems. We were filming several hours south of Bangkok, staying in a city called Hua Hin (nicknamed Whore Hin by the crew for obvious reasons), and I swam in the soothing warm waters of the South China Sea, which glows at night with bioluminescent plankton. During one swim, some terrible creature wrapped itself around my calves, and I ran shrieking from the water to discover that my attacker was a plastic bag used to wrap the beach towels.

The ceiling, floor, even the wastebasket in my room were made of teak, and I kept thinking: *This is where the rain forest is going.* The water in my shower contained some chemicals with interesting special effects. A week into shooting, the director of photography requested a private meeting. "I'm sorry to mention this," he said, "but your hair appears somewhat greenish on camera." I squeezed every available lemon in Southeast Asia on my head and sat in the sun.

When we moved farther south to Bang Sephon, the floor, walls, and ceiling of my hotel bathroom were tiled. There was no shower curtain because the drain was in the middle of the room. I noticed that whatever was deposited in the toilet each morning would still be there at night. Not a good sign. When I returned at the end of the first day of shooting, covered from head to toe with sand and who knows what else from slogging through murky lagoons, I got into the shower and turned on the water. There were a few weak sputters and then nothing. Other crew members confirmed that they were experiencing the same drought, and I placed a call to the producer. "I'm a trooper," I said, "but I draw the line at a hot shower and a functional toilet. If the water isn't restored, I'm leaving for someplace where I know the plumbing works, like Southern California." The next day, in the predawn light, something that looked like a cement truck rumbled into the parking lot and disappeared behind the building. There were noises of plumbing and pipe fitting, and I had a trickly but wet shower.

What I loved best about Thailand was the food: savory soups for breakfast, midmorning snacks of cashews freshly roasted over fires, sticky rice with mangoes that look green but are lusciously ripe. There are a hundred different fruits never seen outside the country, and the familiar ones are as abundant as apples. You can hail a boat coming down the Chaou Praya River in Bangkok and buy a sack of fresh litchi nuts from the farmer (although I never did develop the local enthusiasm for one fruit whose name translates into "tastes like heaven, smells like hell"). What I didn't love about the location was my dressing room: a bus with the seats taken out and furniture that rolled around as if on casters. I literally couldn't fit into its minuscule bathroom, so when I had to use the facilities, I cleared everybody out and stood in the hallway, hoping for the best as I launched my ass back toward the toilet.

PETER BOGDANOVICH HAD THE RIGHTS TO Larry McMurtry's book *Texasville*, a return to the characters of *The Last Picture Show* some thirty years later. (The frontispiece of the 1987 novel reads "For Cybill Shepherd.") Miraculously the entire cast from *Picture Show* was reassembled.

The friendship between Peter and Larry had always been shaky—like two unfixed dogs, they snarled at

each other from separate corners—but Larry and I
were friends for life, or so I thought. A month before I
went to Texas, he stopped returning my phone calls,
essentially vanishing from my life. It was odd to be
filming the book he had dedicated to me and not even
know if I might turn a corner in Archer City and
bump into him. There were other reasons why it
wasn't my happiest experience: I felt like I was con-
fronting the ghosts of the mistakes Peter and I had
made, wreaking havoc in everyone's lives and not even
ending up together. But the worst part of it was a cus-
tody court judge ordering my twenty-month-old twins
to fly back and forth from Dallas to Los Angeles every
other week to see their father, accompanied by a
nanny. This forced separation meant that I had to stop
nursing, which was physically and emotionally traumatic for me and the babies.

Larry McMurtry was the first person who'd ever
sent me lilies, and he used to send them regularly.
About a year after *Texasville*, a huge vase of cut lilies
arrived at my home, and I ripped open the gift card
with excitement, hoping that his long silence was broken. The flowers were from someone else, but they inspired me to write Larry a note about how much I
missed him and our friendship, and he finally responded. That was when he explained why we weren't
friends anymore. He thought I had acted too hastily in
divorcing Bruce, accusing me of "throwing the baby
out with the bathwater" (somehow he turned himself
into the rejected "baby"). When he realized he
couldn't protect me from my "recklessness," he
bolted. I resented his implication that my unhappi-

ness wasn't real. Just because I had a pattern of being with the wrong man didn't mean I should stay with the latest wrong man.

In 1992 I was in Monte Carlo to shoot the feature *Once Upon a Crime*. One day I was sitting across from Sean Young, one of the other actors. Out of the corner of my eye, I noticed something ... missing. *Was it possible? Good God, she wasn't wearing underpants.* I finally said to her, "I'm shootin' squirrel from where I'm sitting." She smiled and crossed her legs, an agreeable colleague.

We were shooting at night, beginning when the last customer had left the grand casino and ending before the first customer arrived the next morning. While we waited for the casino to empty out one night, the cast went gambling. I didn't bet, but every person I stood next to lost. The next night, after I had filmed a scene with George Hamilton, he asked, "How would you like to come with me for breakfast?" The casino restaurant was closed, but George is a high roller, well known to the management, so they opened up just for us. We were still wearing our movie costumes—he in an immaculately cut tuxedo (his teeth blindingly white against his ubiquitous tan) and me in a Versace gown. We had raspberry soufflé and Louis Roederer blush champagne.

As we walked through the restaurant's double doors, there was a roulette table. "I'm going to prove to you right now that you're not a jinx," said George. "Pick a number." I stood next to him, breathless with worry, and watched as he racked up $5,000, $10,000, $25,000, $50,000—in wins, not losses. "Let's go to

Cartier and I'll buy you a watch," he suggested. I declined. I already had a watch.

*A*s spokesperson for Voter's Choice, I was invited—along with many others, including Gloria Steinem, Marlo Thomas, and Whoopie Goldberg—to Washington, D.C., to lead the March for Women's Lives. At the fund-raiser the evening before, I was seated next to a political consultant, born and raised in Chicago, who had stayed in Boston after law school and had become a kind of consigliere to the younger generation of Kennedys. He was a smart, funny, athletic feminist who had massive amounts of curly brown hair with glints of red and gold. I fell.

He was also G.U.—Geographically Undesirable. It was a struggle to find time together, and when I decided to build a house in Memphis, he thought I was insane, suggesting Nantucket or Aspen as more appropriately exciting places. Though I had lots of family and old friends in Memphis, I would have never considered building a home there if I hadn't made new, close friends: one is Sid Selvidge, a brilliant folk singer and songwriter who produced my fourth CD, *Somewhere Down the Road* (which featured a duet with Peabo Bryson, one of the great voices of pop music); the other new friend was Betsy Goodman Burr Flannagan Belz. Like me, she's had three children with two different men. Betsy is a beautiful woman, and I find in her friendship a refreshing lack of envy. With Sid and Betsy, I gained a new brother and sister.

I finally got to build my dream house in downtown

Memphis, up on the bluff overlooking the Mississippi River, and the local newspaper chose my home as one of the three worst eyesores in the city of Memphis. The other two are Pat's Pizza, which has been closed for twenty-five years, and my favorite junkyard on Main Street, filled with old carbine wheels, tow trucks, and patinated pieces of machinery.

In the fall of that year, I agreed to speak in San Francisco at a fund-raiser for Ann Richards, who was running for governor of Texas. The Consultant agreed to meet me there. It was the same day the Giants were playing the A's in the World Series at Candlestick Park. I got to the hotel first and had champagne and oysters waiting in the room. We had just started to make love when the earth moved, literally.

"What's happening?" he asked.

"An earthquake," I said.

"What do we do?"

"Get under the bed." Of course, there was no way to squeeze under a box spring for protection, and we huddled in the doorway until the earth stopped moving. The phone wasn't working, and we didn't know what kind of pandemonium we'd find outside, but my first thought was: _Who knows when we'll get to eat again?_ So we quickly polished off the champagne and oysters before walking downstairs to the lobby, dimly lit with emergency lighting. I looked over at the bar and thought: _If I'm going to die, I might as well die happy._ Several margaritas later, we poked our heads outside, aware that the sounds of the city had been silenced, and saw a long black limousine parked in front of the hotel. I knocked on the driver's side, motioning for him to lower the window.

"Excuse me," I said deliberately, uttering words I had never used in my life, "I'm Cybill Shepherd. You know, the movie star? Could you please let me use your phone so I can call my kids and tell them I'm okay?" From the back of the limo, I heard a man's voice. "Cybill Shepherd? We're from Memphis. We're here for the World Series. Come on inside." We got in the car and saw the collapsed Bay Bridge on the tiny TV. Returning to the hotel, we were each handed a lit candle for the walk up seven flights, and all night long we listened to the repetition of inexplicable noises coming from Union Square: *pop, pop, crash. Pop, pop, crash.* It turned out that many of the windows in the Neiman Marcus building had cracked, and maintenance crews were knocking out the shards of glass before they could fall on pedestrians. The moment it was light, we made it to the airport. San Francisco survived the earthquake; our relationship didn't. But The Consultant will always be my favorite mistake.

Sometime in October 1992 I got a call from a mutual friend involved in the women's movement. There was going to be what turned out to be the largest march in history for gay and lesbian rights in Washington, and I immediately agreed to attend. As the April 1993 date approached, the march began to garner a good deal of publicity. I was told that because Roseanne was planning to charter a jet and bring a plane full of Hollywood celebrities, they really didn't need me. I asked if they had a seat for me on the plane. The answer was no. I called Patricia Ireland, the head of the National Organization for Women, to check to make sure I shouldn't go. She said that I should definitely go and, furthermore, asked if I could attend a major fund-raiser the night before for the Human Rights Campaign Fund. I said sure, and the night of the event we raised a lot of money and lifted a lot of spirits. It turned out that Roseanne and her plane full of celebrities never materialized. The only Hollywood personalities whom I remember being there were Judith Light and myself. On the day of the march I was told that only gays and lesbians would be allowed to carry the banner. I staged my own little protest. I asked them, "Do you think Martin Luther King would have refused to let me carry the banner with him because of the color of my skin?" So I was allowed to carry the banner. It was a great honor, and it was one of my proudest moments as a parent when my thirteen-year-old daughter Clementine told me that since she felt so strongly about the issue, she wanted to march with me.

There had been talk in Memphis for years about someday building an interactive facility around the Lorraine Motel where Martin Luther King was killed. It was to be called the National Civil Rights Museum, and I was invited to speak at the dedication ceremony on January 20, 1992. It took me thirty-four years to actively become involved in the fight against racism. I received a plaque inscribed with the motto "equal opportunity and human dignity," followed by "Thank you Cybill Shepherd for helping break the chain of oppression."

When I arrived in Memphis, my mother picked me up at the airport and said "I've never been as proud of you as I am today." Tears streamed down my face as I spoke of my hope that this museum would give us all a chance to start healing the destructive hatred of the racism that had surrounded us for so long.

Moments before the ceremony began, however, my then-publicist, Cheryl Kagen, appeared, pulling a tall, distinguished-looking man by the arm. She introduced me to Governor Bill Clinton of Arkansas, who had flown in to attend the ceremony but had not been scheduled to speak. When he arrived a few minutes late, he was refused a seat on the podium. No one recognized him. In the coming months, I would speak at three different fund-raisers for the Clinton/Gore campaign. At an event in Little Rock, Clinton and I waited backstage, and I realized, as so many women have, how intelligent, warm, and charismatic he is. I realized I was staring into his eyes and caught myself. "You know what?" I said. "You're entirely too attractive. You better stand on the other side of the room."

IN 1993 CBS OFFERED ME A ROLE AS THE mother of a kidnapped child in a made-for-TV movie called *There Was a Little Boy*. I pushed successfully for the director to be Mimi Leder, a woman whose work I had admired from the series *China Beach*, even though she was not on the CBS "approved" list. (She went on to direct *The Peacemaker*, with a $50 million budget, and *Deep Impact*, at $80 million, becoming one of a handful of women making major action features.) I always explain to colleagues that I have a particular way of trying to develop and sustain a mood that usually involves some quiet and reflection before a scene, but not all actors need to work that way. John Heard, who was playing my husband, can make wisecracking comments right up to the moment the film starts rolling and a moment later have tears streaming down his cheeks. Mimi had been the frequent brunt of his teasing humor, but one day he went a little too far and asked her, "What makes you think you can direct?" She turned to him and said evenly, "When I hired you, I thought I was hiring John Hurt." Mimi was well liked, and the crew applauded.

We were filming at a high school in an area that was considered the drive-by shooting capital of the world. One night, just moments after I'd left, a man was shot and killed half a block away from my trailer. My manager called one of the executives at Lorimar to request a bodyguard for me, and he absolutely refused, so I arranged and paid for an off-duty LAPD officer myself.

It was a good thing. About a week later, we were working in a neighborhood that was the home turf of some notoriously violent gangs. I was waiting for the setup of a scene that called for me to cross the street pushing a baby carriage, when my bodyguard said, "Don't move until I get back," and dashed off to grab a walkie-talkie from one of the crew. I was oblivious to what had caught his eye: a group of men who appeared to be smoking dope on the balcony of a nearby apartment building, one of whom suddenly started waving a gun in my direction. Within moments a police helicopter hovered overhead, and officers on foot entered the building. Filming stopped as the revelers were arrested, but no weapons were ever found.

*I*F THERE'S ONE THING I'VE LEARNED, IT'S THAT the tide goes out and the tide comes in. But I never expected to see Jay Daniels, part of my misery on *Moon-lighting*, washed up on the beach as another piece of flotsam. I was almost struck mute (an uncommon occurrence for me) on the day in 1994 when my manager told me Jay had called, asking to meet with me in hopes of persuading me to go back to television as both star and executive producer of my own show. There was no way I wanted to talk with, let alone work with, a man who had stood by passively while Glenn Caron ripped into me. Jay kept calling, and my manager kept repeating my answer: no. But he claimed to have done a lot of thinking about my troubled *Moon-lighting* experience during his subsequent four years on *Roseanne* and had concluded that I'd been the victim of what amounted to a sexist boys' club. He repeated this to me directly when I agreed to a meeting at my house. And I believed him.

We ended up at Carsey-Werner Productions, a "boutique" studio that had produced *The Cosby Show* and had *Roseanne* and *Grace Under Fire* on the air. In agreeing to do the *Cybill* show, Marcy Carsey (a former actress herself) and Tom Werner were, for the first time, taking on a project developed outside the auspices of their studio. But they hated our first script and asked us to start from scratch, reluctantly agreeing to the original plan of my character being an actress. It felt like the show would never get made.

For several years I had given up singing in public because of all the discouragement. But on a visit to New York in 1994, I saw my good friend Jimmy Viera, who still makes me a blonde with his own two hands even though he's no longer an executive at L'Oréal and I'm no longer the company spokeswoman. "I'm going to take you to hear Dixie Carter at the Café Carlyle," he said, and during her performance, he leaned over and whispered, "You should be back on that stage again." On the next two nights we saw Andrea Marcovicci at the Algonquin and Annie Ross at Rainbow and Stars. Somewhere along the way I had lost the spirit to say "watch me." Jimmy gave me that voice back—and soon there was a microphone to amplify it. I was offered a three-week engagement, five nights a week, two shows a night, at Rainbow and Stars. I hired a new musical director, who brought several new musicians to my home, including one who sang backup, and played sax and keyboards. I will call him "Howard Roark."

I happen to believe that people identify themselves to us within the first days, sometimes within the first moments, of our acquaintance—we often choose not to hear or believe what is patently obvious. It was inappropriate for Roark, at a band rehearsal, to hand me a valentine with a Superman figure he'd altered to be "Safety Man." *Strike One.* On our second date, he told me that when he'd seen *The Heartbreak Kid* years before, he'd vowed, "Someday I'm going to get that babe." *Strike Two.* But it didn't stop me from spending the next three hours in bed. After our romp, we took a walk in a wildlife preserve near my house, still damp after a heavy rain. The light was streaming through the clouds, and two wild mallards flew across our path.

"Maybe that's a good omen," I said, feeling a little mystical. "They're on parallel paths, and they're crossing ours."

"Nah," he said, "that's just two dumb birds." *Strike Three.*

Roark was going through a bitter divorce, living over a friend's garage, and moved into my guest room almost immediately. Only a few weeks later, he announced that he had an offer to go on the road as a backup musician for a rock band. "I understand that you have to make a living," I told him, "but I'm going to date other men while you're gone." A few days later he said that he wanted to turn the job down and stay in town with me, but that would only be possible if he were made musical director of my show. I didn't have a show at that point and made it clear I could never guarantee such a thing. *Strike Four through Thirty-seven.*

Since Jay Daniel was a producer but not a writer, Carsey-Werner suggested that I meet the head writer from *Grace Under Fire*. Everyone warned me that Chuck Lorre, a talented writer, could be difficult. But at our first meeting, he was sweet and funny. When he left, Marcy's mouth was agape. "That was amusing," she said. "I've never seen Chuck so smitten, or so polite."

The arc of Cybill Sheridan's story was closely drawn from my own checkered career and private belly flops: she's a single mother with two ex-husbands, the sort of journeyman actress I would have been had I not been lucky enough to have *The Last Picture Show* or *Moonlighting*. Chuck dissuaded me from making the character a mother of small children, as I was in real life. "It curtails the shooting schedule," he said, "but more importantly you can't get away with adult material. The network doesn't like using sexy double entendres in front of kids."

Jay made many contributions to *Cybill*, one of

which was its use of the Hollywood Walk of Fame as the title sequence. The camera pans the sidewalk stars of Carole Lombard, Lana Turner, Kim Novak, Jean Harlow, and Lassie (all famous Hollywood blondes). I suggested mine be a fake star, drawn in chalk.

My strongest objection to the original pilot script was the absence of any sustaining female friendships. I knew that I didn't want to reprise the icy bitchiness of Maddie in *Moonlighting*, and I insisted on a best friend who was more of an uptight glamour queen so I could be the clown. (You know me, always beggin' for pies in the face.) Chuck created just such a character: Maryann Thorpe, a cynical, hilariously vindictive divorcee who guzzles martinis and refers to her credit card as her therapist, "Dr. Gold." My first choice for the part was Paula Poundstone, a stand-up comedienne with a twisted, wacky charm. I'd met her years before at a party, and as I approached her to shake hands, it looked as if her breasts were motorized. "Just a minute," she said. Then she reached down the front of her shirt and said, "Stop that, Fluffy." I was thinking: *This woman has a real problem. Her breasts are doing figure eights, and she's talking to them*. Then she pulled out a kitten.

But Paula was otherwise engaged, on a variety show, and I began reading with other actresses. It came down to a choice between Sally Kellerman and Christine Baranski. The latter was a Carsey-Werner favorite—she had been considered for their new show *3rd Rock from the Sun*, a role that went to Jane Curtin. Christine has fabulous legs, and she arrived wearing a tight, horizontally striped miniskirt that practically showed goose bumps, but evincing a chilly attitude that I interpreted as "This is beneath me." Since she had a theatrical background in New York, where she'd won two Tony awards, I checked her out with some New York theater friends, and everyone said the same thing: her work was respected, she was serious and talented, but watch your back. So I knew going in, just as I did with Bruce Willis, that this wasn't necessarily Mr. Nice Guy. But when she read for the network, she hit a home run, nailed all the laughs. It was obvious, as it had been on *Moonlighting*, that this was the best person for the part.

We settled on Tom Wopat as the sweetly Neanderthal stuntman ex-husband and Alan Rosenberg as the overwrought Jewish intellectual ex-husband. But we agonized over the role of the younger daughter, Zoey. Even though the titian-haired Alicia Witt was a real-life musical prodigy and had an interesting snotty appeal, she had almost no acting experience. She was already on her way home after the reading at the network, when we decided to call her back and tell her she had the part. The security police stopped her at the gate and sent her back up. I walked out to meet her, put my arms around her, and said, "Congratulations." The role of my elder daughter, Rachel, went to Dedee Pfeiffer (sister of Michelle), and when I suggested, "Why don't we make Rachel pregnant?" Chuck said, "You'd agree to play a grandmother? You're so brave."

Working with Chuck was like a romance without the sex (although if I hadn't just taken up with Roark, we might have crossed that line). He took me out for sushi, he sent me bouquets of out-of-season peonies, he practically moved into my house, and he transcribed my stories as fodder for the show. Much of the pilot was inspired by anecdotes I related, and he asked to have Clementine read the script to make sure the dialogue seemed plausible from a teenager's perspective. A journalist had once teased me about being "an old spotted cow," and Chuck borrowed the phrase to convey the sense of fear about aging in public. Losing cats who wander into the canyons after dark and get eaten by coyotes was my experience too. The set designer even visited my house and modeled Cybill Sheridan's home after it, although the set was too clean, and I kept urging, "It's not like home. Make it messier."

If Cybill Sheridan was the heart of the show, Maryann Thorpe was the sharp tongue. Christine delivered her clever barbs with perfect acerbic timing, but her character was more of a caricature, so it was easier to write her jokes. Every Friday night, I would receive my executive producer's script, and sometimes we needed another pass before it went to the actors— the writers often had to come in on Saturdays to revise. My notes on every script were the same from the beginning: make all the characters smarter. Don't trade their intelligence for dumb jokes. Never underestimate the viewers. Suspense is more interesting than surprise, and a joke is funnier if the audience sees it coming.

It's also true that the rhythm shouldn't be predictable. Sometimes we got into a rut, with my character setting up the joke and Maryann delivering the punch line. When Christine won the Emmy and I did not, it fed a growing conspiracy theory in the press that asserted I was trying to sabotage Christine's lines and enhance my part at the expense of her character. The gossip went something like this: I had been jealous when *Moonlighting* made Bruce Willis a star, and now it was déjà vu all over again. Once a template gets made, the press tends to regurgitate all the old adjectives. The grain of truth in this controversy was that of course I was envious. Who doesn't want to win an Emmy?

My complaints about wardrobe added fuel to the flames of contention. I chose to work again with Robert Turturice, who had won an Emmy for his costuming on *Moonlighting*. For Cybill Sheridan, he often chose the square, shapeless clothes of a septuagenarian librarian, while Maryann's skirts were so short that the world was her gynecologist. Christine didn't need jokey clothes to be funny, and the tackiness of her wardrobe was sometimes distracting.

Nominated for an Emmy for *Cybill*, Turturice became progressively less willing to consider new ideas and was replaced the second season by Leslie Potts, who gave both characters sophisticated and chic wardrobes. When she won an Emmy, you'd think it might have validated my original objections, but the theory, I believe, went: Cybill is jealous that Christine is thinner and wears sexier clothes. Christine once called Leslie into her dressing room and complained about one stunning cocktail sheath that I wore, arguing that Cybill Sheridan wouldn't be able to afford such a dress. She was the victim, I was the monster, and there was little I could do to counter the accusations of self-promoting bitchery.

Almost immediately, the show garnered loyal audiences and dream reviews. I did not take it for granted.

I felt like a phoenix rising from the ashes. And if I didn't have an Emmy, at least I was a figure at Madame Tussaud's Wax Museum in London. The sculptor from the museum came to California with a bowlful of eyeballs, measuring every square inch of my body and every hair on my head—it took him eight hours. When I balked at doing the revolting dental impressions that make you gag, he convinced me to do it by saying, "Tony Bennett did it."

Part of my job satisfaction was working with the man I loved. Chuck and Jay asked Roark to compose some of the "incidental" music for the show. I was very pleased they offered him a job, but keeping to an old pattern, I had fallen in love from the neck down.

Roark could be cruelly insensitive, prone to pick a fight at the worst possible moment, like an opening night. But our biggest source of friction was his allegiance to a pseudo-philosophy called objectivism, promoted by the novelist Ayn Rand and based on the theory that reality is not subjective. There's only one correct point of view, and anybody who doesn't subscribe to it is wrong. In the hope of resolving our conflict, I agreed to finance "couples" therapy, and at our first session, the shrink announced, "This will never work." The relationship was too unbalanced, and Roark was dependent on me for his livelihood. So I made a mental adjustment: Roark's belief was rather like voting Republican—alien to me but something I could overlook. He had recently become my musical director and I thought that music, along with our sex life, was a strong enough bond.

In 1995 both Christine and I were nominated for Emmys. What the public generally doesn't know is that actors have to put forth their own names to be nominated for these awards: the Academy of Television Arts and Sciences sends out a big book with all the names that have been submitted, and then the entire acting membership votes for five in each category. Those nominees each choose an episode that represents their best work from the previous season, and a "blue-ribbon" panel of industry volunteers watches the videotapes in a Beverly Hills hotel suite before voting.

Because I was cohosting the awards that year, I was doing an interview at the back of the auditorium when Christine won for Best Supporting Actress. By the time they got around to announcing Best Actress, I was standing in the wings, listening to my heart beating, hearing people laugh heartily at the footage from my show but applaud more for Candice Bergen's clips from *Murphy Brown*. I was prepared to lose, so when the camera panned to me, I took a swig from a bottle of Jack Daniel's that had been emptied and filled with Snapple. It was history repeating itself. Candice announced that it was embarrassing to keep winning and disqualified herself the following year, but it's pretty damn embarrassing to keep losing too. Actors are telling the truth when they say that the real thrill is to be nominated, but it's only a thrill until thirty seconds after the nomination is announced. Then all you care about is winning because this time you deserve it, more than anyone else. Please, God? (To quote David Addison, God must have been otherwise engaged.) As the winner walks up the aisle, you're smiling graciously and thinking: *Die, bitch, die, it should have been me.*

Every actor has bad habits. I'm sometimes guilty of the kind of shameless mugging that inappropriately comments on the material while pulling the viewer's focus away from the other actors. Orson Welles used to say, "Actors are either getting better or worse. There's no standing still." I was able to do more self-correcting on *Cybill* because for the first time, as executive producer, I had the right to look at dailies. Not so for the others. Alan Rosenberg is a terrific actor, trained at the Yale School of Drama, but he often spoke his lines so fast that it was difficult to understand him, and he made a chewing motion with his jaw after nearly every punch line, like Charlie McCarthy. Christine Baranski went to Julliard, and she breathed fire and magic into her characterization, but she had a couple of bad habits—gazing directly into the camera lens—in movie parlance, it's known as "looking down the barrel." (The camera operator is supposed to let the director of photography know if an actor is doing it.) There's also a bad habit known as "buying it back," laughing at her own joke. Sometimes we had to cut away from her best take at such a moment. The biggest problem was she often refused to hold for laughs, especially when it was my joke. In other words, she would say her lines while the audience was still laughing. As a result, they wouldn't hear the setup for the next joke and wouldn't laugh.

I wanted to have a friendship with Christine, but she turned down so many invitations to visit my home that I finally said, "Look, you'll just have to tell me when you'd like to come over." We were both mothers working outside the home, but she worked in L.A. and her children lived in New York City, which meant that she spent most weekends on the red-eye, usually rushing off after the Friday filming without taking curtain calls. Her wardrobe assistant would come to my dressing room and say, "Christine's so sorry she couldn't say good-bye, but she had to make a plane." Sometimes she returned late on Monday morning, understandably jet-lagged and acting as if the *Cybill* set was the last place on earth she wanted to be. She couldn't have read the script because she was flying cross-country when it was distributed on Sunday night.

Everybody could see when something was troubling Christine—the writers kept asking, "What's wrong with her?" But she never came to me directly to say she wasn't happy. That was not her way. Sometimes I would ask, but there wasn't a lot of time for that kind of solicitation during the craziness of the production week, and when I did have some time, on weekends or during hiatus weeks, she was back East. For both of us, time with our children was the most precious commodity, and just about every moment not working was spent with them. There was little opportunity to develop an off-site camaraderie, even a phony one, which might have been helpful. When performers have some degree of off-camera friendship, it can help develop a basis of mutual trust.

Jay and Chuck never intended to film the show with an audience. From the beginning the plan was to play the finished episode in front of people for the laugh track. The studio audience, they argued, is not a real audience anyway; they're just tourists herded onto the soundstage, and they're weird because they *know* they're being recorded. By not having a live audience,

Jay and Chuck kept control out of the hands of the other executives and actors. It's true that just because an actor gets a laugh doesn't mean it's a good laugh. Christine got some of her biggest ones playing falling-down-dead-drunk. We couldn't use them because then her character would be a serious alcoholic and we'd have to take Maryann back to the Betty Ford Clinic, and that's not so funny.

With a live audience, a show becomes more of an actor's medium—you have the opportunity to say, "See, they didn't laugh. Write me something else." And the buses carry the studio audience away by eleven o'clock, making it imperative to finish by then. Without that limitation, we were at the mercy of Jay and Chuck, who could keep us as late as they liked, while we did take after take.

Even though our ratings were good, Carsey-Werner wanted us to have a live audience. As we approached the second season, they asked for a meeting to talk me into it. "Make sure you say no," Jay instructed. But what the hell, I thought it'd be fun, more like theater. Jay was furious. "You're real popular now," he sniffed. "They call you the 'good witch.'" And Marcy Carsey sent me a Barbie doll dressed as Glinda from *The Wizard of Oz*.

The first time we did the show before a live audience was the second season opener. One of the executives at CBS came to the filming. I said my thoughts out loud to The Suit. "You're an executive at CBS? You're so attractive." He smiled, pleased with the flirtation. That spring I got a call from an assistant to The Suit saying that he wanted to take me to dinner. I assumed it was a pleasant way to have an official meeting. I knew that he was married, and as far as I was concerned, so was I.

I was ten or fifteen minutes late arriving at Pinot, an Italian restaurant in the San Fernando Valley, and The Suit was already at a table having a cocktail. He stood to greet me, said something complimentary about my outfit, and commented on the fact that a driver had brought me.

About halfway through dinner, he asked, "So, are you involved with someone?"

"Yes," I said, mentioning Roark. "We're very committed, very much in love."

We talked about children, his and mine. And then, quite out of the blue, he said, "My wife doesn't really turn me on anymore."

I know there was fish on my plate and a few mounds of vegetables because I looked down for a while, thinking, *I've heard this before.* Those were almost the exact words my dad said to me when he was getting ready to leave my mother. Wrenching myself back into the present, I looked up at him and said, "I'm sorry to hear that."

"Mmmmm," he said, "I've had a number of affairs."

"With whom?" I asked, and he mentioned one well-known actress. I was curious: how much would he spill?

Just as the check came and he was reaching for his credit card, he said, "Why don't you tell your driver to go home and I'll take you?"

I was trying to handle the situation without bruising his ego. It was a bad idea for so many reasons. "You're very attractive," I said, smiling, "but this wouldn't be a good thing. I don't fool around, I'm happy where I am, and we have a really important business relationship here."

There was an uncomfortable pause. As he handed the signed receipt to the waiter and rose to leave, he said, "Maybe you're right. Suppose we broke up and I didn't like you anymore? That might not be good for your show. The network might have to cancel your show."

I don't know what emotion my face registered, but I recovered enough to exchange cordial good-byes. I sent The Suit a handwritten letter, thanking him for dinner and carefully wording a comment about valuing our business relationship. He sent me flowers. I thought we were okay.

But, as John Ford used to say, it was my turn in the barrel. My days at CBS were numbered.

I had not spoken to Bruce Willis since the last days of *Moonlighting*, except in passing at an awards show. Perhaps inspired by the rapprochement with Jay Daniel, another alumnus of the show, I had called him during the hiatus. Neither of us apologized for anything that had transpired between us, but I was empathetic about the difficulty of becoming famous, about how hard it is to have a private life and give your family a sense of normalcy. "Hey," he said when we'd made amends, "if you like, I could come on your show and do a walk-on."

"That would be wonderful," I said. "Would you like to talk to the writers?"

"Nah," he said, "just have them come up with something and send it to me."

They wrote a perfect Bruce Willis cameo into the first episode of our second season. I had suggested that spirituality was a rich area to mine for comedy, and in "Cybill Discovers the Meaning of Life," the writers created a character who was Cybill Sheridan's "spirit guide." It seemed ironically appropriate to have Bruce play the part, since goddess spirituality had become an indelible part of my life as a direct result of my angst during the *Moonlighting* years. I knew that some of my views met with glazed-over eyes and could only imagine what hits I took behind my back—I tended to say "Goddess bless" when anybody sneezed and was probably a little mischievous in directing such a blessing to the most recalcitrant souls. Some people on the show resented any suggestion that we explore these themes, protesting what they considered a soapbox. If the audience laughs, it's not a soapbox.

In the second-season opener, my character is about to become a grandmother, and drags a reluctant Maryann into the Mojave to meditate.

Cybill: "The desert is a power place."

Maryann: "Spago is a power place."

Cybill: "People have been having profound experiences in the desert for thousands of years."

Maryann: "Name three."

Cybill: "Jesus, Moses and Bugsy Siegel."*Cybill is chanting to Mother Earth; Maryann is distracted and bored.*

Maryann: "You're the one who's all screwed up with this self-indulgent, New Age, yuppie crap—meditating, fasting, raising the cone of silence."

Cybill: "It's a cone of power."

Maryann: "It's a cone of crap."

If I had wanted a soapbox, that line would have been cut. It was a way to poke fun at my own beliefs, and I thought it would be even more fun to have "David Addison" show up in the desert. But Bruce Willis's agent said he didn't have time. Read whatever you want into the fact that he did cameos on *Ally McBeal* and *Mad About You* (the latter was head-to-head with my show on Sunday nights for a while).

Second season, second episode: I was thrilled that Tony Bennett was signed as a guest star. I said to Chuck, "Hey, why don't Tony and I sing a duet?"

"We can't change the script," he said. "Tony has already approved it."

That was how I learned that a guest star had read the script before the star and executive producer, namely me. "How did that happen?" I asked Chuck.

He hemmed and hawed, deflecting blame, and said, "If you want him to sing, you'll have to ask him yourself." When Tony Bennett arrived to film his spot and came to my dressing room, he graciously agreed to sing two duets with me, "I Left My Heart in San Francisco" as well as "Nice Work If You Can Get It," the song that I performed over the opening credits every week. Afterward I gave Chuck an ultimatum: "Don't ever send out a script that I haven't approved to a guest star." He rolled his eyes. He had done something inappropriate, and I don't think he ever forgave me for it.

Perhaps my worst infraction was once asking to

swap lines with Christine. In the opening scene of the "Zing!" episode, Cybill and Maryann are relaxing in chaise lounges under a ludicrous camouflage of hats, protective clothes, and sunglasses. Cybill was to say, "I miss the ozone layer," and Maryann was to respond, "What a price to pay for decent hair spray." Chuck interpreted my request as an attempt to steal Christine's joke. Both of us got big laughs, but it was considered the final straw of my evil intent, and Chuck and I would never be the same.

Whenever I argued with Chuck about something that didn't ring true for me, he inferred a hidden agenda. In the third episode of the season, called "Since I Lost My Baby," Cybill goes shopping with her infant grandson, and Maryann absentmindedly leaves with the wrong baby, a girl. She discovers the mistake in the process of changing the baby's diaper and says, "My God, that is the worst circumcision I've ever seen." I hated that line. Referring to the female anatomy as if it is inherently defective because something has been cut off smacks of the most archaic Freudian penis envy. The joke was demeaning and gratuitously disrespectful to all women.

I knew that the line would get a big laugh, but again, audiences sometimes laugh for the wrong reason. Jay implied, none too subtly, that I was simply trying to sabotage a huge laugh for Christine. If they had given me the line, I would have refused to say it. But I was told: too bad, it's staying in. Christine got a big laugh. Looking back, I realize it would not have been uncharacteristic of Maryann's consciousness to say such a thing. The logical fix would have been to simply give Cybill Sheridan a follow-up line that reflected her feminist perspective. Who knows? My response could have been funny. I wish I had thought of that then.

From the beginning Marcy Carsey gave me enormous support. "I was on every show, in every single story session," she defended me in a *TV Guide* interview. "Cybill is smart, she is supportive of Christine. Story meeting by story meeting, she said, 'Can't we do more for Christine here?'" And by the fall of 1995, when virtually every decision with Chuck Lorre involved a fractious disagreement, Marcy was prepared to let him go. Since Chuck is Jewish, she respectfully waited to deliver the bad news until after Yom Kippur, the holiest day of the Jewish calendar, but he still demurred in the press that the timing of his dismissal was insensitive to his religious traditions, without mentioning that his replacement was Jewish too: a kindly-looking bearded fellow named Howard Gould, who'd done an excellent job as supervising producer on the show. When we were looking around to replace Chuck, I kept saying, "Howard can do it, Howard can do it, Howard can do it." Jay Daniel and Carsey-Werner kept responding, "Howard can't do it, Howard can't do it, Howard can't do it." I won that round, and Howard did it.

It was Dedee Pfeiffer who suggested hiring her friend Don Smith as our makeup man, and he soon became buddies with Christine as well, often driving her to and from work. He was let go after one season, but that didn't stop Christine from bringing him as her date to the Golden Globe awards, making an uncomfortable evening for me. (How would you like to have the man you just canned sitting across the dinner table?)

Every few months, there seemed to be a story in the tabloid press, always scurrilous and unattributed, and usually about me. Christine was the target of one particularly obnoxious item, claiming that she was afraid to kiss a homosexual actor for fear of contracting AIDS (her children saw the paper in a store and brought it home, a virgin experience for her but one I've had over and over). It was obvious that someone close to the show was peddling "information." Finally, a well-respected journalist I knew called me and said, "I thought you might want to know that the source of those stories about your show is Don Smith."

When I shared the journalist's information, Christine looked stricken. "I'd heard that might be true," she said quietly, "but I didn't want to believe it." It was the closest I ever felt to her. Dedee was equally dismayed but seemed to put his treachery behind her: When she and a new boyfriend became engaged, she called my assistant and said, "Look, I really can't invite Cybill to the wedding because Chuck Lorre and Don Smith are going to be there."

Howard Gould and I worked like a finely calibrated piece of machinery for most of his first year, but there was something about the first hiatus that changed the dynamics, just as it had with Chuck Lorre. In an episode called "Mourning Has Broken," Maryann is convinced that the lawyer Cybill is dating murdered his wife. The two women sneak into his house, and the script called for us to blacken our faces. This came on the heels of a huge contretemps when Ted Danson was made up in vaudevillian blackface for the Friars Club roast of his then-girlfriend Whoopi Goldberg, and the couple spent weeks in public relations purgatory, defending their odd sense of humor.

"We can't do that," I told Howard. "It's demeaning to black people."

"It's just a little smudge," he argued.

"You know what?" I said. "I am on the advisory board of the National Civil Rights Museum in Memphis. Let's call the museum director and ask what she thinks."

He exploded. "I lost family in the Holocaust," he screamed, "and if anybody knows about discrimination, it's me."

"Why don't we use panty hose pulled down over our faces?" I suggested. "That will look funnier anyway," but he stormed out of the room. The panty hose were hilarious, with the feet dangling like tassels, but Howard never forgave me for my defiance. When he quit the show the next season, he had to be dragged from my trailer, practically foaming at the mouth and shouting, "I'm leaving, but I'm a better person than you are."

Things became Byzantine when Peter Bogdanovich told me his daughters had heard a rumor that my show was too expensive and was about to be canceled. Part of the reason was Jay Daniel, who sometimes demanded extravagant sets and had an expensive predilection for myriad takes of every shot. There's an adage in the business that film is cheap but time is money, which justifies doing it "one more time" to make sure you "get it" and don't have to come back later. But that's not true for a situation comedy with four 35-millimeter cameras moving in a complicated dance across the stage floor between the actors and the audience, each requiring a camera operator riding a dolly, a dolly grip to push, and a focus puller. Video is infinitely cheaper, but film is more aesthetic, more sharply defined, more flattering. We figured out that it cost about $1,000 per foot of film. For at least a year, Carsey-Werner had complained about going over budget and persistently urged that we fire Jay. I defended him but took a stand: "Three takes—that's it. If the actors get the words right and don't fall down, we have to move on."

There was an entire building on the CBS Studio City lot in which every office was filled with people involved in the making of my show. Or so I thought. One day I went in the side door and was walking briskly down the hall, a little late for an editing meeting, when I heard my name called. It was an unpleasant voice from the past, but I didn't identify it until I turned around. What the hell was Polly Platt doing there?

"Cybill," she enthused, "guess what? I'm heading up the new feature film division for Carsey-Werner."

Pause. "How wonderful," I said, knowing that I was up shit's creek without a paddle. Who's the absolutely last person on God's green earth I would want whispering in the ears of the people who sign my paychecks? It is unlikely that I'll ever work in a Polly Platt production. The source of Peter's rumor was apparent, and from then on I used a different entrance to the building, nowhere near her office. A short time later, Polly sent me a handwritten note on Carsey-Werner letterhead, with a little heart drawn next to my name, telling me that her elder daughter, Antonia, an aspiring actress, had submitted a reel of her work to Jay

Daniel, who had promised to get her a small part on my show. "Could you help?" the note pleaded. "It would mean a great deal to her, and of course, to me." The note was signed, "My very best to you Cybill." I passed the note on to Jay.

When I finally insisted on being part of the show's budget meeting, I discovered that Jay was blaming me for the high costs. In his considered opinion, Christine was a Xerox machine—she would say a line exactly the same way no matter how many times she did it. I was the exact opposite. I did it differently every time and took pride in surprising myself and the audience. Jay would say that I didn't even warm up until the fourth take, and he considered himself the master hand, putting together the bits that he liked from each scene. I would often see his choices and remember another, better, funnier take (this was true for all the actors, not just myself). He seldom liked my most outrageous moments and felt that slapstick was appropriate only in isolated incidents. "I will not use your biggest, Lucy-esque takes," he told me. "I will protect you from yourself."

In the fall of 1996, for an episode called "Cybill and Maryann Go to Japan," Jay went over budget creating an unnecessarily large and elaborate Japanese garden, but he said we couldn't afford a pond that would have provided me with a hilarious Lucy-esque moment (my character, dressed in full geisha costume, would fall in) so I finally agreed that Jay should go. When he left, eight episodes into the season, we were over budget. By the end of that season, we were safely in the black.

Caryn Mandabach, the head of production at C-W, said that the only way the show would survive was to "poach" a great head writer named Bob Myer from his development deal at Tri-Star, who had refused to consider her offer until Jay was gone. And Bob did seem heaven-sent, literally the answer to my prayers, from our very first meeting. "I know that part of the problem has been a lack of communication," he said. "But I promise I will be the first person you talk to in the morning and the last person you talk to at night. You will be kept so informed, you will get sick of the information and tell me you don't need to hear any more." Over time we even developed a private code. I hate it when someone says "Be good" as a parting salutation—I always want to say "What if I ain't?" So Bob started signing all his notes to me with "Be bad," "Be so bad," or "Be ever bad."

*I*t WAS ALWAYS INTERESTING TRYING TO DECI-pher the peculiar logic of Standards and Practices at CBS. In the episode "When You're Hot You're Hot" during our second season, Maryann is in denial about the approach of menopause, referring to the herbal potions that Cybill is trying for hot flashes as "bark juice" and "the fungus of many nations."

Maryann: "Thank goodness this will never happen to me."

Cybill: "Probably not. They say alcohol pickles the uterus."

Maryann: "When you say you're premenopausal does that mean your 'Friend' has stopped visiting every month?"

Cybill: "My 'Friend' . . . what are you, twelve?"
Maryann: "You know what I mean, 'Aunt Flo?'"
Cybill: "Just say it out—period, period, period."

In our fourth season, we did another menopause episode called "Some Like It Hot." We were told not to refer to a woman's biological cycle as anything other than her biological cycle, and were forbidden to say uterus, cervix, ovaries, menstruation, period, or flow. And why? Years earlier, Gloria Steinem had pointed out to me that the valentine heart was originally a symbol of female genitalia. When I repeated this to Bob Myer, he was rightfully intrigued and said he'd like to build an episode around it, having fun with a different kind of "V" day. When CBS read the script, Standards and Practices forbade the use of the word *vagina*. I asked Bob to see if they'd agree to let us use *labia*. Remarkably, they said yes. We wondered if CBS knew what the word meant or thought no one else would. Although the episode got some of our biggest laughs and highest ratings, that's when the network began to crack down on any element of the show regarding female anatomy or bodily functions. I had the distinct feeling that they thought we were trying to be lewd or shocking, but our insistence on using those words came from political awareness. Knowing the proper names as well as the slang for body parts is one way for women and children to protect themselves from sexual abuse, as well as open themselves to sexual pleasure. It's astonishing that in daring to describe female anatomy accurately we were breaking new ground in television. At the time, I had no idea that

Eve Ensler had won the 1997 Obie Award for her one-woman show called *The Vagina Monologues*. I didn't know about her hilarious, eye-opening tour into the forbidden zone at the heart of every woman until I read an article in the Arts and Leisure section of the *New York Times* in 1999, a year after my Valentine's Day episode was aired. I rejoiced at the public acknowledgment that her play was an important ground-breaking work, yet I was saddened that similar ground-breaking work on the *Cybill* show had gone unnoticed by the press. But, like menopause, the issue of a woman's identity in regard to her genitals was still taboo in the media at the time we were dealing with it and reaching a huge prime-time audience.

It was Christine's idea to do an episode about mammography, but the show became a source of contention for us. Last-minute changes were not her thing, and she perceived improvisation as ambush. But even flubs often prove to be the funniest moments. In the episode called "In Her Dreams," Maryann goes for a worrisome mammogram. It was scripted that she would cry, but when we came to do the scene, I started to tear up too. Working up the emotion for the scene, I had been listening to "Come in from the Rain," Melissa Manchester's song about friendship ("Well, hello there, dear old friend of mine . . . "). I was imagining a breast cancer scare not for Cybill Sheridan's best friend but for Cybill Shepherd's best friend, and I started to feel the moment for real. I've been there, sitting on turquoise vinyl seats in hospital waiting rooms with loved ones, waiting for scary biopsy reports, and my friends never cry alone — we cry with and for each other. But when Christine saw the tears in my eyes, she went cold. Before the second take, Bob Myer came to me and said, "You know, Christine doesn't like these surprises." Then she had her manager call him. Christine, it seemed, felt quite strongly that we not use the first take when I had cried. In fact, she wanted to participate in the editing to ensure that the first take was not used. Bob denied her request, explaining that we used parts of every take, showing each actor to his or her best advantage.

Early in 1997, Bob came into my dressing room, practically chewing up the furniture and spitting it out with fury. "We've just gotten a call from the producer of *3rd Rock*," he said, "who insists that he needs Christine next week."

"What are you talking about?" I asked.

"Carsey-Werner wants her to do a cameo," he said.

"Why didn't we know about this earlier?" I asked.

"Didn't they tell you?" he said. "Oh, those people don't know how to talk to anybody. I'm going to call them and say they can't have her now."

"You do that," I said, "and furthermore, we want a trade-off: let's get one of their actors to come on *Cybill*."

A few weeks after Christine did her cameo, Marcy and Caryn sent me a note: "If we would have had a brain in our heads, the right thing for us to do would have been to have told you directly about Christine's appearance on *3rd Rock*. . . . We value your work and your friendship more than you know and hope you can forgive us." I also heard from a Carsey-Werner executive known privately as The Executioner because he was always mentioning his uncle Ivan. (If somebody was being rude to you, he would offer, "Uncle Ivan could bury his feet in cement.") His note to me was contrite: "I'm sorry if I caused you any problems regarding Christine and *3rd Rock*," he wrote, signing off, "Your loyal production slave."

One of my concerns with the direction of the show was that Maryann Thorpe had a new romantic interest, while Cybill Sheridan had zippo. Bob kept talking about the difficulty of finding the right actor to play opposite me, so I suggested that my character date lots of men—they might all turn out to be ax murderers, as they often do in real life, but the odyssey would be rich loam for comedy. For the third season closer, he came up with a story called "Let's Stalk" that ends with Maryann fearing she has killed Dr. Dick, but in the first episode of the upcoming season she was to discover she hadn't killed him. Dr. Dick would suddenly appear and be played by a recognizable guest star.

The opening and closing episodes are two of the most important of the year, because of the promotion and media attention, and it's crucial to have a cliffhanger that practically ensures the audience will watch to see the resolution when the new season begins. It was a bad idea to have two such crucial episodes dependent on the casting of a guest star, who might or might not materialize. There was always pressure from the network to have cameos, because such appearances generated good buzz, but I objected to the idea when it came to Dr. Dick. I thought he should be seen only in the imagination of the viewers, a device used successfully throughout television history, from the invisible Sam as the answering service for "Richard Diamond" (it was Mary Tyler Moore's voice), to the off-camera Charlie of *Charlie's Angels* (John Forsythe spoke his lines), to the absent Maris, sister-in-law of *Frasier*. CBS continued to push for John Lithgow to play the odious Dr. Dick, but he had already turned the role down, sending me flowers with a note that said, "Quite apart from feeling wildly overextended these days, I'm following a firm personal policy of concentrating all of my sitcom energies on *3rd Rock*. If I did any other show, it would be yours, but for the moment, I'm doing none. If it's any consolation, you'll never see me turning up on *Friends*."

Timothy Dalton and John Larroquette also declined the honor of playing Dr. Dick. Don Johnson didn't even bother to respond. Just days before we were to begin shooting, I told Bob Myer, "Forget about getting somebody's idea of a name. Just cast the best actor."

"I want you to trust me on this," Bob said. "We'll just shoot the segments that don't require Dr. Dick, and by the time we need him, we'll have somebody great."

Everyone knows the joke about the three biggest lies in Hollywood: "The check is in the mail," "The Mercedes is paid for," and "It's only a cold sore." And they're all preceded by the words: "Trust me." Dr. Dick was never cast, the story was rewritten, and we shot in bits and pieces for several months, never resolving the cliff-hanger. Bob admitted that he had been badly mistaken in building the opening and closing episodes around uncertain casting and sent this note to the cast early in the new season:

Dear Everybody,

Because we waited until we found just the right casting for Dr. Dick to complete the filming of the episode that featured him (#401), we've had to make certain adjustments in the production schedule. If you remember, we preshot two scenes from episode #403 to make room for the two Dr. Dick scenes in #401 that we postponed. Therefore, the following pages represent the scenes from episode #403 that have not been shot, as well as the remainder of the scenes from episode #401 that have not been shot.

Confused? There's more.

The pages that are included under separate cover contain material that needs to be shot, as well as the material that it relates to, which has been shot.

Still with me?

Robert Stack appears in one of the pickup scenes from #401 that formerly featured Dr. Dick. No, Robert Stack is not playing Dr. Dick. He is playing Robert Stack, a friend of both Maryann and Dr. Dick.

What's more . . .

I ask nobody to actually understand this. Just remember, we're having fun.

Trust me,

Bob

P.S. We never did find Dr. Dick, which turned out to be a good thing. Really.

Audiences have always enjoyed seeing me send up my image as a perfectly groomed mannequin. But the network wanted me to be more ladylike: no more burping or spitting olives back into the martini glass. The message, delivered by Bob Myer, was "Can't Cybill leave the sloppy stuff to Drew Carey?" What were they afraid of? That my show might get ratings as high as his? My sloppy eating, talking with my mouth full, and scenes of occasional burping consistently garnered some of my strongest laughs from the studio audience and those episodes always generated the highest ratings.

That November we filmed an episode called "Grandbaby" in which my character becomes a grandmother for the second time and is saddened that her daughter's family is moving away to Boston. I had the idea of using as a lullaby to my new granddaughter "Talk Memphis to Me," a song Tom Adams and I had written about my missing Memphis. I wanted to expand the lullaby moment into a brief music video showing what my character hoped she'd get to do with her granddaughter in Memphis if ever given the chance to take her there. The video included shots of my granddaughter at different ages as we visited our favorite places there. It had already been well established that Cybill Sheridan was born and raised in Memphis like I was. Also, the singing of the song became a reconciliation between my character and her first husband, who was also the grandfather of the newborn girl. That impromptu duet, which reflected their history of singing together, was a creative and emotional resolution to their prior conflict in the episode.

At first, Carsey-Werner refused to finance the video

and I agreed to pay for it myself, but once they saw the footage, they loved it so much I never had to pay. What they and the network wanted cut, however, was thirty-five seconds of a helicopter shot pulling back from a steamboat on the Mississippi River showing a crowd of black and white Memphians rocking out to the song. The studio and the network said that it took us too far out of the story, that nobody would understand who those extras were, even though no one had ever questioned the presence of the extras who sat in the trattoria scenes on the show every week.

This was the seventy-third episode of the show. It was the first and only time I would ever try to pull rank and go higher up to an executive at CBS. I placed a call to The Suit in hopes of getting a chance to explain why that thirty-five seconds of blacks and whites dancing together should stay in. After six hours of waiting with no word from the executive, I received a frantic message that Bob was on his way to the stage and I was not to speak with anyone about this until he had spoken to me. When he arrived there, he told me that it was no longer a creative decision. Standards and Practices, the watchdog department for the network, objected to the use of *all* the Memphis footage, saying it was a conflict of interest (meaning it was blatantly advertising my CD, *Talk Memphis to Me*).

I asked Bob, "So you're saying we have to cut the whole song?"

"No, no. Just any of the footage shot in Memphis."

"That doesn't make sense. It's not logical if their point is conflict of interest. Then they should insist the song be cut in its entirety."

"Well, they're not asking for that," Bob replied.

That's when I realized that it was not really about creative differences or conflict of interest. It was a conflict of power. Who was going to decide what stays in or what is cut out? It was not going to be Cybill Shepherd.

There is never a doubt in any sane person's mind about who really has the power in the television business. It is and always has been the networks. But when an issue begins as a creative one, moves on to become a racist one, and finally ends up as a conflict of interest, it does not bode well for a star/producer or her show. I knew my days were numbered at CBS. I absolutely believe that if I had simply cut the thirty-five seconds that the studio and network representatives originally had requested, the issue of conflict of interest would never have come up and the lovely, moving footage of my character taking her granddaughter to the beautiful landmarks of her youth would have been included in the episode. When I asked Bob if he thought that was the case, he said most likely it was.

"Never ask for whom the bell tolls, it tolls for thee." I began to hear a death knell in my heart for this show to which I had given so much. I knew starting in November 1997 (less than six months before cancellation) that it was only a matter of time. Two things came of this—a constant sense of dread and a constant sense of gratitude that I was getting to do the show at all.

When I returned from the Christmas break, my line producer, Henry Lange, told me he had gone into his office over the holidays to pick up messages and been surprised to see Bob Myer's car on the lot. He was even more surprised when he went in to say hello and was told that Bob wasn't in his *Cybill* office, that he was working on a new Carsey-Werner production starring Damon Wayans.

I was stunned. So much for my getting sick of all his information. "I heard there was a memo about it right before the hiatus," Henry told me.

"Have you seen this memo?" I asked him.

"No," he said, "but I'll see if I can get a copy." Until Henry showed me the memo, dated the week before Christmas, I had no idea my head writer was undertaking a new assignment that would mean being gone more than half the time (while continuing to draw 100 percent of his salary). It was unsigned, and no one would ever admit having been the author. With tears streaming down my face, I confronted him, asking if he was deserting a sinking ship. He didn't dispute the time allocation but pledged his continuing commitment to my show. The only difference, he said, was that he would take my notes from the Monday table reading of the script and give them to the writers, then go to the Wayans show leaving the writers to work out the material.

This was not a good idea. The people who created my dialogue, essentially translated my voice, needed to be hearing my notes directly from me. So I asked for several writers with whom I could communicate personally in Bob's absence. He seemed to be okay with this and asked "Who would you like?" I chose Linda Wallem and Alan Ball, both of whom had been on the show the longest. Bob added two new writers, Kim Frieze and Alan Pourious, and the four choices felt like a good balance. The first story line they pitched involved having the gay waiter at the trattoria come out. I had pitched this story line months before to Bob and he had rejected it because he felt that gay characters coming out was happening so often on television that it was becoming a cliché. What I didn't know was that Alan and Linda had pitched the same thing to Bob and had also been turned down. Bob bowed to the pressure of being outnumbered on this issue and we got our waiter coming-out episode after all. But when it came time to assemble the episode, it didn't seem as good as the others. Editing had always been one of the things Bob did best. We had worked happily side by side for most of our collaboration. Perhaps in this instance he was biased by his original rejection of the material. I felt we needed the input of Alan and Linda, who had actually written the episode, but Bob declared that it was unnecessary. I insisted.

I called Marcy Carsey and proposed that she keep Bob Myer on the new show full-time. We didn't seem to need him anymore, and there was hostility all around for deserting us in the first place. I could justifiably never trust him again because he had broken a solemn promise that he would inform me about everything by not telling me he had begun working on another show.

For the past year or so Alicia Witt had been acting like a spoiled brat, so pouty and truculent that when she wanted time off to have a bump removed from her nose, Bob Myer said, "Get rid of her," and some writers asked if they couldn't write her out of the show. When Peter Krause was hired to play Rachel's husband, he and Alicia became romantically involved and they barely spoke to me.

In April Carsey-Werner received a letter from Alicia's representatives, detailing her "creative concerns" about "character development and participation" and calling me tyrannical, abusive, and demeaning. But her fit of pique turned out to be fair warning for her demand that she have time off to make a film. When we granted her permission and worked around her absence, she wrote me a note, this time detailing my "generosity." I found out later that she got a raise after complaining about me. I also found out, by reading it in the press, that Christine had asked for a secret meeting with The Suit and subsequently got a raise too.

CHAPTER ELEVEN

"To Be Continued"

*T*HERE ARE TWO OR THREE DAYS OF MY LIFE I'd like to rewind and say "I need another take." One was the day that Christine Baranski walked off the set during the rehearsal for what would be the final episode of *Cybill*.

I recognized the first real death rattle of the show quite circuitously when I asked CBS for a raise. Word came back from the network: "We're already paying through the nose for that show. She doesn't get another penny." The rumor was that C-W had made an extraordinary deal in which they didn't pay any money on my show until it went into syndication, making *Cybill* disproportionately expensive for CBS. Two things are curious about this deal: it was made while Peter Torrici was president of CBS Television; he later left to join Carsey-Werner. And it was made at a time when C-W had enormous leverage, having developed a new show for Bill Cosby that had to have been a useful negotiating chip with any network and, in fact, landed on CBS. Toward the end of the 1998 season, Marcy Carsey had assured me that *Cybill* would be picked up. "CBS doesn't have anything else this good," she said, "but Carsey-Werner will have to eat dirt," meaning the company would finally have to pay its share of the bills.

Marcy suggested that the CBS brass wasn't really watching my show, and that the two of us might take some tapes to The Suit to show him how good it was. That never came to pass, although now I'm not sure it would have made much difference.

The Emmy Awards were on CBS that year, and the second highest rated Emmy broadcast of all time had been emceed by Jason Alexander and me three years before. My manager called The Suit and said, "Cybill would love to host again."

"Bryant Gumbel is doing it," he said.

Okay. Bryant Gumbel had a highly promoted magazine-format show premiering on CBS. But this was the first time since my show was on the air that my own network was airing the Emmys, and I wasn't even asked to be a presenter.

"We're not having stars from old CBS shows, only new CBS shows," said The Network Representative. They ended up with five presenters from old CBS shows.

The network had been screwing around with our time slot almost from the start, as networks are wont to do. Twice episodes of *Cybill* were pulled off the air to be supplanted by a new series starring Jean Smart of *Designing Women*, but both *High Society* and *Style and Substance* were dropped after one season. There followed pilots for Faith Ford (of *Murphy Brown*) and Judith Light (of *Who's the Boss?*), neither of which captured the public imagination. But in 1998 there had been relentless preempting: In February *Cybill* was replaced by both the Nagano Olympics and a new Tom Selleck show called *The Closer*. (I read about this change in the *Los Angeles Times*, and a few days later on a talk show, I "accidentally" misspoke and called it *The Loser*.) Three times my show was pulled during "sweeps," those weeks in November, February, and May when the networks schedule their most aggressive programming in an attempt to generate high Nielsen ratings and demand the best rates from advertisers. It was hardly a demonstration of support.

When it seemed manifest destiny that the series was on its way out, Bob Myer came to me and said, "Could you ask Bruce Willis to come on? It might help." I didn't want to leave any stone unturned, but Willis's answer came back: too busy.

During the last hiatus week before the filming of what would be the final two episodes, Christine Baranski's forty-eight-year-old brother dropped dead of a heart attack. She was on the East Coast when it happened, and we didn't know if or when she was returning.

I had no intention of shutting down production. As John Wayne says in *The Searchers*, I knew as sure as the turning of the earth that this would be my last season, and for the sake of the fans I wanted to get in as many episodes as possible. It was not about money—I would have gotten paid anyway. Despite the stress and infighting, *Cybill* provided the best part, the most fun, and the biggest creative opportunity I'd ever had.

I called Marcy and I said, "I've got the best writing staff in the business. Let's put them to work. They can have Maryann on the phone from out-of-town, and her part can be edited in later. We've done this many times before."

"Do you think you can get a good show?" she asked.

"Absolutely."

"Okay," she said.

I wanted to do a story line where my character was a talk-show host with a venomous cohost, a role I thought would be perfectly cast with Linda Wallem, not only a writer but a side-stitchingly funny comedienne. Cybill Sheridan was to lose her job when the talk show is canceled. Joking around with Bob Myer, I said, "Wouldn't it be funny to have a network executive make a pass at me and cancel the talk show after I reject him?" Bob gave a cynical little laugh and said, "Yeah, right." A few days later he relayed a message from CBS that they would never air such a show, and from now on, all plot outlines were to be submitted in advance.

"How did they find out?" I asked.

"I felt that I had to tell the network rep," said Bob. Good ol' "trust me" Bob.

The week before Easter, in order to avoid working on Good Friday (which would have been prohibitively expensive), we were planning to condense the usual five-day workload into four days. That Sunday I was awake all night with stomach pains, but I went to work on Monday morning and later phoned my doctor, who told me to come in right away for some tests. "You don't understand," I said, "this is probably the last episode I'll ever do. I have to finish." Then I took some Maalox. Every single person on the set was fried—the actors, the crew, the writing staff, all in the final stage of burnout—and I was pretty sure my symptoms were stress related.

The final episode called for the talk-show host to break down on camera and walk off the set, leaving my character alone to fill time. My idea was to have Maryann make a grand exit by calling her onstage, from where she was watching in the wings, and have her perform one of her ranting, raving monologues. I also thought that if my character needed to fill another five minutes, we could give Cybill and Maryann an opportunity to sing together one last time. Ever-conscious of budget restrictions, I looked on my list of public domain songs and came up with "Rockabye Your Baby with a Dixie Melody." During rehearsal I asked Christine to sing it with me. She said, "No, you do it." When I finished the song, I turned around to get Maryann's reaction but Christine was gone. Everyone on the set was acting unnaturally calm, as if the elephant in the middle of the room had laid a giant turd. When we got ready to do a second run-through, Christine's stand-in had taken her place.

"My, you look different today, Christine," I said, trying to leaven the moment. Nobody laughed.

The stand-in was looking at her feet. (Clearly abashed, she said, "Christine just left.") I was later told that she went to the wardrobe department with The Executioner, who told her, "Just pick out anything you want—it will make you feel better."

Early in my career, I learned that an actor had better be able to stand and deliver when the director says, "Action." The audience doesn't know that you're inhaling the rancid fumes from frying potatoes in a scorchingly hot Times Square coffee shop, or your leading man is pissed because you rejected his affections, or your costar has walked out in the middle of your song. Before I chose Christine to play Maryann Thorpe, I'd been warned: watch your back. And now there could be no lingering doubt about her feelings toward me.

The night of the final show I greeted the audience during the warm-up with palms upturned, as if I were holding my grandmother's silver tea set, and offering them a gift. I knew it was good-bye. "This is a season of miracles," I said to them, "whether it's Jesus Christ dying on the cross and rising from the dead, or somebody passing over your house and not taking your firstborn. I've been in the business thirty years. When you get a pilot okayed to go on the air, it's a miracle. When you get picked up for a season, it's a miracle. And I really consider eighty-seven episodes a mighty miracle. So like the Lone Ranger said: 'Hi ho, Silver, and away.'"

That weekend was Good Friday, Passover, and Easter. On Monday my manager let me know about a call from The Executioner. "Carsey-Werner is exercising its right to final cut," he informed her.

"Carsey-Werner has always had that right," I said to Judy Hofflund, my manager, when she relayed this conversation. "Why is it being specified now?"

"I don't know," she said.

"Please find out," I asked.

She reported back to me that The Executioner had initially replied, "We want to increase the odds that the show will be picked up for another season." But when Judy persisted, he opened a window into the collective thinking: "In order to protect the rights and interests of Carsey-Werner, and those of Bob Myer and Christine Baranski, Cybill will no longer be involved in the final cut."

Calls to The Executioner and Bob Myer went unreturned for twenty-four hours. When Bob finally called me back, he said angrily, "We have not collaborated in weeks."

"I had no idea you felt this way," I said. "I wish you had said something."

"Oh, come on, Cybill," he said, "you haven't even made eye contact with me all week."

He was right about that. I hadn't trusted him for quite some time. "Is this about money?" I asked. "I'm willing to come down to the editing room right now."

"No, it's nothing to do with that," he said. "I don't want to work with you. I didn't want to come in and do any more work on your show. I wanted to stay home with my kids for Passover, but they made me come in and do the final cut. So I told them, 'The only way I will do this is if Cybill isn't involved.'"

So. Those were Bob Myer's interests. Christine Baranski's interests seemed to involve the increasingly plausible rumors that a series would be developed for her at CBS. Carsey-Werner's interest was making sure the company did not have to "eat dirt" if the show was picked up.

The following Sunday morning I'd planned to hike up in the Santa Monica Mountains with a girlfriend. I put on shorts and a T-shirt, my hair was in a ponytail pulled through a cap, and I was just applying sunblock when I started to feel pain in my abdomen. I crawled into bed wearing everything but my shoes and told my friend I needed to rest. As the morning wore on, the pain intensified. Roark piled me into the car and drove at illegal speed to the emergency room. A battery of tests revealed a spiking white blood count and an obstruction in my small intestine. As I was prepped for surgery, the doctor said, "I'm afraid it's not going to be a pretty scar," and Roark started sobbing.

The doctor made a five-inch vertical incision below my belly button for exploratory surgery. As he passed the length of my intestines through his hands like a garden hose (a procedure called the delivery of the bowel), what turned out to be two twists, untwisted, but the tissue was swollen and bruised—as if I had been kicked in the gut by a horse. I knew the name of that horse. The crisis over, I was sewn back up and awakened woozy, with Demerol dripping into my veins, but otherwise remarkably among the quick.

Once the Demerol stopped dripping, I was dealing with the kind of pain and enervation familiar to anyone who has gone through major surgery. Riding home from the hospital, I was thinking: *I know I can make it, but is it twenty or twenty-five steps up to my bedroom?* When Ariel and Zack got back from their dad's house, I heard Ariel squealing from the kitchen, "Mommy, Mommy, where did you get this adorable puppy!" I didn't know what she was talking about. We didn't have a puppy. I realized how wrong I was when a minute later Ariel came pounding up the steps hugging what looked like a fur covered black slug. Later I learned that Clementine's crisis mode involved purchasing (for $1,200 on my credit card) a female pug dog so pitifully ugly that Clem figured no one else would buy her. Petunia, as she was christened, didn't look like she could possibly survive a week, her legs seemingly too small and skinny to support her weight. "I can't take care of a puppy," I yelled. "I just got out of the hospital." I refused to hold her and insisted Clementine return Petunia immediately. My initial assessment of Petunia turned out to be correct: she had less than one functioning kidney, and the store offered us a replacement puppy if we brought her back. But by then, all of us had fallen in love and wouldn't allow her return, envisioning a pug-size version of the glue factory.

About a week after I got home from the hospital, Roark called from the studio where he was working on the music for the last episode. "The show looks great," he said, "but 'Rockabye Your Baby' was cut. And there's a card at the end that says, 'To be continued. . . .'"

By mid-May, I was officially notified that *Cybill* was not on the fall schedule. For months I had the feeling that somebody was stalking me from behind with a plastic bag that would be placed over my head. I finally felt the moment of suffocation.

The next day I called Marcy Carsey. "Now that the show isn't picked up and nobody could possibly care one way or the other," I said, "it would mean a lot to me if we could put my musical number back in the last episode."

"I thought it *was* in," she said. "We talked about doing it as a tag. But it doesn't make sense because of the 'To be continued' card."

"Can't we take that off?" I asked. "There *is no* 'To be continued. . . .'"

"Let me look into it," she said. A few days later she called back. "It doesn't work," she said. "Christine is just sitting there in the background."

For eighty-seven episodes I always made sure that we had good "coverage" shots, so if an actor (including me) did something distracting or unhelpful to the scene, we could cut it out. I took particular care to do that on the last episode, since Christine had walked out during the rehearsal of my musical number. Out of four camera angles, there were two where she wasn't seen. I'd like to think that if Marcy had actually seen the scene without Christine's scowling, she would have stood up for it. But she said, "No, I like it the way it is."

And that's how the series ended: "To be continued." Maryann Thorpe had her last rant, but Cybill Sheridan did not have her last song. When I was feeling well enough, I called Marcy and asked to recut the scene with the song for my own personal archives.

"I don't see a problem with that," she said agreeably, "especially if you're paying for it." And she suggested that she'd have The Executioner call me back.

"I don't trust him," I told her.

"What are you talking about?" she said. "He's crazy about you."

The Executioner's voice was saccharine sweet. "Cybill darling," he said, "I think I can do it for you cheap."

"How cheap?" I asked.

"Not a penny more than twelve thousand dollars," he said, "but it's going to take a little while. The footage is buried in the salt mines of Utah." Along with, say, my career?

Paul Anderson, the show's editor, had a different idea when he returned my call. "Is this piece of film for broadcasting?" he asked.

"No," I said, "it's just for me."

"Then it won't cost you anything," he said. "I have the whole thing on computer disk. Come on over this weekend and we'll work on it." On a Saturday morning, I pulled into the front gate of the studio. I could see a maintenance man on scaffolding near the roof of Stage 19, spray painting over my name. But the twenty-foot-high CYBILL was such an intense bright blue that it was impossible to completely eradicate it. It will be a ghostly presence until the building is restuccoed.

At its demise, *Cybill* was CBS's highest-rated sitcom for women, number two for young adults, and we finished under budget. The people responsible for the death of a series doing that well should have their heads examined. After the show was canceled, Roseanne called me at home to commiserate. "I knew your days were numbered by the people they kept throwing at you," she said. Roseanne had done a voice-over on my show, and I had always admired her strength.

"Everybody's treating me like a monster," I said, "but I didn't do anything monstrous."

"Well, I did," Roseanne said. "I did everything they said I did, and I don't regret any of it. I just wish I'd done more."

Maybe I should have. If so, my show might still be on the air. Orson Welles once told me a story about William Randolph Hearst. One day when Hearst was getting on an elevator an associate rushed in to join him. "Bill," he said, "so-and-so is saying terrible things about you."

"That's strange," said Hearst, "I never did him a favor."

All through these difficult times, I was writing grateful notes in my journal about the support of "Howard Roark." We'd never taken vows about "in sickness and in health," but the way he rallied his support when I ended up in the hospital actually made me feel more sure of him. We had separate bedrooms in my home, an arrangement that has worked for me ever since I lived with Peter Bogdanovich, but we could hardly have felt more of an erotic connection. Looking back, I see how desperately I was trying to prove my lifelong theory that justified being sexual: if someone makes me feel this good, it must be love. Only in my forties did I begin to see that sex was scariest when I was vulnerable, when I admitted loving someone and waited to see if he would stay and love me back.

When Roark and I went to therapy, I sometimes took a list of petty grievances, and he'd say, "Why do you have to bring up all these little things?" I thought that's what therapy was for—to deal with the little things before they become big things. Five months after my health crisis, Howard said he had issues of his own and wanted to meet with the therapist in private. I paid for that too. Perhaps therapy taught him how to act loving when it wasn't in his heart. His act ended on October 24, 1998. That Saturday, in the middle of our joint session, he said, "I can't do this anymore."

"Do what?" I asked. I thought by "this," he meant therapy.

"Go ahead and tell her, Howard," said the therapist knowingly.

"My feelings have changed," he said.

"What are you talking about?" I asked. "What has happened?"

"It's over between us," he said. "You wouldn't even read that book on objectivism that's been sitting on your coffee table for months. I don't want to be with you anymore."

I felt as if the familiar figure sitting across from me had suddenly sprouted fangs and turned into a werewolf. "All those declarations of love—were they all lies?" I asked.

"No," he said glumly.

"What did you ever love about me?" I asked.

There was a long pause, way too long. "Well, you're a good person," he said.

"Who's going to tell my kids?" I asked.

"I will," he said.

"When?" I asked.

"Now," he said.

The therapist spoke up. "Cybill, I don't want the kids blaming you for this. Would you like me to come home with you?" she asked.

"Yes," I said.

We gathered around the dining room table with my three children. "This relationship between your mom and me isn't going to work," Roark said and started to sob. Whenever he cried in the past, I had thought: *Great, he's more open to his emotions than most men.* But this time he just seemed to feel sorry for himself. We sat in stunned silence watching him. Clementine started to cry and said, "Except for my father, you're the man I've known the longest." Then she turned to me and said, "Men always leave." Roark grabbed his jacket and ran out of the room. Crying myself, I apologized to my children for introducing this man into their life. Ten-year-old Zack asked the therapist, "Does this happen often in your work?"

Somehow the family migrated together outside into the sunshine. When I looked down at my feet, I was wearing socks but no shoes, something I had constantly chided my kids about. We forgot about Zack's tennis lesson, scheduled on the court in our backyard, until we heard the bell at the gate. Zack let him in.

"How are you?" the pro asked.

"Fair to middlin'," I said cheerlessly. You can't tell someone who's come to give your child a tennis lesson that your life has fallen apart.

Afterward somebody said, "Let's go see Howard's room," and we all crept down the hallway, opening the door as if peering over a precipice and looking at the chasm left by an explosion. There at the end of the bed, he had left behind a purple plastic yo-yo Ariel had given him for Christmas. And then I remembered that several days earlier, he had called my business manager and asked to be paid in full for his participation on the *Cybill* show CD, even though his work was not completed. I had sensed that he was low on funds and okayed the entire payment. I hadn't sensed the real reason.

My mother had always defended her marriage to my father as perfect. I didn't find out the truth about his infidelities until I went through the deepest kind of betrayal myself. And I began to wonder: was my life with Roark a model my parents had shown me, presenting to the children and to myself a fantasy good man? That's what wives were supposed to do. Was I a caretaking facilitator, as my mother had been, or just simply fooled? I had told my children: he can't show the affection he feels for you, can't hug you or buy you presents, but he's a good man. He'll always be there. He's solid as a rock. We'd been living with the delusion that this man was honest and loving and committed. Once the impostor left, we all seemed to relax, and my own mother-daughter war had ended. I no longer felt that I had to defend myself in her presence or dodge her zingers. What finally brought us together was that she had been left flat, and so had I.

Comedy writers talk about "schmuck bait": it's when a joke is set up to convince the audience that the actor is playing it straight so the punch line is an even bigger surprise. During my illness, Roark's presence was schmuck bait. He gave me a few months to get better, but once I had physically recovered (and he received his last paycheck) he bolted. Had he stayed, I would have found out eventually that his love and support were just for show, but he made a preemptive strike. I thought I understood how relationships worked out—I had my list, didn't I? But I was wrong. All I know is how *not* to do it.

"Howard Roark" lives with his mother now. I know this because he sold at least one story about our time together to a tabloid, trying to embarrass me with intimate revelations and falsely claiming I owe him money. In the therapist's office, he declared that he was leaving because I hadn't read a particular book. Nine months later there would be a more complete list of grievances in the paper, including the complaint that I was selfish in bed. When I saw his most recent narrative, detailing my fantasy about sex with two women, I tried to warn my ex-husband, who was on vacation with Ariel and

Zack, to stay away from newsstands and supermarket checkout lines. Who knew that a Pizza Hut in Kentucky would sell such periodicals? My twelve-year-old son called saying, "I've seen the article and it's really gross." Long pause. "Mom, a threesome?"

The possession of celebrity looks so desirable from the outside that observers tend to discount the attendant problems, but it's hard to underestimate the awful truth: every private moment in a celebrity's life can become a marketable commodity. I'd made that bargain with the devil: if I can only become rich and famous for doing what I love to do, I'll accept the trade-off, whatever it may be. I thought I'd be able to assimilate the invasion of privacy, the opportunism, the cruel gossip (which is never the truth: I'm both better and worse than what the public believes). It does pain me to know that so many people accept the *National Enquirer* as gospel, just as my grandmother did. (Moma would call my mother anytime there was a story about me, and no matter how outrageous the claims, she'd say, "I can't believe Siboney would do that." When told it was hooey, she'd say, "Oh, I don't think they'd print it if it wasn't true.")

When someone leaves, his ghosts cling to every corner of the house. On the wall outside my bathroom, we had recently measured and marked in Sharpie black ink the heights of the whole family, with me just above Roark at the top of the chart. Noticing this memento mori after he left, I grabbed a red Sharpie off the nightstand to scribble it out, which only made matters worse. When I went away for the holidays, I asked my assistant to hire the best painter in the state of California and erase every trace of Roark's name.

CHAPTER TWELVE

"We'll Make This a Comedy Yet . . ."

ONE OF MY FAVORITE SONGS BY MARY CHAPIN Carpenter relates a universal sentiment, "Sometimes you're the windshield, sometimes you're the bug." Having been squished my fair share, it's time to take stock. If relationships, either personal or professional, keep ending the same way, you'd better examine your own culpability. ("Nothing is more terrible to a new truth than an old error," said Goethe.) After ten years of therapy, four hours a week, I have deconstructed my behavior in every conceivable way, scrutinizing motivation, concerns, the possibility of an unconscious agenda—an excruciating process. Let's see what I bring to the barbecue.

I know this: in a company town, I have never been a company girl. I am too blunt and forthright. I will make noise and take chances. All my life I've been diving off cliffs with wings that I had no assurance would keep me aloft, and I've crashed any number of times. I have adapted behaviors that are maladroit, flippant, or unedited. I've sabotaged other people's marriages, mortgages, promises, diets. I've been ignored or dismissed because of the way I look, and when I think I'm not being heard, my anxiety level rises like the mercury in a thermometer. Growing up, I learned a set of people skills that favored presenting a problem in a flattering light or couching it rather than resolving it, and it's worked both for and against me. I was trained in the southern way of flirting, valued solely for its promise of sexual favor without obligation to deliver. I have definitely taken it to another, more public and more blatantly sexual level. It was, after all, the subtle erotic threat on the cover of *Glamour* that Peter Bogdanovich had recognized, and risqué or ribald innuendo has always been part of my persona and humor, as it was for Mae West. Perhaps the men I worked with so swimmingly at the beginning came to resent a "mere" sexual being having and using power. Perhaps there was some more complex combination of boredom and burnout, cultural or regional misunderstanding, and the kind of sexual politics that makes many men revert to the default position of implied male superiority.

I come from chicken farmers who made it to the country club, and I always felt a kind of numbing despair that my mother was limited to the social imperatives of that set, where the only achievement that counted for a woman was being a homemaker. I've come to understand the inevitable repercussions for the daughter of such a woman. If a mother's life feels uneventful, despite her pleasure in and support of a child's success, she may resent seeing a daughter achieve beyond anything she felt she had the right to expect for herself. But outright envy is unacceptable, so she over-identifies with that daughter, imagining that you and she are one and the same, expecting you to live out her dream. You will inevitably fail to live it exactly as she would have wanted.

Buddhists believe that narcissism is a stage on the way to enlightenment. It's appropriate for a child, who should feel like the center of the universe. Ideally, a mother should hold a mirror up to her child, saying, in effect, "Here you are." My mother couldn't do that for me because her mother hadn't done it for her. The image my mother reflected back to me in the mirror was herself, and I never saw me—the good, the bad, and the ugly. That's a setup for misery, disappointment, and self-doubt. I'm not sure I know how to have a relationship. I'm not sure I know how to maintain friendships. But I do know how to mirror my children back to them.

My mother's competitive edge went away with Howard Roark. When you find a new trust and understanding with a parent, it's like an unexpected gift. I've always wanted to be closer to my brother and older sister—we have that irrevocable common ground of childhood—but our life experiences have taken us in such different directions. There's an emotional gulf that we haven't been able to navigate in adulthood; money and fame seem to impede the strengthening of these fragile relationships. Ancient rivalries and jealousies are resurrected, played out on a different stage. To my sister, a big-hearted country girl, I may always be the "perfect" blonde child plopped down in the middle of her family, inviting odious comparisons. To my brother, a talented filmmaker, I have been both appreciated and resented as a conduit to business opportunities. Each of us has a litany of grievances, which someday I hope to ameliorate.

My grandmother spent the final years of her life confined to a nursing home and heavily sedated. I avoided visiting her because she didn't recognize me and couldn't even acknowledge my presence. But she hung on despite all medical prognostications, and one day I was struck with the thought: *Is it possible that she's waiting to die until I come back to say good-bye?* Sometimes when you ask such a question, you're really answering it. When I went back to Memphis that Christmas, I told my mother I'd like to spend some time alone with Moma, but I didn't tell her what I was going to say—I didn't know myself. Holding my grandmother's hand, I spoke to her.

"I wish you could have protected me more," I said, "from the discomfort I felt around Da-Dee, from my parents' drinking, from the message that women were little more than adornment. But I know you did the best you could. And it's okay, because you've given me so much." She died a week later, on New Year's Day. I hadn't seen many people in coffins, but my grandmother looked so beautiful that I approached the undertaker (who looked young enough that he might outlive me) and said, "When I go, will you do me?" Moma had prepared an un-eulogy called "No Sad Tears for Me" that she asked to be read at the funeral. "I have done these things," it said. "I have held a daughter's hand, I have seen the earth from the sky, I have eaten new white corn on summer evenings, I have heard music that sweetened my heart, I have loved a man and was loved in return. . . ." It only made us all cry more. I just hope it wasn't plagiarized.

IN THAILAND, THERE ARE TEMPLE DRAWINGS OF exquisite young men and women embracing, right next to figures in the exact same position as skeletons—an acute reminder of the ephemeral nature of love and beauty. Outside of my family, I became accustomed to gestures of warmth from people who were responding to my appearance, knowing that the gestures could be as transitory as the gift of beauty. The greatest leap of faith I ever had to make was trusting that love or friendship was predicated on something other than my looks. Beauty tends to be isolating, and people have no qualms about using you because surely you've used that beauty to get where you are. In an annoying shampoo commercial, a vacant young woman intones, "Don't hate me because I'm beautiful." There's no way not to be hated. That's why the evil Queen wanted Snow White dead. Now, whenever people refer to me as "glamorous," I suspect that they're setting me up to tear me down. They needn't have compassion for someone who's glamorous because she's had it easier. And in some ways, no doubt, I have.

THERE ARE ALL KINDS OF EXCUSES FOR SPITE and intolerance, and no one is holding any telethons for fifty-year-old blue-eyed blondes. Last year in the *Jewish Journal of Los Angeles*, a publication distributed free at markets, there was a letter to an advice columnist from a man making demeaning, stereotypical comments about Jewish women. ("Gentile women, by and large, are just happy to be with you. Jewish women have to win.") Illustrating the column was a photograph of me with a caption reading "A prime example of a non-Jewish woman?" Just because in 1972 I played the archetypal shiksa in *The Heartbreak Kid* who steals the Jewish husband from his wife does not give the publication the right to use my image to represent everything Jewish women are not. This is a terrible thing to do to my son and daughter, who will have their bar- and bat-mitzvah next year.

Perhaps I have karmic dues to pay for my participation in the cult of emaciated buffness. I had the serendipity of modeling during a temporary interlude between Twiggy and Kate Moss, when it was actually okay for women to look as if we ate and enjoyed life. I was never emaciated myself, but I did play a role in the tyranny over women about body image, and little has changed in the cultural perception of the idealized female form. When will it ever be okay not to be Barbie? When will we love our female bodies, in all their different sizes and shapes? If we can't do it when we're young, we'll have a hell of a time doing it when we're older. And dare I resist the lure of cosmetic surgery?

This is what fifty looks like, so far not surgically corrected (but never say never). Ancient artifact that I am, my pictures are still on the makeup counter at the drugstore, so I know the response to my lamentations may be: shut up, Cybill Shepherd. But I still have to confront the bathroom mirror—no retouching, no flattering lighting. As an aging beauty in America, I have an interesting perspective. I'm ready for my Shelley Winters parts now, and I have less vanity than you can imagine. My kids beg, "Before you pick us up, could you please comb the back of your hair?"

I've chosen to work in a field that has brought me success and money, much of it by allowing strangers to know the most intimate things about me and by having every private moment examined with the precision of gemstone cutting. Demi Moore was castigated for employing three nannies on a movie set to care for her three children. Nobody asked about Bruce Willis's whereabouts or the boundaries of his responsibility. The list of what's required to be considered a good enough father is about pinky length, but the list for a good enough mother is the interstate. There are times when I don't do a scene as well as I could because I've been up all night with a sick child, and there are times when I miss one of my kids' basketball games because I have to be on the set. Interviewers have always asked me, "How do you do it all?" The truth is, I only *appear* to be doing it all. Every day I fail, but I've developed the ability to improvise. I have to force time to be relative; I have to make five minutes count for five hours. Those balls that I seem to be juggling so effortlessly are, in fact, dropping all around me. What the public sees are moments of perfection, all the balls in the air, frozen for that instant, like in a still photograph.

As a teenager, I was one of the lucky ones. I never had the need to end an unwanted pregnancy because my family doctor provided me with birth control. I had a freedom that many women still don't have today. I'm going to keep speaking out for those girls who weren't so lucky, for my daughters and for other women—if not from the Oval Office, then from a multiplex or Web site or orange-crate podium near you. Watch me.

N OT LONG AGO I READ FOR A PART WITH A young director who asked me, "How does it feel to have been in three great American movies?" (The part went to . . . to be announced.) Yes, that's me in *The Last Picture Show, The Heartbreak Kid,* and *Taxi Driver*. But we are more than the sum of our work, and we're not only as good as the last thing we did.

I was thinking of these things on a trip to Graceland last year, almost thirty years since my last visit. Weeping behind my sunglasses, I stood at Elvis's grave, in the meditation garden that was his pride and joy. At the time he took me there, I did not understand the symbolism in the lotus flower design of his beautiful stained-glass windows. Now I know that the unfolding petals of the lotus blooming in the mud suggest the expansion of the soul through suffering and adversity. Elvis was on to something, but that enlightenment couldn't save him. I wish he were still alive because I think we could be friends now. One of the realms on the Buddhist wheel of life is that of the "hungry ghosts" where beings are tormented by unfulfilled longing and are never satisfied. I think I got stuck in that realm, and tried to resolve my anger and pain with men, taking pleasure as if it had no consequence.

With a girlfriend along as moral support, I decided to check out the plot I'd reserved for myself at Memorial Garden Park, on a wide verdant heath near Moma and Da-Dee. (Actually, I bought four plots, not knowing who might want to accompany me to the great beyond.) The very thought of eternal life made us hungry, so we sat in the cemetery parking lot, stuffing our faces with fried catfish and hush puppies from Captain D's takeout before venturing into the mortuary office, where it took some time to find me.

"How do you spell your name?" the mortician kept asking, eventually recognizing this as a photo op and requesting that I pose in front of a display of headstones.

"What are all those?" I asked, looking at the slabs of marble, the various tints and typefaces.

"Those are your choices," he said cheerfully. "Would you like to make some decisions as long as you're here?" He was enthusiastic about a newly available option: the dearly departed's face in bas-relief on the marker. "We can go look at Charlie Rich," he offered and drove us over to the plot. Poor old Charlie looked exactly like Leslie Nielsen, so I declined.

My friend was mortified, considering it weird and macabre to be hanging out at a graveyard on this clement spring day, discussing whether or not I should be embalmed before being cremated—prettified with a final "hair-and-makeup" for the few moments in the coffin before I turn to ash. But I feel peaceful in this place where my aunt Ruby took me to play when I was a little girl. And I am comforted to imagine that someone in the twenty-first century will remember a big, brassy blonde who tried to use humor as the Krazy Glue for life's necessary reparations, a stranger who will stand with a smile at my final resting place, reading a tombstone that says, "We'll make this a comedy yet. . . ."

Acknowledgments

I OWE THIS BOOK, AND MUCH MORE, TO THE creative juices, tender asylum, and occasional galvanizing cattle prod of many people: to my editor, David Hirshey, who never gave up hope that this undertaking was worthwhile; to Roger Director, who first suggested to David, "Cybill Shepherd—now *that's* a story"; to Jesse Gerstein, for endless overtime patience; the gang at HarperCollins, for going the extra mile; to Peter Bogdanovich, Herma Bogdanovich, Frances Bruno, James Cass Rogers, Stella Adler, Larry McMurtry, and Orson Welles, for incalculable mentoring; to Glenn Gordon Caron, Jay Daniel, Chuck Lorre, Howard Gould, Bob Myer, Marcy Carsey, Tom Werner, Caryn Mandabach, Bruce Willis, and Christine Baranski, for all the great work we did together; to Jane Howard, Linda Wallem, Barbara Harris, Joan Zajac, and James Viera, for their support; to Henry Lange, Heidi Schaeffer, Wendy Morris, Donald

Steele, Walter Teller, and Judy Hofflund, for professional lifelines; to Sid Selvidge and Betsy Goodman, for Memphis grounding; to Myrtle Boone, for her catfish and her generous ministrations to my children; to those children, Clementine Shepherd-Ford, Ariel Shepherd-Oppenheim, and Zachariah Shepherd-Oppenheim, for enduring with good humor the inevitable, unsolicited limelight that comes with having me as a mom; to Jason Martin, for his brilliant assistance; to Aimee Lee Ball, for helping me put into words what was in my heart and giving it gravitas.

Visit Cybill Shepherd's Official Web site at

www.cybill.com

to purchase Cybill's music, movies & books,
for cabaret tour dates, fan club information, and
exclusive downloads.

The Best in Biographies

HAVE A NICE DAY!
A Tale of Blood and Sweatsocks
by Mankind
0-06-103101-1/$7.99 US/$10.99 Can

THE ROCK SAYS
by The Rock
0-06-103116-X/$7.99 US/$10.99 Can

JACK AND JACKIE:
Portrait of an American Marriage
by Christopher Andersen
0-380-73031-6/$6.99 US/$8.99 Can

WALK THIS WAY:
The Autobiography of Aerosmith
by Aerosmith, with Stephen Davis
0-380-79531-0/ $7.99 US/ $9.99 Can

EINSTEIN: THE LIVES AND TIMES
by Ronald W. Clark
0-380-01159-X/$7.99 US/$10.99 Can

IT'S ALWAYS SOMETHING
by Gilda Radner
0-380-81322-X/ $13.00 US/ $19.95 Can

I, TINA *by Tina Turner and Kurt Loder*
0-380-70097-2/ $6.99 US/ $9.99 Can